State Accountability under International Law

This book considers the extent to which states are held accountable for breaches of *jus cogens* norms under international law. The concept of state accountability is distinguished from the doctrine of state responsibility and refers to an *ad hoc* practice in international relations that seeks to ensure that states do not escape with impunity when they violate norms that are considered fundamental to the interests of the international community as a whole.

State Accountability under International Law sets forth a definition of state accountability and establishes a threshold against which the existence, or not, of state accountability can be determined. Using a Foucauldian influenced interpretive methodology, this book adopts a novel construction of state accountability as having legal, political and even moral characteristics. It argues that the international community seeks to hold states accountable utilising a variety of traditional and non-traditional responses that cumulatively recognise that the institutions that comprise and legitimise the state were instrumental in the particular breach. Using case studies taken from state practice from throughout the 20th century and covering a range of geographic contexts, the conclusion is that there is evidence that state accountability, as it is conceptualised here, is evolving into a legal principle.

The book draws together the many academic theories relating to accountability that have arisen in various areas of international law including environmental law, human rights and trade law, before going on to examine an emerging practice of state accountability. A variety of *ad hoc* attempts and informal mechanisms are assessed against the threshold of state accountability established, with emphasis being given to practical examples ranging from the accountability of Germany and Japan after the Second World War to the current attempts to seek accountability from Russia for former crimes of the USSR.

Lisa Yarwood is a lecturer in law at the University of Exeter.

Routledge Research in International Law

Available:

International Law and the Third World
Reshaping Justice
Richard Falk, Balakrishnan Rajagopal and Jacqueline Stevens

International Legal Theory
Essays and Engagements, 1966–2006
Nicholas Onuf

The Problem of Enforcement in International Law
Countermeasures, the Non-Injured State and the Idea of International Community
Elena Katselli Proukaki

International Economic Actors and Human Rights
Adam McBeth

The Law of Consular Access
A Documentary Guide
John Quigley, William J. Aceves and Adele Shank

Forthcoming titles in this series include:

International Organisations and the Idea of Autonomy
Nigel D. White and Richard Collins

Self-Determination in the Post-9/11 Era
Elizabeth Chadwick

The Law on the Use of Force
A Feminist Analysis
Gina Heathcote

International Law in a Multipolar World
Matthew Happold

International Law, Regulation and Resistance
Critical Spaces
Zoe Pearson

Participants in the International Legal System
Theoretical Perspectives
Jean D'Aspremont

Sovereignty, Jurisdiction and Exploitation of the Seas, Polar Regions, Airspace and Outer Space
Legal Criteria for Spatial Delimitation
Gbenga Oduntan

State Accountability under International Law

Holding states accountable for a breach of *jus cogens* norms

Lisa Yarwood

Routledge
Taylor & Francis Group
LONDON AND NEW YORK

First published 2011
by Routledge
2 Park Square, Milton Park, Abingdon, Oxon OX14 4RN
Simultaneously published in the USA and Canada
by Routledge
711 Third Avenue, New York, NY 10017

Routledge is an imprint of the Taylor & Francis Group, an informa business

Typeset in Baskerville by Glyph International

British Library Cataloguing in Publication Data
A catalogue record for this book is available from the British Library

Library of Congress Cataloging-in-Publication Data
Yarwood, Lisa.
State accountability under international law: holding states accountable for a breach of jus cogens norms / Lisa Yarwood.
p. cm.
Includes bibliographical references and index.
ISBN 978-0-415-57783-0 (hbk) – ISBN 978-0-203-83752-8 (ebk)
1. Jus cogens (International law) I. Title.
KZ1261.Y37 2011
341'.1–dc22
2010021659

ISBN 13: 978-0-415-57783-0 (hbk)
ISBN 13: 978-0-203-83752-8 (ebk)

To Judy, who fought with me to be the best apple I could be, to Bruce, who loved me when I tried to be an orange, and to Sally, who daily inspires me in never pretending to be anything other than herself.

Contents

Acknowledgements xiii
Preface xv

Introduction **1**
1. The interpretive framework 2
2. The substantive concept 4

1 Breaking state accountability down to its conceptual parts **9**
1.1 'Accountability' 9
1.1.1 Linguistic interpretation 11
1.1.1.1 The difference between accountability and responsibility 13
1.1.1.2 The relationship between accountability and impunity 14
1.1.2 A trend toward bottom-up accountability? 18
1.1.3 Interpreting accountability in the context of human rights 20
1.1.4 Is there a legal obligation to ensure accountability? 26
1.1.5 A working understanding of accountability 28
1.2 The 'state' 28
1.3 Conclusion 32

2 State accountability as a conceptual whole **34**
2.1 The scope of the ad hoc *accountability practice for analysis 35*
2.2 A tentative set of acountability criteria 41
2.2.1 Is state accountability associated with criminal accountability? 42
2.2.2 Is state accountability associated with state responsibility? 50
2.2.3 Is state accountability associated with the particular law breached? 52
2.2.4 Is state accountability solely associated with legal accountability? 55
2.2.5 Is state accountability associated with political or moral accountability? 57
2.3 Conclusion 59

3 The relationship between state accountability and *jus cogens* norms **61**

3.1 Jus cogens *as the link between conceptual state accountability and established international law 61*

3.2 The debate and attempting to define jus cogens *62*

3.2.1 Distinguishing jus cogens *norms from standard norms 63*

3.2.2 The source and substance of jus cogens *65*

3.2.3 Are states under a positive duty to comply and ensure compliance with jus cogens *norms? 67*

3.2.4 Which norms are jus cogens *norms? 68*

3.3 A working definition of jus cogens *70*

3.4 Conclusion 73

4 The relationship between conceptual state accountability and doctrinal state responsibility **74**

4.1 An introduction to the doctrine of state responsibility 74

4.2 State responsibility under the ILC's Draft Articles 78

4.2.1 Can the international community as a whole invoke state responsibility? 79

4.2.2 Is state responsibility for violating an erga omnes *obligation effectual in terms of holding states accountable for breaching the underlying* jus cogens *norm? 82*

4.2.3 How effective is reparation under the Draft Articles in holding states accountable? 84

4.3 Juridical support for state accountability in the context of the state responsibility doctrine 89

4.4 Conclusion 93

5 State accountability in state practice **94**

5.1 Setting the scene to analyse state accountability in practice 94

5.1.1 Who determines whether a state breached international law? 95

5.1.2 What forms of redress ensure the breaching state is held accountable? 99

5.1.3 Is state accountability solely a state prerogative? 100

5.2 Case studies 100

5.2.1 Armenian massacre 1915 100

5.2.2 Crimes against humanity by the USSR – Holdomor famine 1933 and the Katyń Forest massacre 1940 110

5.2.3 Apartheid in South Africa 120

5.2.4 Comparing responses to state aggresion in the 20th century 129

5.2.4.1 Invasion of the Republic of Korea 1950 130

5.2.4.2 Bombing of the Osiraq Nuclear Reactor 1981 133
5.2.4.3 Invasion of Kuwait 1990 135
5.2.4.4 Conclusions on the responses to state aggression 140
5.2.5 Australia's 'stolen generation' 142
5.3 Conclusion 152

Conclusion: An accountability epoch? 155

1 State accountability has no normative standing 158
2 State practice is indicative rather than determinative of state accountability 158
3 State accountability is a legal, political and moral concept 159
4 State accountability represents a continuum of answerability 160
5 State accountability is sought on the basis of a norm's substance, not its jus cogens *status 161*
6 Characteristics of state accountability 162
6.1 A mix of motivations 162
6.2 A mix of accountability seekers 163
6.3 A mix of responses 163
7 Moving from lex feranda *to* lex lata? *164*

Bibliography 166
Index 181

Acknowledgements

This book is adapted from my doctoral thesis and the acknowledgements here are in appreciation for the support I received throughout that arduous journey.

Foremost, I wish to thank my family, in particular my parents, Judy and Bruce, my sisters Anita, Sally and Deana and my brothers Shane and Richard, all of whom have never once questioned anything I do and never once doubted I could do anything I want … not to mention my nephews Dom and Fin who never cease to put things in perspective. I also want to thank extended family and in particular Liz and Heath for allowing me to imagine myself a real author in a Parisian garret, Dave for the hard yards early on and Jenny for telling me there are no rules – a mantra to live by.

I want to thank those who gave professional support both to me and to the project: Dr Chris Gallavin for telling me to do a PhD; Scott Davidson for being the best referee always (and his wife Olivia for the many bottles of vino and laughs); Sir Colin Keating for keeping in touch with a lowly student; Professor Christian Tomuschat for giving me an afternoon of his precious time; Dr Andrea Sudbury for giving me 'How to Write a Phd' and making the thing seem accessible; Dr Caroline Fournet for seeing the big picture; Dr Greta Bosch for pointing out the small details; Dr Aurel Sari for giving me clarity; Dr Mike Addo for telling me either 'to get a life' or 'we have a problem' at the appropriate time; Dr Helene Lambert for the kick-start; Dr Amandine Garde for explaining the EU to me; Sarah Roberts for listening; Barb Powell for wiping the tears; Bob Drury for looking shocked and then thrilled at the appropriate times; Patrick Overy for satisfying 'urgent' information requests; the Cornwall crew with their helpful suggestions – indeed the entire staff at the Law School, University of Exeter for their continued support. And especially to Liz Dwomoh and Paul Clemence for reading drafts with infinite patience and the hugs.

I met some amazing people during my studies in the UK (and overseas). These people supported me throughout the PhD despite not having known me until this time and I can only promise them a much more relaxed and easy-going friend in the future: Liz, Annalotte, Sarah and the entire ICTR gang for sharing a vision; Paul and Frances who gave me the chance to talk about 'Nuuezillan'; Clotilde and her French way of keeping it real; Elaine and Kendra for allowing me to vent but keeping 'mum' … never forgetting the inimitable Judith, Jax and Zoe because from the very start you gave me a home away from home.

Then there are those friends who have always been there from the days of Girls and Boys High – they know who they are and that I love them all. I especially want to mention a few kindred spirits who have loved and believed in me unconditionally from the day we met: Sara McMillan-Bower, Steve and Lynsey Robinson, Emily Gillam, Sienna Pat, Katie Dunlop and Rachel Hebden. You are cherished more than you will ever know.

Finally, in addition to the formal dedications I wish to acknowledge my grandfather, Professor John Ritchie, who said to me when I fell that the bastards didn't know what they were talking about … but just in case there was anything in what they had to say then best pay attention and follow their advice. A gentleman's academic!

Preface

In 2007 Koskenniemi wrote of 'the project of modern international law',[1] when he gave an overview of 20th-century developments relating to how public international law is conceptualised, discussed and studied. This book, and the concept of state accountability that is discussed here, seek to make a contribution to that project by adopting the 'language of universal reason' and arguing from the outset that 'although statehood [is] important it [is] also problematic'. The premise on which this book is based is that an overly technical approach to public international law – which Lauterpacht explained in terms of being a self-contained legal system that establishes and relies on its own precedents – undermines the efficacy of the legal framework as a means for managing and regulating states.[2] Instead, this work is an academic inquiry as to whether, irrespective of the fact that public international law has traditionally developed in an overly technical manner, a principle of state accountability has managed to evolve – or is currently in the process thereof.

This book is based on my doctoral thesis, which was awarded in March 2010. I consider the arguments here contribute to a much wider discussion – but discussion that is largely oral and infrequently captured in writing. In particular, conference presentations by Edith Brown-Weiss and Richard Falk, meeting with Christian Tomuschat of Humboldt University and many, many useful talks with colleagues – notably Dr Michael Addo – were hugely influential in helping me to articulate what can be described as an accountability instinct. Consistent throughout those discussions has been the perception that the manner in which states are made to answer for grievous breaches of state power is in the process of – and must – change.

Accountability is widely and openly discussed – whether as part of the grander, long term international law project that Koskenniemi referred to or whether because a concept of state accountability is emerging as a contemporary political response to events in the new millennium (as diverse as climate change, the escalation in displacement of asylum seekers, meeting the perceived threat of global terrorism and nuclear proliferation). Thus, the limited space here is dedicated to presenting a

1 M. Koskenniemi, 'The Fate of Public International Law: Between Technique and Politics' (2007) 70 *The Modern Law Review*.

2 H. Lauterpacht, *The Function of Law in the International Community* (Oxford: Clarendon Press, 1933).

distilled version of the longer argument made in my thesis and to give an insight into the scope and nature of the accountability debate occurring worldwide.

The focus on *jus cogens* is arguably a narrower consideration of the broader question of accountability for human rights breaches, given the strong association between them. The election to focus on *jus cogens* was owing to the legal language that surrounds the concept, which is an appropriate foil to the highly theoretical nature of accountability discussed here. It is submitted that the strongest link between conceptual state accountability and established international law, and the primary indicator that there may be an evolution of the concept to *lex lata*, is that *jus cogens* have been widely recognised by states as norms that are non-derogable. Thus, and adopting Koskenniemi's view that law can be used to make sense of reality,[3] *jus cogens* is applied here as a tool to make sense – to identify and analyse – any practice of state accountability. An analogy that further illustrates the rationale for this argument can be drawn from the point by Malcolm Evans, who examined my thesis, that 'the language of state responsibility has been used ... quite deliberately to broaden the scope of substantive legal obligations'.[4] Here the question is whether the language of state accountability can be used to broaden the scope of substantive legal *jus cogens* related obligations.

There are three things that the research presented here will not do. This book does not seek to provide a magic solution where established commentators have failed, or traverse ground that has already been covered in the many previous studies of how states are made to answer for breaching public international law; in particular, this book is not advocating that criminal state responsibility, collective security or international intervention are the sole means by which states can be held accountable. Furthermore, this work is not intended to provide commentary on instances when states have breached international law or the reasons why. This book is not concerned with the interpretation or implementation of accountability by states in the domestic sense. And, finally, no new normative conception of *jus cogens* will be attempted. Rather, the working definition of *jus cogens* that is adopted here will be based on an analysis of the current consensus (if found to exist) and discussion on the topic.

What this book does intend to do is to define what accountability means in relation to states and in the context of public international law, using the language of *jus cogens* norms that represent the fundamental interests of the international community – and therefore more likely to inspire calls for accountability when breached – as a vehicle for this discussion. State practice and the feasibility of accountability as a legal norm are analysed in order to draw a conclusion as to the current status of state accountability. The extent to which the conclusion reached here is subsequently borne out in international relations will then require future and further research.

3 M. Koskenniemi, *From Apology to Utopia – The Structure of International Legal Argument* (Cambridge: Cambridge University Press, 2005).

4 M. Evans, 'State Responsibility and the ECHR' in M. Fitzmaurice, *Issues of State Responsibility before International Judicial Institutions* (Oregon: Hart Publishing, 2004) 139, 149.

Introduction

An introduction to the notion of state accountability as a novel academic concept has been constructed by the author as a vehicle to argue that an emerging 21st century epoch of accountability has influenced, and is continuing to influence the evolution of a norm of state accountability, in particular where the breach in question threatened the fundamental interests of the international community as a whole. In addition, the methodology that draws upon the Foucauldian tradition is explicated.

There is little doubt that public international law has undergone radical change in the past century, but one development that has yet to crystallise – at least as a legal principle – is state accountability. However, the modern recognition by states that certain norms are so fundamental that they are non-derogable (often called *jus cogens* norms) proves that more than just state interests influence both the development and implementation of contemporary public international law. The argument presented here is that if state accountability is understood as a sometimes legal and – probably in part – political or even moral response, which recognises that the institutions that comprise and legitimise the state were instrumental in the particular breach, then a typology of accountability can in fact be identified in state practice. In turn, it will be suggested that there is evidence that state accountability, as it is conceptualised here, is evolving into a legal principle.

Viewing accountability as more than a strictly legal concept, while arguing its evolution towards possessing normative legal status is not as controversial as may first appear. Bernard Röling, a prominent Dutch jurist and member of the International Military Tribunal for the Far East, expressed the view 'that the link between international law and politics is much closer than in national relations' and that the task of international lawyers, which he believed focused upon issues of *lex feranda,* was to employ a 'multi-disciplinary approach' in order to determine the 'adaptation and regulation needed'.[5] The International Court of Justice (ICJ) likewise recognised that a legal principle of public international law will crystallise

5 B. Röling and A. Cassese, *The Tokyo Trial and Beyond: Reflections of a Peacemonger* (Cambridge: Polity Press, 1994).

'even though the basic elements thus recognised need a consequential apparatus of rules dealing with related problems'[6] – inevitably legal principles start life as political constructs. The question here is whether a concept of state accountability has, or is in the process of, evolving as *lex feranda* and whether there is any evidence in international jurisprudence and/or practice that a norm of state accountability may one day be identified as *lex lata*?

This book seeks to build on the myriad of previous studies in which state accountability is articulated in a variety of conceptual and theoretical forms and presumes, based on prior research, that any inquiry into state accountability as *lex lata* would not withstand rigorous textual legal analysis. The methodological approach taken is therefore to eschew conventional approaches to the study of public international law and instead borrow from Foucauldian theory. An interpretive framework will be constructed in order that accountability can be conceptualised as a legal, political and even moral construct – thus, the term state accountability is employed as a normative conception rather than a unitary definition. Adopting an interpretive framework for the analysis also allows a broader range of state practice and indicators of juridical support (rather than established legal principles) to be taken into account. Furthermore, the political and moral context can be referred to in assessing the momentum toward state accountability crystallising as a principle of public international law, although such factors will be analysed through a legalist lens; thus, a quasi-legal methodology is being used. Support for mixing legal and non-legal methodologies is controversial in the conventional study of public international law. For example, in Kelsen's pure theory of law 'to comprehend something legally can only be to comprehend it as law' and 'mental processes, physical events' or other non-legal factors that may help 'cognize [legal] norms' are irrelevant.[7] However, a pure theory of law is concerned with how public international law is created while this work is concerned with its identification and evolution so that issues with employing *Methodensynkretismus* are justifiably set aside. Instead, this book is an academic inquiry into current state practice and juridical thinking relating to the question of how states are made to answer for breaching public international law. This inquiry seeks to identify a typology of accountability particular to states and to consider the possible evolution of state accountability as a normative response to the breach of *jus cogens* norms.

1 The interpretive framework

Some words are needed on the rationale in adopting an interpretive framework, which draws on critical theory and especially the work of French philosopher

6 *North Sea Continental Cases (Federal Republic of Germany v Denmark; Federal Republic of Germany v Netherlands)* (Merits 1969) ICJ Reports (1967) paras 61–64 as interpreted by I. Brownlie, 'General Course on Public International Law' (1995) *Hague Recueil* 9, 47.

7 H. Kelsen (translated by B. Paulson and S. Paulson), *Introduction to the Problems of Legal Theory* (USA: Clarendon Books, 1992) discussing H. Kelsen (trans M. Knight) *Pure Theory of Law* (New Jersey: The Law Book Exchange Ltd, 2002) 11.

Michel Foucault, who is best known for challenging the nature of knowledge and his analysis of the knowledge/power nexus in the context of government and the self.[8] Foucault is widely associated with Jürgen Habermas and the Frankfurt School of theory that argued the analysis of practice should not be undertaken to the exclusion of theory. Combining 'textualism with universalism' provides a greater range of analytical tools better to equip the investigator when faced with chaos.[9] Thus, in the study of international law, which has likewise been described as 'chaos',[10] factors that influence the implementation and evolution of the law (universalism) are equally as important as analysing the precise doctrines of law (textualism). It may seem ironic to develop a methodology for studying the normative evolution of international law by referring to Foucault, who argued that legal doctrine is just one factor at work in constructing normative frameworks, but it is precisely because Foucault was instrumental in illustrating that methodologies were not bound to the lens of legal formalism that the interpretive framework model is ideal. Foucault championed the interpretive framework in his thesis on the decentralised spread of power, where he argued that strength was equated with knowledge so that power is neither institutionalised nor constitutionalised.[11] The study of international law inevitably focuses on states, but Foucault was of the opinion that the state should not be seen as central to such analysis. Instead, the state should be viewed as 'part of a matrix of power assertions that allows for the incorporation of a variety of actors and their contributions to the development of international law'.[12]

A Foucauldian approach is ideal because firstly, the state is viewed as only one influential force in the evolution of public international law. Secondly, the state is recognised as various manifestations of power rather than an autonomous actor, thus, the discussion of state accountability extends in application to all the various manifestations of power that comprise the state – in contrast to other works that treat the state as a unitary legal entity. Thirdly, the inconsistencies in terms of how accountability is implemented in practice do not displace the hypothesis that a concept of state accountability may be evolving in terms of *lex feranda*. On the contrary, discrepancies between theory and practice give a more accurate picture of the typology of state accountability – each case study is treated *sui generis* and the similarities and differences between them allow a picture to be drawn showing how the concept is evolving. Finally, developments in international law, including the recognition of *jus cogens* norms and other social, political and cultural

8 T. McCarthy, 'The Critique of Impure Reason: Foucault and the Frankfurt School' at 243 in M. Kelly (ed) *Critique and Power: Recasting the Foucault/Habermas Debate* (Cambridge: MIT Press, 2004).

9 *Ibid*, 248.

10 J. Wouters, 'Perspectives for International Law in the Twenty-First Century: Chaos or a World Legal Order' (2000) *Ethical Perspectives* 1, 17.

11 M. Foucault, *Discipline and Punish: The Birth of the Prison* (New York: Vintage Books, 1995).

12 L. Hammer, *A Foucauldian Approach to International Law: Descriptive Thoughts for Normative Issues* (London: Ashgate, 2007) 16, 18. A similar interpretation of Foucault's work is given in L. Amoore and P. Langley, 'Global Civil Society and Global Governmentality' in R. Germain and M. Kenny (eds), *The Idea of Global Civil Society: Politics and Ethics in a Globalizing Era* (UK: Routledge, 2005) 147.

factors influencing the practice of accountability, are able to be taken into account.

Legal formalism presumes that states construct, and are the primary subjects of, international law. It addresses established legal doctrine, rather than normative and policy concerns, and treats law as a discrete scientific discipline, rather than as part of an integrated discourse that includes politics and morals – thus a formalist methodology would be unsuitable here where the argument is being made that the typology of state accountability is not only legal, but also political and moral. There is certainly support for discounting a formalist approach and adopting a broader methodology in the study of international law. Koskenniemi, Hammer and Berman are just three highly respected academics who argue that the study of international law cannot be undertaken by doctrinal analysis alone and must draw on the practice or 'concreteness'[13] of the law, rather than its juridical expression. Berman notes 'the overall vision of the international community is not solely a unitary State choice regarding rational choice'[14] and that social policy and moral concerns are influential in the construction, implementation and evolution of international law. An investigative methodology was used by Alston in the context of human rights[15] and by Schwarzenberger in his studies on sovereignty. In Schwarzenberger's opinion, as long as a 'phenomenon remain[ed] amorphous, it may prove impossible or difficult to understand its character and implications. Once the various sides of the problem are separated, the phenomenon as a whole becomes easier to comprehend'.[16] Thus, and assuming there is a generalised understanding that states should be held accountable when they breach international law, it is rational for this book to conceptualise state accountability with regard to non-legal factors and then examine state practice to determine the concept's evolutionary (and normative) status. A Foucauldian methodology means that practice and theory are equally relevant and the indeterminacy of the substantive concept is dealt with, in Koskenniemi's words, through the language that is international law.[17]

2 The substantive concept

Holding states accountable for breaching international law is difficult, primarily because it relates to the complicated relationship between the power of states and the authority of international law. The state is seldom identified in terms of being liable for its own acts and omissions. Instead, the liability of states is usually derived from the acts and omissions of its various organs and from forms of collective liability,

13 M. Koskenniemi, 'The Politics of International Law' (1990) 1 *European Journal of International Law* 4.

14 P. Berman, 'Seeing Beyond the Limits of International Law' (2006) 84 *Texas Law Review* 1265.

15 For example see the approach of P. Alston in P. Alston (ed), *Human Rights Law* (Aldershot: Dartmouth, 1996).

16 G. Schwarzenberger, 'The Forms of Sovereignty' (1957) 10 *Current Legal Problems* 264.

17 M. Koskenniemi, *From Apology to Utopia* (Cambridge: CUP, 2006) 568.

such as criminal organisation theory developed at the Nuremberg Trials and the state responsibility doctrine (that aggregates breaches by individuals to attribute to the state). However, certain developments in international law mean that accountability in the comprehensive rather than representative sense (ie the accountability of states for their separate acts and omissions) is desirable. In particular, there is said to be a body of *jus cogens* norms that are recognised as being in the interests of the international community as a whole[18] and not merely those of states. Thus, the international community as a whole has a direct interest in accountability when *jus cogens* norms are breached. Furthermore, a breach of *jus cogens* norms is often associated with large-scale human rights breaches and atrocities, given that the most widely accepted peremptory norms are the prohibition on genocide, aggression and crimes against humanity so that not only is there an arguable legal duty to account for the breach but there is also a moral imperative. On the basis that the traditional approaches to ensuring states are made to answer for breaching international law serve discrete functions (such as reparation for the breach of obligations owed between states) and do not necessarily satisfy the interest held by the wider international community as a whole or respond to moral imperatives, then the question of how to hold states accountable remains unanswered.

From the outset it is acknowledged that any argument that a concept of state accountability has crystallised into an established legal principle, as a parallel development to the recognition of *jus cogens*, is weak – so instead the focus here is on illustrating that there is legal space into which such a norm has started to evolve. The legal space referred to does not require the creation of new rules or the relinquishing of established doctrines in public international law – it is simply a readjustment of already existing principles to ensure that states are held accountable for breaching *jus cogens* norms. The first step in identifying whether such a legal space exists is to conceptualise state accountability for the purposes of the subsequent analysis.

Chapter 1 examines the term 'accountability' from the perspective of determining whether the term is legal, political, moral or a combination; whether there is any relationship to responsibility or other synonyms for answerability; whether accountability would prevent impunity and how accountability is more broadly conceived in international relations – indeed the focus here is on accountability in the context of international law and relations rather than domestically. The objective in understanding what accountability means in this context is to determine why state accountability is different to other forms of accountability in terms of

18 The term 'international community' is used to represent not only states but all legal persons recognised as having rights and obligations under international law, even if those persons are not direct participants in creating international law. The term 'international community' originates in German legal language that brought the concept of universalism to international law through theorists such as Lauterpacht and Oppenheim and that view the world as a international community both in a descriptive and a legal sense. See A. Paulus, *Die internationale Gemeinschaft im Völkerrecht* (Munich: Beck, 2000). In contrast, Tomuschat is one example of a theorist who considers that the term is not instructive (C. Tomuschat, 'Die internationale Gemeinschaft' (1995) 33 *Archiv des Völkerrechts* 1, 4).

both the party being held accountable (ie why does the state need to be held accountable in a separate capacity rather than simply conflating accountability between the state and its various manifestations and organs) and the nature of the accountability (for example, why does domestic law not seek to hold states accountable in the same way it holds individuals accountable). It is similarly important to unravel the structural, legal and institutional layers that comprise the nation 'state' in order to identify exactly what entity is being made to answer – separate from those individuals or organs that are independently made to answer for their respective role in the breach. It is important that the state is viewed as more than just its government in the context of this argument, as otherwise there is little utility in arguing that the state's accountability is a separate consideration. Conceptualising state accountability requires more than, for example, the prosecution of individual government authorities. It is crucial that state accountability pierces the institutional layers surrounding the state – in order that the institutional infrastructure that allowed the breach to occur is then disabled.

Chapter 2 reunites the constituent elements to explore state accountability as a conceptual whole. Consideration is given to whether state accountability should be viewed as a discrete outcome to be measured against certain evaluative criteria; an entire process (the response to the breach, why the response was selected, by whom and for what purpose); or whether the analysis of state accountability is both as a process and an outcome. The focus will then turn to identify some evaluative criteria against which instances of state accountability, if they exist, can be identified in state practice. These criteria are identified by determining whether there are any common associations, in the context of international relations, in the sense of what is needed to make states answer for grievous breaches of international law. This analysis includes an inquiry into whether state accountability is associated with criminal accountability.

The main objective in Chapters 1 and 2 is to obtain as great a degree of specificity as possible in conceptualising state accountability. The interpretive framework that is established will provide a basis for analysing state practice and seeking evidence of juridical support, while the evaluative criteria permit tentative conclusions to be drawn about the future normative standing of state accountability. The purpose of Chapter 3 is then to explore the debate surrounding *jus cogens* to determine the status of these norms under international law and as a link between conceptual state accountability and established legal doctrine.

Jus cogens norms are pivotal to this discussion, because it will be argued that these norms are the link between conceptual state accountability and established public international law. It is from the perspective of how the international community should respond when *jus cogens* norms are breached that it becomes credible to argue that the theory, canvassed in Chapters 1 and 2, is juridically feasible and has practical state support.[19] It is not the intention to endorse one definition

19 The term 'juridical feasibility' was adopted from N. Jorgensen, *The Responsibility of States for International Crimes* (Oxford: OUP, 2003) and synonyms used in this work include 'legal viability'

of *jus cogens* above another or argue that a certain norm is or is not *jus cogens*, because the focus here is on accountability for the breach, rather than development of the law. However, without greater clarity as to what *jus cogens* norms are it cannot be argued that there are unique properties relating to *jus cogens* that are instrumental to, and indicative of, the evolution of a principle of state accountability. In addition, it may be assumed that if *jus cogens* norms are distinguished from standard norms of international law, then there is a definitional reason why this is so. Furthermore, if it is shown that there is a distinction without understanding why, it is impossible to determine if so-called *jus cogens* norms have been breached and accordingly whether there is any practice of states being held accountable for such breaches.

The second approach in determining whether state accountability is a legally viable concept is to compare it with the state responsibility doctrine, as a formal legal framework that already exists for the purposes of making states answer for breaching international law. To the extent that a parallel exists between state responsibility and conceptual state accountability then there is a stronger argument that the latter is *lex feranda*. The state responsibility doctrine, in its contemporary guise, embodies decades of interpretation by international and domestic courts, contemplation by jurists (notably its codification by the International Law Commission) and express and implied implementation in a range of legal contexts, from international human rights to trade law. Despite or perhaps because of this it will be argued that engaging a state's responsibility is not necessarily the same thing as holding a state accountable. In order to justify this argument, Chapter 4 considers the ways in which the responsibility doctrine overlaps with the accountability concept and what characteristics of the responsibility doctrine mean that accountability will not always be achieved, especially when the breach is of a *jus cogens* norm. Chapter 4 seeks to assess the normative standing of conceptual state accountability when international law already makes provision for responding when states breach international law. It determines what juridical indicators exist or have emerged in the context of the development and implementation of the state responsibility doctrine that support the argument that state accountability is viable under international law.

Chapter 5 then uses a series of representative case studies to assess whether there is an informal practice of state accountability, analysing the various responses when states breach international law against the evaluative criteria established in Chapter 2. The case studies seek to illustrate how the complexities in holding states accountable are (or are not) dealt with in practice, including what is an effective response, is accountability the prerogative of states or are non-state actors instrumental in the process and, finally, how is it determined that the breach has occurred in the first place. In order to determine that practice is indicative of

and 'juridical support'. All three expressions refer to evidence that public international law expressly acknowledges, permits by implication or is evolving in such a way as to accommodate the concept in question.

an evolving accountability norm, evidence is sought that both the response per se and the specific form of redress reflect the objective of holding the particular state accountable – and whether the choice of response was influenced by the fact the breach was of a *jus cogens* norm. It would be impossible to be comprehensive in the scope of this inquiry (although the potential for supplementary studies conducted on a variety of themes such as geographic or temporal location or studies of responses to a particular norm is phenomenal). Instead, the five studies prioritise depth of analysis and in addition seek, first, to offer both high profile and less well-known case studies. The 'high-profile' case studies include apartheid in South Africa, which is a breach of international law known at a global level. Case studies of 'less well-known' breaches, such as the forcible removal of indigenous children by the Australian Government, may be readily identifiable in the particular geographic or temporal context but tend to have a lower global profile. The second priority influencing the selection was to include case studies where the response to the breach would not typically be seen as seeking redress from the state. A typical response might be to use force against an aggressive state as when, for example, North Korea invaded South Korea in 1950, while an atypical response may be the threat to block Turkey's membership of the EU as an *ex post facto* response to the alleged Armenian massacre during the First World War. It is on the strength of analysing these case studies in the context of the interpretive framework developed in Chapters 1 and 2 that this book will be equipped to conclude whether state accountability, at this time, has reached the giddy heights of *lex lata*, is growing in credibility as evolving *lex feranda* or remains the fantasy of academic speculation.

1 Breaking state accountability down to its conceptual parts

Chapter 1 examines the term 'accountability' to determine that it is legal, political and moral in nature. It can be distinguished from responsibility and other synonyms for answerability and is not necessarily the opposite of impunity. Chapter 1 also unravels the structural, legal and institutional layers that comprise the nation 'state' and identifies the entity being made to answer – the state as more than merely its government, individual leaders or organs. The objective is to show that state accountability is different from other forms of accountability in terms of both the party being held accountable and the nature of the accountability.

1.1 'Accountability'

The question of how parties are made to answer for abusing their power is of contemporary relevance beyond the context of state accountability. Corporate accountability is topical in the context of the current financial recession, as seen with the Enron scandal in 2001, where allegations of accounting fraud led to the collapse of the professional services firm Arthur Andersen, which had been responsible for auditing the Enron Corporation. Environmental accountability continues to be a key agenda item in many domestic and global political forums, as seen with the compliance mechanism for the Kyoto Protocol, which is comprised of a Compliance Committee represented by 10 Member States, which determine the consequences when states fail to satisfy their responsibilities under the Protocol. Furthermore, an epoch in individual accountability dating from before the Nuremberg Trials has meant that national leaders are no longer able to hide behind political institutions, as seen with the 2009 expenses scandal requiring British MPs to resign or repay overpaid expenses claims. Likewise, heads of state increasingly find that they are unable to hide behind their respective national government amid public scandal, as with former US President Richard Nixon, who ultimately resigned his presidency or find that they cannot exercise immunity, as with former Presidents Milošević of Serbia and Charles Taylor of Liberia, who were both indicted before international courts. From just these few examples it can be seen that in practice accountability is not only legal but also political and moral, while the stakeholders in accountability appear similarly varied, rather than being restricted to just a few direct victims.

However, it is 'premature to speak of a revolution in favour of accountability'[20] under international law, given that the term 'accountability' is legally indeterminate. Without some agreement as to its meaning, accountability has the potential to traverse a number of related, but distinct, forms of answerability. For example, the establishment of the International Criminal Court (ICC) is certainly a development in terms of individual criminal accountability but this development has little relevance in arguing that there is an emerging norm of state accountability – unless accountability has the same meaning regardless of whether the object is an individual criminal or state. The study of accountability, both in relation to states and in the broader framework of international law, is topical because it feeds into the increasing cross-disciplinary emphasis on accountability. On the one hand, international law may be described in terms of having certain entrenched normative characteristics, such as state sovereignty; while, on the other hand, international law is dynamic and redefines itself as it interacts, influences and is influenced by disciplines, such as politics[21] – so that international law is both independent and co-dependent with respect to international relations. Thus, it is rational to anticipate that the way that accountability is conceived in the framework of international law could be both as a discrete concept and as a concept that draws on related disciplines. To the extent that accountability is understood in a cross-disciplinary sense, even though it applies in the context of international law, then the question is whether accountability is a constant objective, which applies when states breach international law, individuals contravene corporate governance rules or organisations infringe industry environmental standards. Accordingly, the approach here is to see what accountability means in a variety of contexts.

First, a linguistic interpretation will identify what accountability means from an etymological perspective, consider how influential cultural perspectives are and determine whether accountability is universally understood or if Western conceptions of answerability predominate. A comparison with responsibility will also be undertaken, given that the terms are used interchangeably in international law. In addition, the relationship between accountability and impunity will be explored. Specifically, it will be determined whether calls to end impunity for breaches of international law, such as those by the Commission on Human Rights as part of the Vienna Programme for Action in 2005, are the same as a call to hold all culpable parties accountable. Secondly, the way in which accountability is interpreted in the context of international relations generally and human rights, specifically, is examined. This context is specifically chosen because while human rights norms, as a corpus, are not recognised as *jus cogens*,[22] there is an inevitable

20 S. Ratner and J. Abrams, *Accountability for Human Rights Atrocities in International Law* (3rd edn Oxford: OUP, 2009) 16.

21 P. Weil, 'Le Droit International en Quête de Son Identité' (1992) 237 *Recueil des Cours de L'Académie de Droit International de La Hague*.

22 On this point see G. Christenson, 'Jus Cogens: Guarding Interests Fundamental to International Society' (1988) 28 *Virginia Journal of International Law* 585 and K. Parker and L. Neylon, 'Jus Cogens: Compelling the Law of Human Rights' (1989) 12 *Hastings International and Comparative Law Review* 411.

overlap given that human rights also relate to the interests of more than just states. To the extent that a wider stakeholding has influenced the way in which accountability is understood in the human rights context, then it can be anticipated that the nature of accountability for breaching *jus cogens* norms will have similar characteristics.

1.1.1 Linguistic interpretation

Lister notes that the word 'accountability' is not easily translated into many languages,[23] which links the etymology of accountability with the constructs and traditions of justice in Anglophone, usually Western, countries. Western associations with accountability emphasise 'individualistic values and the emotional state of guilt',[24] rather than collective fault that is seen for example in Asian and African cultures.[25] The potential for a clash of cultural perspectives relating to the source, substantive content and the application of international law is clearly apparent, yet so is the reality that cultural relativity permeates many aspects of international relations. For example, democratic governance and social order, which are also underpinned by the belief that parties with power must be publicly accountable for the exercise of that power, are key organisational mechanisms in not only Western society. The United Nations (UN), which adopts a representative framework and emphasises the promotion of democracy in its work (despite the word democracy never appearing in the UN Charter), prioritises collective, rather than unilateral, action when states breach public international law in a way that threatens peace and security. Given that the organisational structure of international relations is itself Western dominated, it therefore would not be inappropriate to adopt a Western construct of accountability.

This is not to say that cultural relativism is not pertinent to the study of accountability generally, or irrelevant in the study of accountability under international law specifically. An analogy is with the meaning of human rights that likewise differs widely amongst states,[26] but the scope of perspective does not mean that states are not committed to some form of universal human rights system as evident in the adoption of instruments such as the Universal Declaration on Human Rights. A Western interpretation of accountability (or indeed a non-Western interpretation if it was more compatible with the structure of international relations) simply provides a baseline for studying accountability, even if only to determine that in practice accountability is understood – and implemented – in a variety of fashions.

23 S. Lister, 'NGO Legitimacy: Technical Issue or Social Construct?' (2003) *Critique of Anthropology* 175, 175–92.

24 S. Velayutham, 'The Discharge of Accountability and Responsibility in Asian Societies: An Evaluation' (1999) 27 *Asian Profile* 361.

25 J. Cobbah, 'African Values and the Human Rights Debate: An African Perspective (1997) *Human Rights Quarterly* 323; Velayutham (n 24).

26 For a discussion on human rights and relativism see U. Baxi, *The Future of Human Rights* (New Delhi: OUP, 2002).

As is also the case with human rights, although there is no universal consensus as to what accountability specifically means in the context of international relations, there is affirmation of accountability at a broader, conceptual level. Western and non-Western states who are parties to the 1998 Rome Statute of the ICC, which is a commitment to holding individuals accountable for international crimes, are also parties to instruments such as the 1973 Convention on the Suppression and Punishment of the Crime of Apartheid, which criminalises racial discrimination that constitutes apartheid to imply that a suitable response is required when the Convention is breached. These Western and non-Western states are parties to establishing accountability processes in their own communities that meet with international standards, as for example with Cambodia and Sierra Leone that both established courts to deal with international crimes. If there is a generalised consensus among states that certain breaches of the law warrant consideration beyond the domestic framework, it seems rational to suppose that some form of consensus exists as to what accountability means in relation to those breaches.

The word accountability requires parties to account for their actions or, put another way, where a party is determined to be liable it must provide redress. This interpretation is not isolated to the context of legal accountability and can be seen more broadly in social and business frameworks. For example, Naqi defines accountability in the context of commercial enterprise as 'acts justifying one's actions or inaction to an audience that has reward or sanction authority and where rewards or sanctions are dependent on an audience's evaluation'.[27] Balint describes institutional accountability in terms of recognition of the role played by the institution followed by systemic reform of the institution – a formula that would seem to apply equally to corporations, governments and, it is argued here, to the state itself.[28] In terms of holding individuals criminally accountable, redress is generally linked to punishment after a judicial finding of guilt, and the party with the right and power to impose punishment is the state. The investigation of UN staff over allegations of abuse is just one example of how accountability was comprised of a determination of liability followed by punishment as a form of redress. Resolution 62/63 demanded due process in the investigations but once it was established that the abuse had occurred, the General Assembly considered that the individuals in question could not be 'exempt from the consequences of [their] criminal acts'.[29] Accountability required both a determination of liability and redress based on liability.

27 S. Naqi, 'The Process of Accountability' (2008) *International Business Management* 1, 2 and see also A. Ammeter et al, 'A Social Relationship Conceptualization of Trust and Accountability in Organizations' (2008) *Human Resource Management Review* 343; P. Tetlock, 'The Impact of Accountability on Judgment and Choice: Toward a Social Contingency Model' (1992) *Advanced Experimental Social Psychology* 331.

28 J. Balint, 'The Place of Addressing Internal Regime Conflicts' (1996) 59 *Law and Contemporary Problems* 103.

29 'Criminal Accountability of UN Officials and Experts on Mission' General Assembly Resolution 62/63 (2008).

Therefore, accountability can be described as a two-step process involving, in Keohane's words, both 'information and sanctions'.[30] Redress is not limited to punishment and may take many forms, as seen with the increasing number of transitional justice mechanisms that eschew forms of punishment in favour of providing some contextually appropriate form of justice.[31] Redress may include acts of retribution, sanctions to compel performance, apologies, explanations and other commemorative acts.[32] Furthermore, interpreting accountability as a two-step process is appropriate regardless of whether the perpetrator was an individual, state or other party. This approach accommodates Western and non-Western perspectives as to the form of redress required to hold the party accountable; the nature of accountability may be legal, political or moral; and this interpretation is applicable to business, social and international relations.

1.1.1.1 The difference between accountability and responsibility

The words accountability and responsibility are used interchangeably in international relations, although responsibility also has a separate meaning when referred to in the context of the state responsibility doctrine. A comparative assessment is required to determine whether the difference is not only semantic but also substantive and whether accountability is a broader (or narrower) category of answerability, which includes responsibility. Non-legal dictionaries, such as the Merriam-Webster, define accountability as 'an obligation or willingness to accept responsibility or to account for one's actions' and responsibility as 'being the cause or explanation; able to answer for one's conduct or obligations'.[33] Thus, accountability does not merely seek to identify the responsible party; accountability seeks to make the responsible party account for its actions. Accountability will 'ensure the discharge of responsibility',[34] while the reverse does not necessarily apply. Accountability is similarly defined in the Merriam-Webster legal dictionary as an 'oblig[ation] to accept responsibility',[35] implying that a determination of liability is not enough; the party in breach must accept that determination. Bassiouni is just one commentator to argue similarly that accountability is a much broader concept, defining it

30 R. Keohane, 'The Concept of Accountability in World Politics and the Use of Force' (2003) 24 *Michigan Journal of International Law* 1121, 1124.

31 The extent to which punishment does not necessarily equate to justice is apparent in a recent survey in Northern Uganda, which asked community participants what associations they had with justice. While only 1 per cent identified punishment, 18 per cent nominated reconciliation (P.N. Pham et al, 'Forgotten Voices: A Population Based Study on Attitudes About Peace and Justice in Northern Uganda' International Centre for Transitional Justice and the Human Rights Centre, University of California Berkeley (2005).

32 J. Borneman, 'Events of Closure, Rites of Repetition: Modes of Accountability' (2004) *Conference on Settling Accounts: Truth, Justice and Redress in Post-Conflict Societies* Harvard University.

33 *Merriam-Webster Collegiate Dictionary* (11th edn USA: Merriam Webster, 2003).

34 Note 24 above.

35 *Merriam-Webster's Dictionary of Law* (UK: The Book Service Ltd, 2000).

as an 'acknowledgment of responsibility',[36] while the use of the respective terms in the context of international relations confirms the definitional and semantic distinction noted.

The state responsibility doctrine is premised on the principle stated in the *Chorzów Factory* case that states have an obligation to make reparation for the breach of a specific engagement, and reparation is only granted to the extent necessary to rescind the breach, without an additional punitive element being factored in. The distinction between responsibility and accountability, which is broader in scope, can therefore be illustrated by referring to the jurisdiction of the ICJ that is limited to matters of state responsibility. For example, in 2007, the ICJ entered judgment in the *Application of the Convention on the Prevention and Punishment of the Crime of Genocide*[37] (the *Genocide Convention* case), which concerned Serbia's responsibility for alleged breaches of obligations owed under the 1948 Genocide Convention. Serbia was found responsible for breaching Articles 4 and 5 of the Convention, but this finding was not the same as holding Serbia accountable. It is somewhat trite to say that Serbia was not held accountable, given that the ICJ can only exercise its jurisdiction in relation to alleged breaches of legal obligations owed between states, rather than order redress for breaching international law per se. The Court itself implicitly highlighted that the state responsibility doctrine may leave a gap in answerability, when it noted that other sources of international protection are contemplated within the Genocide Convention while recognising that these forms of protection currently arise at a 'political level rather than as a matter of legal responsibility'.[38] There is nothing to indicate that the Court was expressly referring to a gap in legal accountability; however, this statement illustrates that the responses to a breach of international law are viewed by the Court as broader than just a finding of legal responsibility.

1.1.1.2 The relationship between accountability and impunity

Although linguistically the origins of accountability arise within Western constructs, the word is often associated with the regulation of power and accountability is widely viewed as part of a broader category of answerability whereby something more is required in addition to determining that a party caused or was liable for the breach. The idea that 'something more' is required for accountability than mere recognition of responsibility needs, and is afforded, further discussion throughout. The first method of discovering the unknown quality that distinguishes accountability is to ask whether it has an opposite – namely, impunity. The prevention of impunity is linked to accountability, for example in the preamble to various resolutions the UN General Assembly 'stress[es] the need to

36 C. Bassiouni, 'Searching for Peace and Achieving Justice: The Need for Accountability' (1996) 59 *Law and Contemporary Problems* 9, 19.

37 *Application of the Convention on the Prevention and Punishment of the Crime of Genocide (Bosnia and Herzegovina v Yugoslavia (Serbia and Montenegro))* (Judgment 2007) ICJ Reports (1993).

38 Ibid, para 159.

ensure accountability for all violations of international humanitarian law and international human rights law in order to prevent impunity',[39] but without understanding what is meant by impunity it cannot be determined, first, that the only means by which to prevent impunity is to ensure accountability; secondly, whether there are additional means by which to prevent impunity; or, thirdly, whether impunity will always mean a failure to hold the liable party accountable.

Calls to end the impunity of individuals have certainly influenced the development of international criminal law, which seeks to hold individuals criminally accountable. The preamble of the Rome Statute, for example, noted the intent of state parties to end 'impunity for the perpetrators of crimes', the Statutes for the International Criminal Tribunal for the Former Yugoslavia and the International Criminal Tribunal for Rwanda likewise declared an end to impunity and the objective was omnipresent during the negotiations preceding establishment of both tribunals and subsequently reaffirmed in their respective jurisprudence.[40] Whether the desire to end impunity is as influential in terms of a normative evolution of state accountability, as it is with individual accountability, is not as clear-cut. The 1993 'Principles for the Protection and Promotion of Human Rights Through Action to Combat Impunity', adopted under Resolution 2003/72 by the Commission on Human Rights, is a useful reference because the document was part of a wider discussion seeking an end to the abuse of power by states, in this case, human rights abuses. Although non-binding, the Principles were drafted as part of the Vienna Programme for Action, which was in turn the outcome of the World Conference on Human Rights that involved participants from over 171 countries and 8000 NGOs, and can therefore be seen as representative of the opinion of the broader international community. The Principles defined impunity as the failure to provide 'appropriate penalties', which were described in the First Principle as 'effective remedies' for the party that was affected by the breach in question. Thus, there is a link to accountability, as the prevention of impunity required redress, as well as a determination of liability. A second association arises because the Principles envisaged that redress would be determined contextually rather than according to an inflexible doctrinal precedent. The wording of Special Rapporteur Louis Joinet in his 1996 report on the 'Question of the Impunity of Perpetrators of Human Rights Violations', which preceded the Principles, confirms this interpretation as 'appropriate penalties' were defined to include reparations, disarming paramilitary groups and 'measures repealing emergency provisions, legislative or otherwise, which are conducive to violations'.[41] The extent to which any of these measures are penal in nature, or amount to a strictly legal sanction,

39 For example see Resolution 64/10 (2010).

40 For example see the 'Annual Report of the International Tribunal for the Prosecution of Persons Responsible for Serious Violations of International Humanitarian Law Committed in the Territory of the Former Yugoslavia Since 1991' UN Doc E/95/III/P/2 (1994) and *Prosecutor v Kambanda* (Sentence) IT-97-28-S (1998) para 28.

41 Principles 34, 36 and 37 'Question of the Impunity of Perpetrators of Human Rights Violations (Civil And Political) Revised Final Report Prepared by Mr Joinet Pursuant to Sub-Commission Decision 1996/119' UN Doc E/CN.4/Sub.2/1997/20/Rev.1 (1997).

is arguable and instead we see that the particular circumstances of the breach were considered to be relevant in determining the nature of the redress.

The view that preventing impunity is less about punishing the violator as it is about ensuring there is an appropriate response to the breach was likewise adopted by the Economic and Social Council in its 2004 'Report on the Protection and Promotion of Human Rights: Impunity',[42] while some commentators can only be described as vehement in their claims that there is a link between accountability and the prevention of impunity. Bassiouni considered accountability as the 'antithesis of impunity'[43] and Cohen stated that impunity 'was conceived as the opposite' to accountability.[44] Similar parallels between accountability and impunity also arise in the context of international relations. Scholars cite the 1915 Armenian massacres as an example of state impunity[45] because even though, for example, 10 out of 26 NATO states have labelled the violence as genocide[46] (a quasi determination of liability), there has never been any form of redress and the Turkish Government has never officially acknowledged that the massacres in 1915 were genocide.

More recently, the ongoing humanitarian crisis in Zimbabwe was described by the World Health Organisation and the UN Office for the Coordination of Humanitarian Affairs in terms of impunity, owing to the lack of effective response following the failure of the Government of Zimbabwe to respect 'civil, cultural, economic, political and social rights',[47] in particular by breaching Articles 11 and 12 of the International Covenant of Economic, Social and Cultural Rights 1966 and Article 25 of the Universal Declaration of Human Rights.[48] UN Special Rapporteur on the Right to Health, Anand Grover, the Special Rapporteur on the Right to Food, Olivier de Schutter and the Special Rapporteur on the Situation of Human Rights Defenders, Margaret Sekkagya collectively brought to the attention of UN Members the closure of public hospitals, the failure to provide infrastructure for the distribution of health care, the lack of clean water supply, hyperinflation that meant people did not have money to buy food, the unjustified use of force and civil rights abuses.[49] In terms of a response to the atrocities, South Africa blocked a resolution condemning Zimbabwe that was introduced before

42 'Report on the Protection and Promotion of Human Rights: Impunity' (Special Rapporteur Diane Orentlicher) UN Doc E/CN.4/2004/88 (2004).

43 Note 36 above, 19.

44 S. Cohen, 'State Crimes of Previous Regimes' (1995) 20 *Law and Social Inquiry* 6, 28.

45 T. Akcan, 'A Shameful Act: The Armenian Genocide and Turkish Responsibility' (Metropolitan Books: 2006); Balint (n 28) 118; M. Kielsgard, 'Restorative Justice for the Armenians, Resolved: It's The Least We Can Do' (2008) *Connecticut Journal of International Law* 1.

46 Belgium, Canada, France, Germany, Greece, Italy, Lithuania, the Netherlands, Poland and Slovakia: The Armenian Genocide Museum (2009) available at http://www.genocide-museum.am/eng/states.php.

47 'UN Experts Call for Rebuilding Zimbabwe's Health/Food Systems' (2008) available at http://www.un.org/apps/news/story.asp?NewsID=29385&Cr=zimbabwe&Cr1=.

48 World Health Organisation and the UN Office for the Coordination of Humanitarian Affairs (2009) available at http://www.rinnews.org/Report.aspx?ReportId=82370.

49 Note 47 above.

the Security Council,[50] sanctions imposed by the USA and the European Union (EU) were directed at the Mugabe Government rather than Zimbabwe per se;[51] and sporting sanctions imposed by states such as Australia affected only the relevant individual citizens.[52] Simplistically, the lack of redress directly from Zimbabwe would suggest the state escaped with impunity. Yet, without a clearer understanding of who or what Zimbabwe is in this context, for accountability/impunity purposes, it is difficult to determine whether or not redress was in fact sought from the state. Indeed, it may be more accurate to comment that the reason Zimbabwe was not perceived to have been held accountable was due to misunderstanding in identifying the State of Zimbabwe as the liable party – rather than claiming that Zimbabwe escaped with impunity owing to the lack of effective penalties available. Sanctions were certainly imposed against individual government ministers and individuals in positions of authority. By 2009, the targets included Robert Mugabe, as head of state, and his associates,[53] including Al Shanfari with 'ties to the Government and implicated in activities that seriously undermine democracy, respect for human rights and the rule of law', the present and former Police Commissioners and the Minister for Industry and International Trade. The fact that these individuals collectively embodied the power and authority of the culpable regime makes it problematic to argue that accountability was not being sought from the state when sanctions were imposed on those individuals.

If appropriate redress is available, in terms of seeking accountability, but cannot be imposed because the state cannot be distinguished from its organs, then it is argued here that the outcome is not one of impunity – it is a gap in accountability. Clearly, the conceptual difficulty in deciding where the liability of the state's agents ends and the liability of the state begins must be dealt with in order to seek accountability; however, this issue should not be misconstrued as leading to a risk of impunity. Thus, it cannot be said, in absolute terms, that ensuring accountability would eradicate impunity or vice versa – for example, accountability (or even partial accountability) may be achieved through amalgamating the impact of a number of responses, but accountability in such cases would not be the same thing as preventing impunity. A second illustration of the distinction between accountability and impunity is that the means for achieving accountability may be political or quasi-legal while impunity is prevented through the imposition of legal penalties; thus, there can simultaneously be political accountability and legal impunity. It appears more appropriate to describe the relationship between accountability

50 'South African Opposition Blocks UN Condemnation of Mugabe' Associated Foreign Press (2009) available at http://www.france24.com/en/20081216-un-plan-condemnation-mugabe-fails-because-south-african-opposition-zimbabwe.

51 'Commission Regulation of 26 January 2009 Amending Council Regulation (EC) 314/2004 Concerning Certain Restrictive Measures in Respect of Zimbabwe' EC Doc 77/2009 (2009) and see also 'Obama Renews Zimbabwe Sanctions' (2009) available at http://www.news.bbc.co.uk/1/hi/world/africa/7925240.stm.

52 J. Farrall, *United Nations Sanctions and the Rule of Law* (Cambridge: CUP, 2007).

53 Note 51 above.

and impunity in cautious, rather than uncategoric, terms. As such, there is little that can be taken from this discussion in terms of furthering our understanding as to why and how accountability is a distinct and unique form of answerability.

1.1.2 A trend toward bottom-up accountability?

Historically, any response to a breach of international law (in terms of legal accountability) has been made by states and from what Brown Weiss describes as the 'top down',[54] whether horizontally between states, or vertically when imposed by states. Pursuant to the top down framework that has dominated international relations, states have had both the political and legal power to impose legal accountability – either vertically (states regulate the power of non-state actors through domestic law) or horizontally (states regulate the exercise of power by other states, albeit only to the extent that the exercise of one state's power negatively impacts on the exercise of another state's sovereignty). However, developments in international law, notably for these purposes the increasing recognition of *jus cogens* norms and *erga omnes* obligations, have encouraged a shift away from a top down imposition of legal accountability. Because of the broader interest in accountability that is implicit to these concepts, there has had to be a reconsideration of what accountability mechanisms can best meet the interests of an expanded pool of stakeholders. Thus, Brown Weiss argued that in the context of international relations accountability is increasingly sought from the 'bottom up',[55] as can be seen at the European Court of Human Rights (ECtHR) where individuals have the right to bring claims against a state and the Court has the jurisdiction to deliver a judgment against that state accordingly. The limited practical effect of a judgment from the Court, owing to difficulties in enforcement, requires the caveat to be added that a principal characteristic of bottom up accountability must be that it is not only legal but also political and moral in nature – depending as it will on the adverse publicity and criticism of the state in terms of redress.

Brown Weiss describes state accountability as arising from the bottom up when 'individuals, NGOs and private entities are able to hold states accountable for their actions', which she links to a global trend seeking 'to hold leaders accountable' as well as developments in trade and corporate responsibility, such as the International Centre for Settlement of Investment Disputes that permits foreign investors (working with the international organisation) to bring a claim against a host state indirectly.[56] The principal difference between top down and bottom up accountability is that the relationship between the party seeking accountability and the party being held accountable is no longer described in terms of actual power – which had previously meant that states were able to hold individuals accountable but not vice versa. Instead, bottom up accountability views the maintenance of the law as being

54 E. Brown Weiss, 'Bottom Up Accountability' (2007) 37 *Environmental Policy and Law* 259.
55 Ibid.
56 Ibid.

so crucial that the capability to seek accountability is extended beyond the most powerful parties – there is de facto power for accountability purposes. The stakeholder/s in accountability include all those parties protected by and subject to the relevant regulation/law/rule – whether shareholders in a company, voters in a constituency or the international community as a whole – so that in theory accountability is just as likely to come from the bottom up as it is from the top down.

Practice may show that Brown Weiss is correct given that there are an increasing array of forums in which accountability can be sought from the bottom up, even though there are a number of issues associated with bottom up accountability that may be seen to frustrate rather than facilitate the evolution of a state accountability norm. For example, the greater the number of parties with an interest in accountability, the more burdensome the task in achieving accountability could be, largely due to the greater number of views that need to be taken into consideration. If, as discussed earlier, accountability is relational, then a variety of perspectives must be brought to bear on what constitutes an appropriate response, identifying the state and determining the specific breach – making it difficult to resolve these questions to the satisfaction of all parties. The problems in trying to accommodate a number of stakeholder perspectives in the process of seeking legal accountability is also apparent with regard to the emergence of forums, such as the Inter-American Court of Human Rights, that permit individuals to seek redress from states where the practical reality is that the sheer volume of applications means that progress is limited. As of 2007, the ECtHR was faced with more than 20,000 cases pending against Russia alone,[57] illustrating that even where a specific forum exists prima facie to facilitate legal accountability, there is no guarantee that this will occur.

A further issue in terms of relying on a broader range of accountability forums is illustrated in the context of Germany's claim against Italy before the ICJ in 2008.[58] Germany sought declarations that Italy had violated its sovereign immunity by allowing individuals to seek compensation from Germany for loss incurred during the First World War. On the basis that the Entente powers had already sought redress from Germany for those acts and omissions pursuant to the 1919 Treaty of Versailles then there would appear to be a doubling up of accountability. This raises the question of whether a trend toward bottom up accountability in international relations suggests that states are not only to be held accountable for the specific breach, but could potentially be held accountable multiple times, because accountability is owed to every party with a stake in the relevant law. Furthermore, if accountability is to be sought in a variety of forums is preference to be given to legal accountability (which is what an award of compensation would

57 C. Tomuschat, 'The European Court of Human Rights Overwhelmed by Applications: Problems and Possible Solutions' in R. Wolfrum and U. Deutsch, (eds) *The European Court of Human Rights Overwhelmed by Applications: The Problems and Possible Solutions'* (Berlin: Springer-Verlag, 2009) 1, 10.

58 *Jurisdictional Immunities of the State (Germany v Italy)* (Application of the Federal Republic of Germany) ICJ Reports (2008).

be) as opposed to a mix of legal, political and moral accountability (which was imposed by the Entente powers)? While there might be a trend toward bottom up accountability throughout international relations, it is apparent that the exact implications in terms of holding states accountable for breaching international law need further consideration.

1.1.3 Interpreting accountability in the context of human rights

In considering the interpretation and implementation of accountability in the specific field of human rights, evidence is sought as to whether accountability is sought from the bottom up when it is more than just state interests that are at stake. In addition, is accountability within the human rights context solely viewed as legal in nature or can accountability be a mix of political and legal responses? A large number of international conventions and treaties deal with human rights both as a body of rights, such as the Universal Declaration on Human Rights, and individually, such as the UN Convention on the Rights of the Child. Cumulatively, these instruments provide a comprehensive human rights code, yet there is no equivalent universal code that determines how parties that breach human rights are to be held accountable. Like accountability, 'human rights' is an indeterminate term that is subject to cultural and disciplinary relativity, to name just two interpretive lenses that may be influential. Despite issues of relativity, which are set aside for the purposes of this discussion, the majority of states have recognised that certain human rights are so fundamental that a breach is deemed to be criminal, and accountability for that breach is dealt with under international criminal law; for example, the Rome Statute of the ICC recognises breaches of human rights prohibiting torture, genocide and the arbitrary deprivation of life as crimes. Individual accountability for human rights violations is sought in accordance with the same two-step process that has underpinned the discussion thus far (a determination of liability being the judgment of a criminal court and commensurate redress that typically is imprisonment), while the status of the norm clearly influences the manner in which liability is sought and the nature of redress. The historic development of international criminal law likewise confirms that human rights accountability (albeit of individuals) is norm specific. The principle of universal jurisdiction (whereby the 'universal character' of certain norms, for example the prohibition on genocide, requires universal cooperation to punish perpetrators[59]) and the obligation on states to extradite or prosecute are both means to ensure that perpetrators of 'criminal' human rights breaches are held accountable. Furthermore, accountability for 'criminal' human rights breaches is so crucial that

59 *Advisory Opinion on Reservations to the Convention on the Prevention and Punishment of the Crime of Genocide* ICJ Reports (1951) para 23 and *Application of the Convention on the Prevention and Punishment of the Crime of Genocide (Bosnia and Herzegovina v Yugoslavia (Serbia and Montenegro))* (Preliminary Objections 1996) ICJ Reports (1993) para 31.

the failure to hold an individual accountable gives other states, and even non-state actors such as the ICC pursuant to the principle of complementarity captured in Article 17 of the Rome Statute, the right to assume this role.

A second development within the context of human rights illustrating that accountability is both a two-step process and viewed by states as a priority, is the proliferation of forums that seek human rights accountability – including the accountability of states. These bodies seek accountability in a variety of ways ranging from the legal, such as the European and Inter-American Human Rights Courts; to the quasi-legal, such as truth and reconciliation commissions including the National Commission on the Disappearance of Persons established in Argentina in 1983; and even the political, such as the Universal Periodic Review mechanism for reviewing the fulfilment by UN Member States of their human rights obligations as introduced by the Human Rights Council in 2008. The proliferation of a range of accountability forums illustrates that accountability is understood to be context specific, to require more than mere recognition of the breach and is not always legal in nature. The establishment of the Human Rights Council, which complements the work of human rights monitoring bodies such as the Committee on Economic, Social and Cultural Rights, is a prime example. The Universal Periodic Review mechanism and the establishment of the Human Rights Council in 2008 represent a new breed of human rights review and monitoring – the ethos of which is compatible with the way that accountability has been identified in this discussion. Human Rights Council Resolution 5/1 (2007) stated that the mandate of the Council is to review the 'normative and institutional framework, for the promotion and protection of human rights' in states – a process akin to investigation and determination of compliance. 'After exhausting all efforts to encourage, rather than compel, a State to cooperate with the universal periodic review mechanism' the Council reserves the right to 'address, as appropriate, cases of persistent non-cooperation' – or, in other words, to seek some form of redress.

The work of the Council illustrates how this mandate bears out in practice. Thus, for example, having expressed concern 'at the fact that perpetrators of past and ongoing serious violations of human rights and international humanitarian law in Darfur have not yet been held accountable', the Human Rights Council urged the Sudanese Government to 'thoroughly investigat[e] all allegations' (determination of liability) and then to seek 'justice' from 'the perpetrators of those violations' (redress).[60] In the broader context of how human rights were to be protected in countering terrorism, the Council stated that both 'a proper judicial review and reparation for the victims of violations of economic, social and cultural rights [wa]s crucial to ensure the accountability of States'.[61] In both cases accountability

60 'Group of Experts on the Situation of Human Rights in Darfur' Human Rights Council Resolution 6/35 (2007) para 4.

61 'Report of the Human Rights Council on the Promotion and Protection of Human Rights While Countering Terrorism' UN Doc A/HRC/12/22 (2008) para 50.

was equated with a determination of liability and redress; indeed, the Council has even referred to these two limbs as 'indicators' of accountability. The Council listed the 'number of investigations; number of prosecutions [and] number of convictions' as indicators that liability had been effectively determined, while 'findings of investigation committees made public' and the 'number of compensated and rehabilitated victims' were viewed as indicators of redress on the basis of liability.[62] A further point of overlap with the characteristics of accountability that has emerged in this discussion is that the Human Rights Council likewise viewed the mode of redress to be relational and context specific. Redress can be 'through legal or political means', provided that the steps taken are in accordance with 'applicable international law'.[63] Indeed, and provided that redress is within the bounds of what is legally permissible, human rights monitoring bodies tend to adopt both flexibility and pragmatism in terms of seeking accountability. For example, the Committee on the Elimination of Racial Discrimination recommended that the USA and Canada 'explore ways to hold transnational corporations registered in Canada accountable',[64] where there was a perceived risk that such companies could enjoy impunity for misdeeds. The Universal Peer Review (UPR) mechanism could also be viewed as a viable means of redress, given that states face political condemnation and criticism from their state peers when they are found not to have complied with their human rights obligations.

The reference to the work of the Human Rights Council and the development of the UPR not only confirm that accountability is a two-step process, relational and not solely legal in nature; it expands our understanding by linking accountability with transparency. It has already been noted that traditionally the top down approach to accountability in international relations excluded non-state actors and made it extremely difficult to penetrate the state's façade or require a sovereign entity to answer for its acts and omissions. UPR is the investigation of states by states, but the information under review is both the country's report and information compiled by the Office of the High Commissioner of Human Rights (OHCHR), including relevant decisions of human rights bodies and submissions by other stakeholders, such as indigenous peoples and non-governmental organisations. This process goes a long way to breaking down the structural layers that

62 'Report of the Special Rapporteur on the Situation of Human Rights in the Sudan: Addendum Status of Implementation of the "Compilation of Recommendations of the Experts Group to the Government of the Sudan for the Implementation of Human Rights Council Resolution 4/8" Pursuant to Human Rights Council Resolutions 6/34, 6/35, 7/16, and 9/17' UN Doc A/HRC/11/14/Add.1 (2009) para 53.

63 'Report of the Special Representative of the Secretary-General on the Issue of Human Rights and Transnational Corporations and Other Business Enterprises, John Ruggie: Addendum State Obligations to Provide Access to Remedy for Human Rights Abuses by Third Parties, Including Business: An Overview of International and Regional Provisions, Commentary and Decisions' UN Doc A/HRC/11/13/Add.1 (2009) para 54.

64 'Concluding Observations for Canada' UN Doc CERD/C/CAN/CO/18 (2007) para 17 and 'Concluding Observations for the United States' UN Doc CERD/C/USA/CO/6 (2007) para 30.

obfuscate the state and protect it from having to account for its actions to the wider international community. In Human Rights Council Resolution 7/11 on the 'Role of Good Governance in the Promotion and Protection of Human Rights', accountability and transparency were specifically listed as preconditions for good governance – on the basis that where accountability and transparency were the norm then the state's power structure could be regulated and improved if necessary. The link between accountability and transparency was also made by the Committee on Economic, Social and Cultural Rights in General Comment No 19 when it stated that the 'effective implementation of all human rights' relied on 'the principles of accountability *and* transparency'[65] – an association supported by the fact that the Human Rights Council referred to 'accountability and transparency' three times in its Eighth Session Report alone.[66] From the perspective of the Council and monitoring bodies such as the Committee on Economic, Social and Cultural Rights, accountability is more than merely responding to the breach; it requires an understanding of why the breach occurred, which in turn requires insight into the preconditions within a state that facilitated the breach. Ideally, a link between accountability and transparency means that the reasons for the breach are identified and applied to prevent future breaches; for example, a loophole in the law may be closed, a particular scenario may subsequently constitute a permissible derogation from the law or a massive overthrow and systemic rebuilding of the state is undertaken. Evans describes the work of bodies such as the Committee on Economic, Social and Cultural Rights as being not 'to hold states to account for wrongs' but to 'assist the State in the fine tuning of its internal apparatus, scrutinising compliance and indicating deviance'.[67] However, these two functions are not exclusive if accountability is considered more broadly than simply finding that a breach occurred. Investigating the specific state's practices and subsequently levelling criticism where the state was found to be lacking has the prerequisites of determining that a breach occurred and redress as a result – thus providing a form of political or even moral accountability.

Ratner and Abrams argued that the proliferation of forums that seek human rights accountability is evidence of a normative obligation to ensure accountability for human rights infringements.[68] Certainly, it can be said that there are references to accountability as a principle of international law in the human rights context, as with General Comment No 19 and Resolution 4/5, when the Human Rights Council listed accountability as a 'fundamental principle that underpin[s] the corpus of human rights'.[69] The issue, however, is whether mere reference to

65 'General Comment No 19: The Right to Social Security Under Article 9' UN Doc E/C.12/GC/19 (2008) para 70 (emphasis added).

66 'Report of Human Rights Council on the Eighth Session' UN Doc A/HRC/8/52 (2008).

67 M. Evans, 'State Responsibility and the ECHR' in M. Fitzmaurice, *Issues of State Responsibility before International Judicial Institutions* (Oregon: Hart Publishing, 2004) 139, 149.

68 Note 20 above.

69 Adopted without a vote: 'Globalization and its Impact on the Full Enjoyment of All Human Rights' Human Rights Council Resolution 4/5 (2007) 45.

accountability as a legal principle is sufficient to give the concept normative standing, or to establish a legal obligation to ensure accountability in the human rights context.

The way the question is approached here, where the discussion is centred on the human rights context, is to ask whether a legal obligation to seek accountability is a corollary to the right that victims of human rights breaches hold. This right is captured in Article 2(3) of the International Covenant on Civil and Political Rights (ICCPR), which provides that parties must 'ensure that any person whose rights or freedoms as herein recognised are violated shall have an effective remedy' and Article 8 of the Universal Declaration of Human Rights, which cites the active steps that states must take to ensure 'the right to an effective remedy', including the provision of 'competent national tribunals ... by the constitution or by law'. This question of a legal obligation to ensure accountability is not only relevant to the discussion of accountability in the human rights context but before the argument is subsequently widened; the focus here is on how the right to redress is interpreted within regional frameworks for the protection of human rights. In particular, the focus is on whether the elements required to satisfy this duty are the same as (or similar to) the two-step approach to accountability. If the right to redress requires more than a determination of liability and redress as a result, then it is pertinent to investigate whether that something extra is relevant to and expands on our understanding of accountability.

Article 1(1) of the American Convention on Human Rights requires states to 'respect' and 'ensure' the human rights contained therein and where states fail to do so then Article 25 provides for 'the right to simple and prompt recourse ... to a competent court or tribunal for protection against acts that violate fundamental rights'. The Inter-American Commission on Human Rights interpreted Article 25 to require an investigation of the breach within a judicial forum; fair trial protections and redress; and that the court or tribunal give its judgment with reference to the particulars of the breach, including how and why the breach occurred.[70] The right to redress was interpreted by the Inter-American Court of Human Rights in the 1988 *Velasquez Rodriguez* case, in which Honduras was alleged to be responsible both for breaching the relevant human rights per se and for failing to comply with its duty to 'ensure'[71] a right to redress. The victim disappeared between 1981 and 1984, at a time when individuals who were considered to hold views that were a threat to the state's security were being abducted. A complaint was lodged with the Inter-American Commission on Human Rights, after which the Honduras Government delayed for four years before reporting to the Commission that all officials were cleared of blame. The Commission then joined the application to two

70 The need for full reasoning was confirmed in a series of decisions by the Inter-American Court of Human Rights: *Godínez Cruz* Inter-American Court of Human Right (1989); *Fairen Garbi and Solis Corrales* Inter-American Court of Human Rights (1988); *Velasquez Rodriguez* Inter-American Court of Human Rights (1988).

71 *Velasquez Rodriguez* (n 70).

similar cases against Honduras and filed a successful claim before the Inter-American Court of Human Rights alleging a breach of the victim's human rights under the Convention. The Court held that Honduras had breached the victim's rights under Articles 4, 5 and 7 of the Convention and that the last was entitled to redress on the basis that 'the abduction together with the failure to investigate' was in violation of the state's legal obligations under Articles 1(1) and 4(1) of the Convention. The Court considered that Honduras should have taken 'all means of a legal, political, administrative and cultural nature' in order to 'prevent, investigate and punish any violation of the rights recognised by the Convention' – although a detailed list of all such measures was not possible 'since they vary with the law and the conditions of each State'.[72] The failure by Honduras to 'to provide effective judicial remedies to victims of human rights'[73] was held to be in breach of the state's legal obligations under the American Convention on Human Rights 'to take reasonable steps to prevent human rights violations and to use the means at its disposal to carry out a serious investigation of violations committed within its jurisdiction, to identify those responsible, to impose the appropriate punishment and to ensure the victim adequate compensation'.[74] Clearly, there is a parallel between the right to redress, as interpreted by the Inter-American Court in this case, and accountability, as conceptualised here, because there must be a determination of liability and, in addition, some form of response that reflects the actual breach. However, it is tenuous to stretch the similarities between redress and accountability any further in order to argue the existence of a legal duty to ensure accountability, especially given that it is unclear who the duty holder would be. For example, it would be absurd to claim that Honduras was under a legal obligation to hold itself accountable and simply unpractical to argue that states would ever recognise they were under a legal obligation to seek accountability (in the formal legal sense as with the right to redress) for every human rights breach.

In contrast to the American Convention on Human Rights, which expressly refers to both remedies and recourse to a court or tribunal, the European Convention on Human Rights does not. Article 13 simply provides that 'everyone whose rights and freedoms as set forth in this Convention are violated shall have an effective remedy'. This discrepancy between the Conventions was remedied in a series of decisions by the ECtHR finding that the right to an effective remedy was breached unless the state in question both investigated the abuse and provided compensation.[75] Thus, in the European framework, the right to redress is likewise associated with the requirement for information and sanctions that characterise accountability in the broader human rights context. Article 7 of the

72 Ibid, para 188.

73 Ibid (Preliminary Objections 1987), para 91.

74 Ibid, para 174.

75 *Aksoy v Turkey* European Court of Human Rights (1996); *Aydin v Turkey* European Court of Human Rights (1997); *Assenov v Bulgaria* European Court of Human Rights (1998); *Ilhan v Turkey* European Court of Human Rights (2000); *Keenan v UK* European Court of Human Rights (2001).

African Charter on Human and Peoples' Rights provides that 'every individual shall have the right to have his cause heard', which is a right to access the courts, rather than a right to redress or a remedy. Article 7 is narrower than the European Convention on Human Rights but the African Commission on Human and Peoples' Rights has also sought to expand the express wording of Article 7. In *Zimbabwe Human Rights NGO Forum v Zimbabwe*[76] the Commission interpreted the requirement in Article 1 to 'recognise the rights, duties and freedoms enshrined [therein] and to give effect to them', meaning that states would breach their obligations under the Charter by failing either to investigate or to provide redress for human rights abuses, including either punishment or compensation.

A brief overview of the right to redress in regional human rights instruments shows that both investigation and redress are required in answering for breaches of human rights, but there is no indication that the relevant regional instruments and courts have interpreted this right to amount to a legal obligation to ensure accountability. Indeed, there is not even consistency as to what an entitlement to redress means, as further seen with reference to Article 9 of the Arab Charter on Human Rights, which provides 'a guaranteed right to a legal remedy' (and only in relation to domestic laws), rather than redress. In terms of furthering our understanding of accountability, the recurring theme is that accountability is associated with information and sanctions (that are determined contextually) but in terms of being *lex lata*, the indeterminacy of accountability means that the concept has some way to go.

1.1.4 Is there a legal obligation to ensure accountability?

While it cannot be said that the right to redress gives rise to, and establishes the parameters of, a legal obligation to ensure accountability for human rights breaches, is it rational to consider whether there is a broader obligation to ensure accountability under public international law? An affirmative answer establishes a presumption that any response to the breach of international law is to a degree seeking accountability, while a negative answer suggests that in practice accountability may only be the unintended consequence of, for an extreme example, an act of retribution.

The first approach is to consider whether there is a legal duty on states to hold individuals accountable (that is not derived from the right to redress), which could then infer an obligation to ensure states are held accountable. There is certainly a lacuna in the treaty law and no express legal obligation on states to hold individuals accountable. Commentators such as Balint and Bassiouni, who were mentioned previously in terms of their respective works on accountability, argue that states are under a duty to prosecute individuals who commit international crimes

76 *Zimbabwe Human Rights NGO Forum v Zimbabwe* Communication No 245/2002 (2006) para 144.

(or permit extradition of those individuals for prosecution elsewhere),[77] but it is difficult to conclude that a duty to extradite or criminally prosecute individuals is the same as a legal obligation to ensure accountability. This is especially so given that criminal prosecution may not always be an appropriate response to the breach and can even be counter-productive: for example, in a fragile post-conflict state that depends on the continuation of its government (rather than prosecution of the leaders) in order to ensure stability, as with post-apartheid South Africa. In such situations accountability may take a completely different form, such as apologies or acts of remembrance and acknowledgement by the individuals in question, and arguably the beauty of international law (not to mention the Foucauldian approach to conceptualising state accountability here) is that it is dynamic enough to accommodate these contextual vagaries, rather than adopting a one size fits all response to breaches of the law. The argument that there is a duty to prosecute was made by Bassiouni and Balint on the basis that international crimes such as genocide, crimes against humanity and torture are based on *jus cogens* norms and therefore the fundamental interest in their protection and non-derogable character dictates a response when breached. Whether this approach is more broadly correct, in that breaches of *jus cogens* norms demand a response, will be dealt with when unpacking the *jus cogens* debate subsequently. However, to the extent that Bassiouni and Balint are correct and there is a legal obligation to hold individuals criminally accountable because international crimes are based on the breach of *jus cogens* norms then there is no reason to suppose that such a duty would not likewise apply when it was a state that breached the *jus cogens* norm.

The second approach is therefore to consider whether there is any legal obligation to hold states accountable for breaching laws recognised as arising from *jus cogens* norms. The German Federal Constitutional Court seems to answer the question positively, arguing that 'States are increasingly subjected to a duty to terminate and remove grave violations of peremptory international law', given that 'modern public international law is characterised by a continuous increase in the severity of the legal consequences which it attaches to the violation of particular central norms'.[78] However, any judicial optimism cannot overcome the lack of support in practice or the fact that there is sufficient uncertainty surrounding *jus cogens*, discussed subsequently, to make it difficult to determine what the juridical basis of the obligation would be. Victims have a right to redress under international law but the extent to which there is an obligation to hold states accountable is far less certain. Uncertainty exists as to whether any such obligation would relate to the underlying norm, whether states would be the only duty holders, whether other actors, such as the UN, would likewise be bound and whether the nature of

77 Note 22 above at 111 and argued in M. Bassiouni, and E. Wise in *Aut Dedere, Aut Judicare* (Boston: Martinus Nijhoff Publishers, 1995) and M. Bassiouni, *Crimes against Humanity in International Criminal Law* (Boston: Martinus Nijhoff Publishers, 1992).

78 *East German Expropriation Case (Order of the Second Senate of the German Federal Constitutional Court)* BVerfG 955/00 (2004) para 119.

accountability would be solely legal in nature. A finding that there is no legal obligation, at this time, does not mean that such an obligation will not crystallise in the future. The conclusion is simply that there is no express legal obligation to ensure states are held accountable and that it cannot be assumed that when states respond to a breach of international law, the objective is to seek accountability.

1.1.5 A working understanding of accountability

This discussion of accountability, as a broader notion that applies regardless of whether the subject is a state, individual or other party, has not sought to define the word. Instead, the goal was to identify any consistency in the way accountability is interpreted from a linguistic, cultural, legal and international relations perspective. What has emerged is that while the form of accountability is context specific (both in terms of the factual and disciplinary context), the objective in seeking accountability is consistent. Accountability can be distinguished from other forms of answerability because some form of response or redress is required in addition to determining the party's responsibility (or potential responsibility if accountability was pre-emptive). Where accountability is not possible in the legal sense, then we have already seen that political, and even moral, forms of accountability are contemplated, as with the UPR mechanism. Accordingly, this argument proceeds on the understanding that accountability for breaches of public international law is not just legal in nature and that more is sought from the liable party than merely a determination that the breach occurred.

1.2 The 'state'

In order to claim that accountability must be sought directly from the state, and not just indirectly from its agents or organs, there must be a greater understanding of how and why the state is a separate entity from its organs and agents. If the state is viewed merely as a structural apparatus that encompasses its individual citizens then state accountability is a misnomer because any breach of the law could, logically, only be committed by those individuals or state organs. Viewing the state as an independent legal entity requires the adoption of an artificial construct, but then this is no different to how people are viewed in both international and domestic law. For legal purposes, individuals are typically white, rational, male contractors regardless of the context, and oblivious to the diverse reality of the human population. Similarly, states are legal entities constructed for a specific function, which is to recognise the existence of other states as the protagonists of and participants within the international legal framework. Given that states, which in reality are a form of societal and structural organisation, can be legally conceived for the purposes of granting rights and duties (and irrespective of the artificiality in so viewing the state as an autonomous entity) it is equally feasible legally to conceive of the state for the purpose of seeking accountability.

In order to pierce the state's complex façade – so that the state is identified as the party that committed the breach, independent of its individuals and organs – the work of Foucault is heavily relied on.

The Foucauldian approach accords with much of the earlier discussion; whereby accountability was viewed as a means to regulate, and prevent the abuse of, power. Foucault viewed the state as a 'mechanism of power'[79]and thus any abuse of that power must be the state's own. In other words, and given the scope of power that only a state can possess, it would be irrational to suggest that an individual or organ could ever, single-handedly, commandeer and misapply that power. For example, the atrocities of the Nazi regime depended on the acquiescence of the population, assistance of the SS and armed forces and even the law itself, which legitimised the regime; thus, Hitler's individual crimes could never have been committed without the systemic support provided by Germany as a whole. On the basis that the breach in question was different, a separate search for accountability from the state is justified. Thus, the state's accountability is conceptually complementary to, and distinguished from, the individual accountability of the component organs complicit in the respective breach – even if in practice the accountability of the state and its organs will in fact overlap.

It is easier to conceptualise the state as a 'mechanism of power' for accountability purposes, but before focusing on those characteristics that give the state its power (in other words those aspects of statehood that can only be expressed by a state, as opposed to any other party), the theoretical Foucauldian approach should be reconciled with how the state is defined in international relations and under public international law. The word state is derived from the Latin *status* and implies physical attributes, such as territory and non-physical attributes, such as sovereignty, which was the approach taken by theorists such as Machiavelli,[80] Locke[81] and Weber[82] in defining the state. The most widely accepted legal definition is found in Article 1 of the 1933 Montevideo Convention, which defined states as having '(a) a permanent population; (b) a defined territory; (c) government; and (d) capacity to enter into relations with other States'. The question is whether the indicators of statehood in the Montevideo Convention could be employed to identify both the legal and the accountable state.

Certainly, the legal definition of the state has adapted to take into account the political reality, to highlight that the express elements of the Montevideo Convention are not exhaustive. An indication that the Montevideo Convention is authoritative, rather than definitive, is that states do not cease to exist just because there is a lack of effective governance. The variety in how governance is practised within contemporary international relations illustrates that the concept is flexible and subject to contextual adaptation. Theories of governance include 'network governance', typified by the EU model, and 'governance without government', whereby international treaties arguably amount to 'new forms of governance'.[83]

79 M. Foucault, *Power/Knowledge: Selected Interviews* (Sussex: Harvester Press, 1980) 72.
80 In *The Prince* (1513) and *The Discourses* (1513–19).
81 F. Pollock, 'Locke's Theory of the State' (1904) 2 *Proceedings of the British Academy* 237.
82 M. Weber, '*The Profession and Vocation of Politics (Lecture 1918)*' (Cambridge: CUP, 1994).
83 See J. Crawford, *The Creation of States* (Oxford: OUP 2006) and K. van Kersbergen and F. van Waarden, '"Governance" as a Bridge Between Disciplines: Cross-disciplinary Inspiration

Typical of both these theories and practice generally is that they are pluricentric and involve inter- or intra-national relations whereby governance is not exercised by the authorities in isolation. This was seen with the grant of UN membership, which Article 4 of the UN Charter limits to states, to Bosnia and Herzegovina in 1992 despite the ongoing conflict affecting the authorities' capacity to govern effectively. Another example was Kosovo's 2008 declaration of independence that has been recognised, for example, by a majority of the Member States of the EU and the USA. In anticipation of the declaration, the UN adopted its Comprehensive Proposal for the Kosovo Status Settlement, which recommended that the international community supervise Kosovo's 'independence'. The Special Envoy to the UN Secretary General concluded that 'Kosovo's capacity to tackle the challenges of minority protection, democratic development, economic recovery and social reconciliation on its own' was 'limited' and that 'international supervision' was required.[84] From the perspective of the Special Envoy and those states that adopted the findings, the Government of Kosovo was merely a constituent element of the state so that the capacity to govern was unrelated to Kosovo's statehood.

A second illustration of the legal definition bending to the political reality when identifying the state is the rise in regional forms of governance, such as the African Union and the EU. States confer certain competencies to these organisations, including aspects of their sovereign prerogative, rather than delegating statehood.[85] When the German Constitutional Court was required in the *Maastricht Judgment* to consider 'whether legal acts of the European institutions and organs are within or exceed the sovereign powers transferred to them',[86] it concluded that states can and do cede sovereign rights, within the terms of Article 5 of the EC Treaty and domestic law, without delegating statehood. Indeed, membership of the EU can even be seen as an indicator of statehood because the Copenhagen criteria that sets out the accession criterion, provides that only a 'European *State* ... may apply to become a member of the Union'.[87] Thus, the State of Macedonia was acknowledged as a candidate for EU membership in 2005 despite lingering questions on the extent to which it is fully sovereign given the ongoing financial and political support provided by Serbia.

These points do not mean that the Montevideo Convention definition is redundant in identifying the state for the purposes of accountability. Certainly, the

Regarding Shifts in Governance and Problems of Governability, Accountability and Legitimacy' (2004) *European Journal of Political Research* 143, 149–52.

84 'Letter dated 26 March 2007 from the Secretary-General Addressed to the President of the Security Council' UN Doc S/2007/168 (2007) Annex I para 11.

85 Sarooshi argued there are three types of conferral in evidence being agency, delegation of powers and full transfer or ceding of power that is irrevocable: D. Sarooshi, *International Organizations and Their Exercise of Sovereign Powers* (Oxford: OUP, 2005).

86 *Maastricht Judgment* (BVerfGE 89, 155 (1993)) 188.

87 Maastricht Treaty on the European Union (1992) art 49 (emphasis added).

requirement that a state may enter into international relations is particularly useful in identifying the state as a 'mechanism of power', because the ability to participate in international relations depends on other states perceiving that the state in question had the requisite power to do so.[88] This is illustrated in the case of Taiwan, which has historically enjoyed recognition as the Government of China from states such as Japan and the USA. Today Taiwan still has territory, a population and some form of government but what is less clear is the extent to which Taiwan has the ability to enter into relations with other states in particular since 1971 when the UN General Assembly passed Resolution 2758, which recognised the People's Republic of China as 'the only legitimate representative of China to the United Nations' and expelled the representatives of Taiwan. The shift in support has occurred as the People's Republic of China assumed an increasingly powerful position in international relations, while that of Taiwan has arguably declined. Thus, while the Montevideo Convention is authoritative, political pragmatism is increasingly influential, even to the extent that adopting a broader interpretation of those parties that constitute the state may lead to a greater number of parties escaping the consequences of their actions. Article 2(1) of the United Nations Convention on Jurisdictional Immunities of States and Their Property extends state immunity to 'organs of government'; 'constituent units of a federal State or political subdivisions of the State'; 'agencies or instrumentalities' and 'representatives of the State acting in that capacity'. The view is taken here that if the state can be viewed as an aggregate of its substantive parts for the purposes of granting immunity, it is surely rational to argue that the same approach can be used to identify the state for the purposes of seeking accountability.

Article 1 of the Montevideo Convention uses the four elements listed to 'qualify' an entity as a state but, in terms of seeking accountability, it is more useful to view the state as a systemic framework in which individuals, society and government exist, because this interpretation gives the state a discernible form – and thus the acts and omissions that are unique to the state in that form can be identified. The question becomes whether the relevant breach could only have been committed by the state, rather than the government, individuals in power or other organs? For example, Germany was held accountable after the Second World War, irrespective of the change in government regime and findings of individual criminal liability that occurred. In Pella's opinion, 'the natural persons who decided upon and ordered the commission of the crimes' were punished at the Nuremberg

88 Article 3 of the Montevideo Convention in fact provides that the 'political existence' (rather than the legal existence) of the state does not depend on recognition. However, two points can be noted: first, the state's political existence is not the same as its legal existence and, secondly, without recognition by other states there will be no other states to enter into relations with. Thus, recognition is necessary.

Trials, but in addition there needed to be accountability from the 'passive element' for its role, which was 'reached by imposing suitable penalties on the State'.[89]

The argument that the state must be made to answer for providing the structural and institutional framework that facilitated the breaches/crimes of its various organs also highlights one of the differences between state accountability and other forms of answerability, such as state responsibility. In the *Genocide Convention* case, which involved a determination of state responsibility, the ICJ considered that 'the degree and nature of a state's involvement in an armed conflict' can 'without logical inconsistency, differ from the degree and nature of the involvement required to give rise to that state's responsibility for a specific act in the course of the conflict'.[90] This comment recognised that the state assumes different manifestations for different purposes. The responsible state is one that exercises a certain level of control over its organs and is thus required to make amends for the acts and omissions of those organs; in contrast, a state at war will include all those individuals providing some form of assistance on behalf of the state but that does not make the state liable for the acts and omissions of every one of those individuals (unless there was the requisite level of control in relation to the breach and the respective individual was also an organ). Thus, it is not irrational to argue that the accountable state is different still and constitutes the systemic framework that allows its organs to perpetrate breaches and sees the state as a whole go to war.

1.3 Conclusion

This chapter has broken down the constituent elements of state accountability to consider how 'accountability' and the 'state' are defined or, at least, understood – in the general proximity of international law, politics and relations. Accountability is only one form of answerability but is distinguishable because there must be a determination of liability and, in addition, there must be redress – Keohane used the phrase 'information and sanctions'. In order to overcome the indeterminacy of accountability, regard was paid to linguistic, cultural and cross-disciplinary interpretations to establish if any consensus exists. It emerged that accountability is a tool for regulating and responding to the abuse of power and that, in order to do so, the concept is relational and context specific. However, it cannot be denied that the concept still lacks definitional clarity and greater specificity will be attempted in the next chapter by analysing the broader term 'accountability' specifically in terms of 'state accountability'. Unlike accountability, there was a legal standard that could be referred to in discussing the state, namely the Montevideo Convention. But, as with accountability, it was apparent that an isolated legal definition was insufficient for the purposes here. Namely, the issue was how to

89 Pella's 'Memorandum Concerning a Draft Code of Offences Against the Peace and Security of Mankind' UN Doc A/CN.4/39 (1950).

90 Note 37 above, para 405.

extract the state as an autonomous entity from its various organs in order to hold the state separately accountable. In order to overcome this issue, it was argued that for accountability purposes the state should be identified as a systemic framework that facilitates the breach of individuals, the government or other parties that are likewise culpable. In other words, but for the existence of the 'state' the individual/government/other party would not have breached international law. Foucault's moniker of the state as a mechanism of power helped to identify why the accountable state is a separate entity from that of its constituent parts and distinguished from the state as the legally autonomous actor defined by the Montevideo Convention. Ultimately, accountability must be sought from the state for abusing its power – power that could have only been exercised by the state as a whole and not by its constituent parts.

2 State accountability as a conceptual whole

Chapter 2 reunites the constituent elements to explore state accountability as a conceptual whole. It argues that state accountability should be viewed as a discrete outcome to be measured against certain evaluative criteria, before turning to identify those evaluative criteria being: (1) that the response will exceed the scope of the state responsibility doctrine; (2) that any response capable of holding states accountable for breaching public international law would not be illegal; (3) that any response would reflect the specific law breached; and (4) that state accountability could be legal, moral and, in all probability, political in nature.

Having broken state accountability down to its conceptual elements in Chapter 1, the objective in Chapter 2 is to provide some clarity as to the concept as a whole. The variety in formal and informal responses when states breach international law confirms that, at a minimum, there is an *ad hoc* practice of seeking accountability from states. The aim here is to develop a conceptual framework in which such *ad hoc* accountability practices can be analysed in order that conclusions may then be drawn as to the current normative status of state accountability. The first step in constructing this framework is to set limits on the scope of *ad hoc* practice to be analysed: namely, can responses that are not strictly legal and responses that seek to hold the organs of the state accountable in lieu of the state be taken as evidence of state accountability. The second step is to identify a 'tentative set of [accountability] criteria'[91] against which the attainment of accountability can then be measured.

The word 'tentative' is used consciously because, in keeping with the Foucauldian philosophy permeating this discussion, the attempt to develop objective evaluative criteria cannot be ignorant of subjective factors that influence the pursuit of accountability in a given context. This point can be illustrated by referring to incidents where states impose amnesty laws that arguably violate public international law in the view of UN human rights bodies – as expressed in the 2000

91 T. McCarthy, 'The Critique of Impure Reason: Foucault and the Frankfurt School' at 243 in M. Kelly (ed) *Critique and Power: Recasting the Foucault/Habermas Debate* (Cambridge: MIT Press, 2004).

Report on the Right to Restitution, Compensation and Rehabilitation for Victims of Gross Human Rights Violations – and in accordance with the jurisprudence of regional human rights courts – for example in its 2001 decision in *Chumbipuma Aguirre v Peru* the Inter-American Court of Human Rights expressly stated that amnesty laws were incompatible with the American Convention on Human Rights. Such inconsistencies and differences in opinion make it difficult to identify any form of objective evaluative criteria against which to measure accountability practices. Certainly, amnesties may at first glance appear to be anathema to accountability but, in certain cases, they have arguably facilitated accountability for the broader community. For example, the 1978 Decreto Ley No 2.191 in Chile and the 1986 Law No 23.492 in Argentina instituted amnesties for the purpose of rehabilitating the national community following the collapse of the respective oppressive government, rather than as a means to deny individuals the right to redress. Similarly, South Africa's amnesty for a confession scheme that was established under the 1995 Promotion of National Unity and Reconciliation Act did not lead to trial and punishment of individuals – but the respective parties were required to acknowledge their role, provide information and were publicly exposed (thus also satisfying the two limbs associated with accountability, being determining liability and redress). Thus, the way states interpret – and seek – accountability may differ in practice from the views of human rights monitoring bodies and courts, which are more jurisprudentially based. On that basis, any tentative set of evaluative criteria will be subject to change once applied to state practice and references to state practice in this chapter (for the purpose of identifying what associations exist in terms of holding states accountable) are determinative, rather than authoritative, and subject to amendment once they have been tested in the subsequent case studies.

2.1 The scope of the *ad hoc* accountability practice for analysis

Bassiouni argued that just as there is no one manner in which states breach the law so there is no one manner by which to hold states accountable.[92] The range of potential mechanisms for redress, when states commit grievous breaches of international law, has always been significant – as evident in Pella's 'Memorandum Concerning a Draft Code of Offences Against the Peace and Security of Mankind', which was drafted in 1926 under the guidance of the International Association of Penal Law and in the midst of a growing debate on state criminality. The recommendation was for the Permanent Court of International Justice to have criminal jurisdiction over crimes of aggression and that redress (to be imposed by the League of Nations) could include 'the destruction of strategic railways and fortifications, prohibiting military production, the confiscation of armaments, the limitation of

92 C. Bassiouni, 'Searching for Peace and Achieving Justice: The Need for Accountability' (1996) 59 *Law and Contemporary Problems* 9, 23.

the size of armed forces, complete disarmament, [and] the formation of demilitarized zones on the territory of the state'.[93] It would truly be a remarkable feat if the law was viewed as the sole source and means of seeking accountability, especially given that the law may have even been used as a tool in the breach, as occurred in Nazi Germany where the discrimination of Jews was legalised. But does this mean that any analysis of potential accountability mechanisms should be undertaken without any restriction as to what may or may not qualify as a means for holding states accountable? In particular, two points require express clarification in order to determine how wide this inquiry will extend in analysing the *ad hoc* practice of, and approach to, state accountability: whether non-legal responses should be taken into consideration and whether responses that seek to hold individuals or state organs accountable, in lieu of the state, likewise relevant?

To the extent that the concept is understood in terms of what it seeks to achieve, and not in terms of the process used to achieve that objective, then it is even possible that state accountability could be achieved regardless that the response preceding the outcome did not comply with public international law. For example, and strictly speaking, military intervention is in breach of Article 2(4) and (7) of the UN Charter; however, it cannot be doubted that military intervention was effective in ending aggression and arguably holding North Korea to account after it invaded the Republic of Korea. Irrespective of such cases, the UN has consistently emphasised that states are under a legal obligation to comply with human rights, humanitarian and public international law, regardless of the circumstances and even the increase in counter-terrorist measures after the terrorist attacks in New York and Pennsylvania on 11 September 2001 to meet a supposedly increased threat of global terrorism, has not altered this stance.[94] Certainly, there is an implied moral advantage if the response complies with international law, especially where, as Alexidze noted, it was a *jus cogens* norm that was breached.[95] But even though illegal responses would risk undermining the validity of the legal framework, the question remains whether a response that does not comply with black letter public international law – or, in Balint's words 'extra-legal'[96] – is likewise precluded. In other words, and given the dynamic nature of public international law, the question is to what extent are evolving practices of answerability evidence of state accountability in practice?

The balance and tension between what is expressly legal and what is impliedly permitted under public international law is highlighted with reference to the

93 Pella's 'Memorandum Concerning a Draft Code of Offences Against the Peace and Security of Mankind' (UN Doc A/CN.4/39 (1950)) cited in N. Jorgensen, *The Responsibility of States for International Crimes* (Oxford: OUP, 2003) 174.

94 B. Nacos, Y. Bloch-Elkon and R. Shapiro, 'Post-9/11 Terrorism Threats, News Coverage, and Public Perceptions in the United States' (2007) *International Journal of Conflict and Violence* 106.

95 L. Alexidze, 'Legal Nature of *Jus Cogens* in Contemporary International Law' (1981) *Recueil des Cours de L'Académie de Droit International de La Hague* 219, 226.

96 J. Balint, 'The Place of Addressing Internal Regime Conflicts' (1996) 59 *Law and Contemporary Problems* 103, 115.

prohibition on intervention. The Declaration of Principles of International Law Concerning Friendly Relations Between states provided that 'no State or group of states has the right to intervene ... in the internal or external affairs of any other State', including through 'the use of economic, political or any other type of measures'. The Declaration is not a binding legal instrument but it helps to expand upon how the purposes and principles of the UN Charter are to be understood and thus is indicative that the prohibition on intervention in the UN Charter is absolute. Scholars including Charney,[97] Meron[98] and Schachter[99] disagree, arguing that the prohibition on intervention is derogable because public international law demands that states respond to human rights violations. In the case of grievous human rights breaches the question of whether intervention was legitimate, even if not expressly legal, would be determined by referring to the objective of intervention. The ongoing debate as to whether state intervention may be legitimate – although not legally endorsed – parallels the issue of whether states could ever be justified in responding to breaches of international law if the response itself failed to comply with international law. This was arguably the exact same question faced by the Independent International Commission on Kosovo, which described the NATO bombing of Kosovo as 'illegal but legitimate' as a result of what the UK Secretary of Defence at the time described as the 'humanitarian catastrophe'.[100] To the extent that some form of intervention on humanitarian grounds is tolerated by states, it seems rational then to consider whether intervention could, in addition, be accepted as a means to hold states accountable for breaching *jus cogens*.

In exploring the possibility of an evolving norm of humanitarian intervention, it is noted that consistent amongst the many declarations that intervention is not permitted under international law, is the implication that the prohibition on all forms of intervention is not in fact absolute. For example, in the *Military and Paramilitary Activities In and Against Nicaragua* (the *Nicaragua* case) the ICJ clarified that the prohibition on intervention is *jus cogens* – but the Court was talking about intervention solely through the use of force.[101] Similarly, Article 2(4) of the UN Charter states that 'all Members shall refrain in their international relations from the threat or use of *force* against the territorial integrity or political independence of any state'. The prohibition on intervention set down in Article 2(7) is broader as it prohibits any form of intervention 'into the internal affairs of a Member State', but then both Article 2(7) and 2(4) only prohibit intervention into UN states. Furthermore, Article 2(7) would not seem to accord with state practice, as

97 J. Charney, 'Third State Remedies in International Law (1989) 10(1) *Michigan Journal of International Law* 57, 60.

98 T. Meron, 'On a Hierarchy of International Human Rights' (1986) 80 *American Journal of International Law* 1, 11.

99 O. Schachter, 'International Law in Theory and Practice' (1982) *Recueil des Cours de L'Académie de Droit International de la Hague* 175, 185.

100 I. Johnstone, 'The Plea of "Necessity" in International Legal Discourse: Humanitarian Intervention and Counter-Terrorism' (2005) 43 *Columbia Journal of Transnational Law* 337, 365.

101 *Military v Paramilitary Activities In and Against Nicaragua* (Merits 1986) ICJ Reports (1984) para 190.

in 1991 when the UN Security Council 'insist[ed] that Iraq allow immediate access by international humanitarian organizations'.[102] Clearly, there is recognition that exceptions to the broader prohibition on intervention, namely in terms of intervention for humanitarian reasons, may exist. The ICJ, again in the *Nicaragua* case, acknowledged that 'humanitarian aid cannot be recognised as unlawful intervention',[103] while in the 2007 judgment in the *Genocide Convention* case the Court considered that a combination of state practice and the wording of the 1948 Genocide Convention arguably amounted to a legal obligation on states to protect – that Milanovic described as closer to a '"responsibility to protect" than any other judicial pronouncement so far'.[104] In terms of state recognition, Article 4(h) of the Charter of the African Union allows intervention in 'grave circumstances, namely war crimes, genocide and crimes against humanity'. And, more recently, the 2001 final Report of the International Commission on Intervention and State Sovereignty (ICISS) was compiled by human rights experts including representatives of relevant UN bodies seeking to capture the concept of humanitarian intervention as part of a broader 'responsibility to protect', or R2P, principle.[105]

The ICISS concluded that 'sovereign States have a responsibility to protect their own citizens ... but when they are unwilling or unable to do so, that responsibility must be borne by the broader community of States',[106] which would thus effectively permit a form of intervention on humanitarian grounds. In terms of state practice, Security Council Resolution 1706, which attempted to deploy 17,000 peacekeeping troops to Darfur in 2006 referred to paragraphs 138 and 139 of the 2005 Summit Outcome Document, whereby states accepted they were under a responsibility to protect and committed to act in accordance with that responsibility. The Darfur Government blocked the peacekeeping mission but this was to mark an increase in references to the principle and, in the same year, Security Council Resolution 1674 generally reaffirmed the R2P principle. By 2008, the response of the international community to violence after elections in Kenya that resulted in thousands of deaths and estimates of 290,000 displaced, was expressly couched in R2P rhetoric; for example, then French Foreign and European Affairs Minister Bernard Kouchner called on the UN Security Council

102 UN Security Council Resolution 688 (1991).

103 Note 101 above, paras 106 and 268.

104 M. Milanovic, 'State Responsibility for Genocide: A Follow-Up' (2007) 18 *European Journal of International Law* 669. The Court did in fact limit the scope of this obligation to the parameters of established international law recalling that there is a prohibition on physical intervention (*Application of the Convention on the Prevention and Punishment of the Crime of Genocide (Bosnia and Herzegovina) v Yugoslavia (Serbia and Montenegro)*) (Judgment 2007) ICJ Reports (1993) paras 428–38).

105 Humanitarian intervention is in fact only one aspect of the broader R2P doctrine, which includes restructuring, rebuilding, capacity building and prevention that are not necessarily coercive in nature. For the purposes of this discussion, however, the focus is on the extent to which the R2P doctrine is a vehicle for allowing what were traditionally prohibited forms of intervention on the grounds of alleviating humanitarian crisis.

106 International Commission on Intervention and State Sovereignty '*The Responsibility to Protect*' (Canada: International Research Centre, 2001) viii.

to act 'in the name of the responsibility to protect'.[107] Likewise, former UN Secretary General Kofi Annan described the attempts to mediate the violence when the Kenyan Government was unable to react as a form of non-military intervention and described Kenya as 'a successful example of R2P at work'.[108]

Despite significant commitment to the R2P principle within the political arena, there is also scepticism. For example, when the UN General Assembly included a thematic dialogue on the R2P principles in its 2009 programme of work, General Assembly President Miguel D'Escoto argued that 'those who might abuse the right that R2P would give nation-states to resort to the use of force against other states' outweighed the best intentions of 'authors and proponents of R2P'[109]. In particular, President d'Escoto referred to the 2003 invasion of Iraq, labelling the UK and the USA as 'self-appointed saviours who arrogated to themselves the right to intervene with impunity in the name of overcoming nation-state impunity' before disputing 'whether we are ready for R2P'. While these are the comments of one individual, they capture the perceived tension in needing to respond when states breach international law when there is limited, formal means to do so, with the risk in tolerating *ad hoc* practices for this purpose. The need to overcome this tension was instrumental in framing the R2P principle as a responsibility on states to protect (and thus states were compelled to act) – rather than a right of states to intervene for humanitarian purposes (and therefore optional); however, the continued distrust of R2P suggests that critics fear that the distinction is only semantic. As with all normative developments, time is required to determine the extent to which the vocal expressions of support for an emerging responsibility to protect principle are conclusively reflected in practice to the point that R2P is considered custom. The conclusion that can be drawn, however, is that humanitarian imperatives are influential in the evolution of international law and, in particular, the response when states breach what can arguably be described as fundamental *jus cogens* norms. Therefore, to the extent that intervention on humanitarian grounds (in the guise of R2P) is tolerated by states (if not viewed as having normative value), it is equally rational to expand the analysis here to forms of accountability that are not strictly legal but that are tolerated due to the grievous nature of the breach.

On the basis that international law is dynamic and responds to changing policy goals,[110] as evidenced by the increased popularity of the R2P principle and the

107 B. Kouchner, 'Violence in Kenya' (31 January 2008) available at http://www.diplomatie.gouv.fr/en/country-files_156/kenya_209/situation-in-kenya-2008.

108 R. Cohen, 'How Kofi Annan Rescued Kenya' 55(13) *The New York Review of Books* (14 August 2008).

109 'Statement of the President of the UN General Assembly At the Opening of the Thematic Dialogue of the General Assembly on the Responsibility to Protect' (2009) available at http://www.un.org/ga/president/63/statements/openingr2p230709.shtml.

110 Yasuaki describes international law in terms of being an interaction between policy and morals and says that international law has a 'determinative' characteristic that reflects the interaction of interests and opinions' in O. Yasuaki, 'International Law In and With International Politics: The Functions of International Law in International Society' (2003) 14 *European Journal of International Law* 105, 112.

emergence of *jus cogens* norms, the approach taken here is to contemplate a 'mosaic' of 'legal and extra-legal'[111] responses when states breach international law. Responses, which may not yet be legally sanctioned, can still be effective in holding states accountable and may be indicators of the future development and evolution of state accountability as a principle of public international law. In the framework of international relations where the development of international law is preconditioned on political will, the evolution of state accountability – or the acceptance of a doctrine of humanitarian intervention as part of a broader R2P principle – and acquisition of legal status depends upon states adopting it as a priority. It is being argued here, in light of the above discussion, that interfacing the language of state accountability into the debate on humanitarian intervention may contribute to a more institutionalised treatment and change in the legal status of both – given the shared focus on states being made to answer when *jus cogens* norms or fundamental human values are breached. Until that time, and on the assumption that there is sufficient evidence to argue that humanitarian intervention cannot be discounted as a means for holding state to account, the potential that accountability is achieved with a combination of legal and extra-legal responses is not excluded.

The second aspect for clarification in terms of the scope of *ad hoc* practice that may be referred to in analysing state accountability in practice is the extent to which holding a state's organs/individuals accountable can also be interpreted as holding the state accountable. If the state's liability can be identified with regard to the acts and omissions of its organs then logic suggests that the state's accountability may also be ascertained by referring to the accountability of those same state organs. To a degree, this rationale is an extension of the attribution principle, employed within the context of the state responsibility doctrine. The analogy also allows the point to be noted here that any reference throughout the book to a state's organ(s) (or agent(s)) is in accordance with how the term is used in public international law rhetoric generally. In short, a state's agents or organs are those individuals or bodies that exercise power on behalf of the state and whose acts and omissions can be aggregated and cumulatively viewed as the acts and omissions of the state. There are, however, three caveats arising from the reverse-attribution analogy, which help to illustrate why ultimately the accountability of the state remains a separate question from that of its agents/organs, despite the overlap in other ways.

First, a state's organs are not always held to account for their acts and omissions and thus the analogy can only apply in limited circumstances. For example, the effect of the functional immunity doctrine, which attributes the acts of the organ to the state, is that the organ is no longer seen as liable for the breach. In that case, redress is never sought from the organ that was granted immunity so there is no measure of individual accountability that could then be attributed to address the state's accountability. Secondly, it is not argued here that seeking redress from the

111 Note 96 above at 115.

state's organs eradicates the need to seek redress from the state. Rather, redress from the state's organs would be more appropriate in terms of addressing any gap in accountability arising because of the practical difficulties in holding states accountable. An example of where attribution of redress would be appropriate include where the breaching state's resources were wiped out after conflict, making compensation impossible. Indeed, the concept of individual state accountability is premised on the fact that there are two distinct breaches (one by the state and one by the state's organs) and thus accountability of the state's organs cannot automatically and comprehensively address the accountability of the state. Referring back to the example of legalised discrimination in Nazi Germany illustrates this point because separate accountability was sought from the state for establishing a legal framework that meant that groups and individuals could commit the various atrocities, for which they were subsequently held individually criminally accountable, with impunity. Finally, a form of reverse-attribution is inappropriate where the respective breach of each party was unrelated, as in the *Nicaragua* case. The ICJ held that the USA was responsible for breaching obligations that were different to those breached by the Contras, even though the breaches were contextually linked. Where the state's liability arose irrespective of the other party, as in the *Nicaragua* case where it was the acts of the government and military that were attributed to the USA and not the acts of the Contras, then it is nonsensical to claim that the state could in any way be held accountable by referring to redress sought from the Contras.

2.2 A tentative set of accountability criteria

Thus far it has been argued that any principle or norm of state accountability identified as evolved or evolving throughout international relations must be sufficiently broad to adapt to the geographic, temporal, cultural and even political context. In addition, the possibility was noted that accountability might only be an indirect aim in responding to the specific breach. The accuracy of these claims is apparent in comparing the consequences imposed on Germany at the end of the two World Wars. After the First World War, the Allied powers imposed significant reparations on Germany pursuant to the 1919 Treaty of Versailles, which required Germany to accept its responsibility for the damage caused (Article 231) and imposed reparations as a means for redress. The reparation was designed to reduce Germany's capability for aggression (Articles 231 to 247) – but also constituted a deterrent, denounced the state's actions and sought to prevent future aggression. A similar approach was initially taken at the end of the Second World War under the Potsdam Agreement (including the reduction or destruction of all industry with war potential, notably shipbuilding, machine production and chemical factories pursuant to the so called 'Level of Industry Plans for Germany'); however, the different political and social context soon necessitated a change in tactics. The reduction of civilian industry was rapidly seen to be counter-productive to restoration and there was a perceived risk that the burden placed on Germany could have led to individuals, who were struggling as a result of the drastic economic measures, being swept up in the communist wave sweeping through Europe at that time. Accordingly, the decision was taken to relinquish the restrictive terms imposed under the Potsdam settlement and the Restatement of Policy on Germany was adopted instead. Thus, while in both cases the breaching state was Germany and the breach can be superficially summed up as aggression and grievous breaches of human rights, the mode of accountability was specific to the historical, political and social context.

Acknowledging that state accountability is a contextually specific phenomenon provides little value in terms of objectively conceptualising the notion (beyond a determination of liability and redress as a result) so that the concept may be recognised in practice. Accordingly, a set of evaluative criteria are needed so that these can be referred to in analysing a particular context and concluding whether the situation in review is an example of state accountability in practice. Given the contextual vagaries involved, however, it is more likely to be the broader associations with accountability that provide the most accurate set of evaluative criteria – as Bassiouni argued in relation to individual accountability which he claimed was associated with 'cessation ... prevention ... deterrence ... rehabilitation of the society as a whole and of the victims ... and reconciliation'.[112] The second part of this chapter is therefore occupied with identifying whether there are likewise any broad and objective associations that exist in terms of what it means to hold states accountable.

2.2.1 Is state accountability associated with criminal accountability?

It would be simple to bypass the issue of whether state accountability has any associations with criminal accountability, first, given that the Nuremberg Court explicitly rejected state criminality and, secondly, based on the presumption that criminal redress must be punitive and thus state criminal accountability would be impossible because states cannot be imprisoned. However, such a simplistic treatment can be easily displaced. First, the Nuremberg Tribunal was not even concerned with whether Germany was to be held legally – or criminally – accountable as the focus was on individual liability. Indeed, the tribunal recognised that 'the involvement of the State d[id] not modify or limit the guilt or responsibility of the individual'.[113] Secondly, it is arguable that the pejorative connotations in labelling the state as criminal and the resulting injury to state dignity, could go a long way in terms of a form of penal redress. Thus, dismissing the idea that states may be criminally accountable requires greater justification than merely the lack of precedent as to how such a determination would be made and what the legal consequences would be.

112 Note 92 above, 23.
113 *Trial of Friedrich Flick and Five Others* US Military Tribunal LRTWC Volume IX 1 (1947) 18.

Certainly, commentators such as Bruck have argued that criminal redress can be sought from states, citing the 1919 Covenant of the League of Nations as an example.[114] Where states have committed an act of aggressive war – which the Draft Treaty of Mutual Assistance 1923 and the League of Nations Protocol for the Pacific Settlement of International Disputes 1924 determined was 'an international crime' – Article 16 of the Covenant dictated 'the severance of all trade or financial relations ... the prevention of all financial, commercial or personal intercourse between the nationals of the covenant-breaking state and the nationals of any other state' and that the state was no longer a member of the League of Nations. If, as Bruck suggested, the Covenant constituted a criminal code then the issue of how to punish the state was overcome because punishment meant more than just imprisonment. However, given the ineffectiveness of the League of Nations and the fact that no doctrine of criminal state liability has crystallised on the basis of the precedent set down by the Covenant, then Brownlie's claim that Article 16 was a 'police measure rather than punishment'[115] had weight. Brownlie also noted that penal forms of redress would not always be appropriate in terms of requiring states to answer for grievous breaches of international law, because imposing sanctions or boycotts, as a form of punishment, could lead to a threat against international peace and security. Regardless of whether the reason was political or owing to a lack of legal feasibility, it is clear that public international law has maintained a distance from the criminality framework throughout the 20th century.

The Nuremberg Tribunal considered it was not rational to hold states criminally accountable – in the legal sense – because 'crimes against international law are committed by men, not abstract entities'.[116] However, the tribunal did 'not warrant the view that a state cannot be a criminal'.[117] In order to understand why, for example, the International Law Commission (ILC) therefore rejected the notion of state crimes in the context of working on the Draft Articles on State Responsibility (the Draft Articles),[118] the approach taken here is to refer to the three elements required to establish criminal accountability under the law (being designation of the breach as a crime, an adjudicating forum and some form of redress). To the extent that these prerequisites in fact exist – in order to hold states criminally accountable under international law – then there can be no legal justification for altogether excluding the criminal accountability of states.

The first requirement is that the breach is recognised as a state crime under public international law. Clearly, without some determination that certain breaches of public international law amount to crimes and elucidation of the definitional

114 O. Bruck, *Les Sanctions en Droit International* (Paris: A. Pedone, 1933) 101.

115 I. Brownlie, *International Law and the Use of Force by States* (Oxford: Clarendon Press, 1963) 153.

116 *Judgment of the IMT for the Trial of German Major War Criminals* (London: HMSO, 1946) 223.

117 Ibid, 56.

118 Taken from G. Gilbert, 'The Criminal Responsibility of States' (1990) 2 *International and Comparative Law Quarterly* 345, 352.

elements that comprise such crimes, a state cannot be branded a criminal in the legal sense. The primary obstacle is that even if the acts and omissions of states can otherwise be criminalised, for example with genocide and apartheid, there remains the difficulty in proving some form of *mens rea* requirement, which arguably justifies the imposition of a harsher penalty because the perpetrator acted with some sort of knowledge or intent. At Nuremberg, Prosecutor Shawcross argued that the state could be viewed as an accessory to the crimes directly committed by individuals and that such an approach would displace the need to show any intent. The bench, led by Justice Jackson, disagreed and considered that all crimes have a *mens rea* element, which cannot be established if the alleged perpetrator is a state. States are considered to act with fault when breaching international law but that is different to intent and the *mens rea* standard that would be required for criminal state accountability. For example, Article 4 of the 1972 Convention on the International Liability for Damage Caused by Space Objects determined that states are liable for damages to 'the extent to which they were at fault'. Thus, in 1981 the USSR was required to pay damages for environmental damage suffered by Canada only after it was established that the USSR had launched the relevant materials into outer space.[119] The ILC did not consider fault a necessary element to engage state responsibility, if 'fault' was interpreted to mean 'an intention to harm'.[120] Although state responsibility is civil rather than criminal the ICJ adopted the same view in the *Genocide Convention* case, when considering Serbia's responsibility for complicity in genocide, which is a crime under the Genocide Convention. The Court stated that a complicit state must be 'aware of the special intent of the principal perpetrator',[121] but did not go so far as to say that the state was required to possess that intent itself.

The second element required to establish criminal accountability under the law is that there must be an adjudicating forum with the authority to determine that the breach was a crime under international law and impose a criminal sanction as a result. The primary difficulty here is that, at present, the international courts including the ICJ do not have the power to punish a state, even though former Special Rapporteur Arangio-Ruiz had thought that the ICJ would be a suitable forum to decide on questions of criminal state responsibility.[122] The criminal framework is hierarchical and, at both the international and domestic level, it is states that vest courts with the power to impose criminal sanctions on individuals. Given that the framework of international relations presupposes the equality of states, it is unlikely that in practice a consensus could be reached and an international court granted criminal jurisdiction over states, let alone the power to impose

119 'Settlement of Claim between Canada and the Union of Soviet Socialist Republics for Damage Caused by Cosmos 954' (2 April 1981).

120 'Report of the International Law Commission on the Work of its Fifty-Third Session' UN Doc A/56/10 (2001) Commentary on Article 2 para 10.

121 Note 104 above, para 421.

122 International Law Commission Seventh Report on State Responsibility UN Doc A/CN.4/469/ Add.1 4.

criminal punishment. The issue of identifying a suitable adjudicating body is not limited to the question of criminal state accountability and will be discussed in more depth.

The third element that would need to be satisfied in order to show a link between state accountability and criminal accountability is that the form of redress must establish that the state's liability was more than civil (in other words beyond the scope of general state responsibility) – and it will be argued here that where the breach is of a *jus cogens* norms the sanction must illustrate global condemnation. In the current state of affairs, any declaration that a state is criminal is a political declaration and likely to reflect the outcome of a conflict or constitute censure for a particular act, rather than be a reasoned legal judgment that the state contravened black letter criminal law. A political condemnation of state criminality can still be effective in terms of political accountability – especially given that the potential diplomatic fallout means that the likely frequency of such allegations is rare.[123] But does the impossibility of imprisoning a state mean that criminal condemnation of states could instead be viewed as political? Although Nuremberg focused on individual accountability the prosecutors for the US, the UK and France considered that the Tribunal's judgment at the same time effectively condemned Germany; Prosecutor Taylor stating that the trials led to 'extensive moral responsibility' for all 'German society for the laws and the practices of the Nazis'.[124] Yet, to the extent that the consequences of finding a state criminally liable were only ever political – or even moral – then why bother with a legal determination of criminal liability in the first place?

When the ILC dealt with the problem of how to seek criminal redress from states, in codifying the law relating to state responsibility, the view was taken in Draft Article 19 of the 1980 Draft that certain breaches of international obligations by a state were criminal. Although Draft Article 19 identified what would amount to a state crime, it did not list any form of penal sanction beyond what was already available within the standard scope of the state responsibility doctrine – which in all probability contributed to its ultimate exclusion from the final 2001 Draft Articles. This was despite former Special Rapporteur Arangio-Ruiz speculating as to the possible consequences of state crimes, including 'acceptance of observation teams, adoption of laws affording adequate protection for minorities and establishment of a form of government not incompatible with fundamental freedoms, civil and political rights'.[125] Gilbert was of the opinion that additional consequences were not in fact necessary to hold a state criminally responsible, beyond those arising when standard state responsibility was engaged. 'In a flight

123 P. Dupuy, 'A General Stocktaking of the Connections Between the Multilateral Dimension of Obligations and Codification of the Law of Responsibility' (2002) 13(5) *European Journal of International Law* 1053, 1060.

124 T. Taylor, 'Guilt, Responsibility and the Third Reich' *Churchill College Overseas Fellowship Lectures* (1970).

125 'Seventh Report of the Special Rapporteur Gaetano Arangio-Ruiz' UN Doc A/CN.4/469 (1995) para 36.

of academic fantasy',[126] Gilbert argued that a declaratory judgment could be equally effective where the breach was criminal, citing the *South West Africa Cases*[127] in support. Liberia and Ethiopia sought a declaration that South Africa was in breach of its mandate in South West Africa having introduced apartheid policies. The application was dismissed on procedural grounds, but Gilbert considered that had it been decided on the merits the effect would be a determination of guilt for committing the international crime of apartheid. Gilbert's argument presumed that a determination of criminality is, of itself, an effective sanction but since the time of writing in 1990, the decision in the *Genocide Convention* case may provide some support for his hypothesis. Rather than compensation, the ICJ obviously considered that a declaratory judgment was more effective in terms of condemning Serbia for failing to comply with provisional measures and breaching the state's obligation under the Genocide Convention to prevent genocide. The breaches in question are not expressly defined crimes pursuant to the Convention but there is undoubtedly a high level of stigmatisation as the failure to prevent genocide was listed alongside acts and omissions of genocide.

The conclusion here, in terms of whether state accountability could be criminal without the capacity to imprison a state, is twofold. First, in relation to breaches most likely to be deemed criminal due to the gravity such as massive human rights breaches, there is credence in arguing that stigma alone holds weight in terms of redress. Secondly, because the consequences envisaged in terms of state crimes have never progressed much further than censure and denunciation, the effectiveness and nature of redress would be implicit (creating political and moral awareness of the breach) rather than overtly legal (such as damages to compensate for loss incurred). Clearly, there are very real obstacles in terms of declaring a state to be criminal, namely whether it is possible to punish a state, and if so, how. From a political perspective, branding a state that commits atrocities as criminal is an attractive proposition, but there is little juridical support to suggest that there is any legal association with state accountability, even in its nebulous form as conceptualised here. However, it would be unwise entirely to dissociate state accountability from criminal accountability until further regard is had to state practice, when it is examined below.

Given the obstacles in terms of giving practical effect to a finding of criminal liability, why then are advocates so dogged in continuing to insist state criminality is legally feasible? And what is the purpose when international law already makes provision under the doctrine of state responsibility for dealing with states for breaching their legal obligations? Recourse to the historical emergence of state criminal liability suggests that the notion of state criminality was really a convenient euphemism in response to the complex issue of seeking redress for more aggravated forms of liability – inescapable in light of the atrocities of the two World Wars – than was possible within the parameters of the traditional state

126 Note 118 above, 353.
127 *South West Africa Cases (Ethiopia v South Africa; Liberia v South Africa)* ICJ Reports (1962).

responsibility doctrine. The end of the First World War was significant because the Allied powers sought to distinguish between the individual fault of the German Kaiser and the fault of Germany as a whole. The terms of the 1919 Treaty of Versailles sought to bring the Kaiser to trial but its wording laid the greater proportion of legal, as opposed to moral, blame with Germany. Article 227 charged the Kaiser with 'a supreme offence against international morality and the sanctity of treaties', linking the breach to the immorality of the war. In contrast, Article 231 stated that Germany's liability was for aggressive war – a breach of international law. Kelsen argued that charging the Kaiser with a breach of 'international morality' rather than 'international law' was intended to capture the gravity of the breach but avoiding the fact there was a dubious legal basis for bringing the Kaiser to trial.[128]

It was not only the fault of individual and state that were kept separate. In terms of redress, Article 232 required Germany to pay reparations 'for all damage done ... by such aggression', which implied a penal element in diverting funds from the internal reconstruction of Germany after the Second World War to impose a burden on the state. Article 231 also required that Germany 'accept' responsibility for the loss caused by any of its allies over which it had control, requiring the state to admit its fault, rather than simply accepting that the other parties to the Treaty considered Germany was at fault. The nature of the redress sought from Germany was different to any redress that could theoretically have been sought from the Kaiser following a criminal trial, creating an anomaly in that Germany was charged with the crime of aggression but the nature of redress was not criminal. In contrast, the Kaiser was charged with breaching morality because there was perceived to be no crime of aggression by individuals, but if found guilty then he would inevitably have faced criminal punishment.

The anomaly noted here highlights that at the end of the First World War the accountability of individuals was frustrated by a deficit in the expression of crimes by individuals under international law, while the accountability of states was frustrated by a lack of effective redress with which to respond to the state's liability. Thus, there were two potential directions that the development of international criminal law was likely to have taken, either to codify the criminal accountability of individuals or to identify some way to seek criminal redress from states. History shows that the former path was taken. The practical issues in relation to seeking an aggravated form of accountability from either the Kaiser or Germany were noted by the Commission on Responsibility that was established in 1919 to consider the issue of liability for the First World War. Even before the consequences of imposing post-war reparations on Germany were apparent so as to dissuade against future use of what proved to be crippling reparations against the state as a whole, the conclusion of the Commission was that individual accountability was the priority. The recommendation was that in the future there should be 'penal sanctions' 'for such grave outrages against the elementary principles of

128 H. Kelsen, *Peace Through Law* (Chapel Hill: University of North Carolina Press, 1944) 89.

international law'.[129] Indeed, in the aftermath of the Second World War it was the criminal punishment of the individual perpetrators of international crimes that was sought.

The focus at the Nuremberg Trials on individual accountability was not to the prejudice of addressing the role played by Germany (or Japan in the context of the Far East Tribunal); even Colonel Bernays, who had conceived the idea of the Nuremberg Trials, was conscious that 'behind every Axis war criminal … lies the basic criminal instigation of the Nazi doctrine'.[130] The difficulty lay in determining how to capture the gravity of Germany's offending when the idea of criminal state accountability had been rejected as a consideration for the Nuremberg Trials and reparations had fallen out of favour owing to the extent to which the German people had suffered in the aftermath of the First World War. Arguably, there were two responses that show the intent to hold Germany accountable in its separate capacity and in a manner commensurate to the aggravated nature of the breach.

The first response was to view Germany's culpability as a form of collective criminal liability, replacing the need to seek criminal accountability directly from the state, on the basis that either the accountability of various individuals counted toward the accountability of the state or the state was a derivation of the collective population. The Charter of the International Military Tribunal supports this interpretation as Articles 9 to 11 provide that an individual would be liable for membership of a criminal organisation such as the Gestapo as well as incurring separate liability for breaches committed in a personal capacity. This approach in distinguishing the forms of liability influenced the subsequent development of international criminal law, seen for example with the Rome Statute of the ICC. Article 25 declares that, on the one hand, individuals are liable when they knowingly contribute to crimes 'by a group of persons' and, on the other hand, that no provision in the Rome Statute 'relating to individual criminal responsibility shall affect the responsibility of states under international law'. Similarly, Article 5 of the ILC's 1991 Draft Code of Offences Against the Peace and Security of Mankind provided that the 'prosecution of an individual for a crime against the peace and security of mankind does not relieve a state'[131] of liability. Thus, the liability of the

129 Commission on the Responsibility of the Authors of the War and the Enforcement of Penalties 'Conclusions' (1920) *American Journal of International Law* 95 and presented at the Paris Peace Conference 1919.

130 B. Smith (ed), *The American Road to Nuremberg: The Documentary Record 1944–1945* (New York: Basic Books, 1982) 35.

131 The wording of Article 5 differs from that of the final Article 4 (1996 Draft) but it is apparent that the nature of the redress envisaged was based on attribution. In the Commentary to the 1996 Draft the ILC noted that: 'an individual may commit a crime against the peace and security of mankind as an "agent of the State", "on behalf of the State", "in the name of the State" or even in a de facto relationship with the State, without being vested with any legal power'. The ILC further considered that reverse attribution could not be used to permit a state to escape liability. It said that the state was 'unable to exonerate itself … by invoking the prosecution or punishment of the individuals who committed the crime' ('Report of the International Law Commission on

group is quite distinct to that of its individual members – the difficulty being that the liability of the group's members is still applied, to varying degrees, to wipe out the need to address the liability of the group.

The more convincing argument of a response that sought to and, in the opinion of Tomuschat,[132] did hold Germany accountable was the cumulative measures imposed on – and assumed by – the state in the following decades. The Potsdam Agreement required the division of Germany's territory amongst the Allied powers as well as the reduction or destruction of all industry with war potential, including shipbuilding, machine production and chemical factories, under the so-called Level of Industry Plans for Germany. In addition, a reparations deal was agreed with the German Government and negotiated with international Jewish organisations and the Israeli Government, which has resulted in excess of US$60 billion being paid to survivors.[133] Finally, in 1990 an apology was made by the Government of the Federal Republic of Germany on behalf of the German state for the crimes of the Nazi regime.[134] Taken in combination, these responses illustrate that the focus on individual criminal accountability at the Nuremberg Trials was not a replacement for seeking redress from Germany. Instead, the means for seeking redress were not solely those mechanisms within the framework of international criminal law. In the context of both World Wars the need to respond to atrocity, the likes of which had not been seen before, meant that the difficulties in seeking some form of legal accountability from the state that was commensurate with the aggravated nature of the breach were avoided. Instead, the focus shifted to individual accountability, which was readily dealt with under the framework provided by international criminal law. This did not mean that Germany's liability was ignored; rather, redress was sought by alternative, largely political, and even moral means of redress.

The more developments there are in terms of broadening the modes of redress when public international law is breached, especially when the breach in some way implicates the state, the stronger the indicator that a principle of state accountability exists or is evolving. Thus, it is rational also to consider the implications of international criminal law in terms of state accountability. The first point is that the development of international criminal law has established a precedent whereby effective accountability is sought commensurate to the gravity of the norm breached. The second point is that international criminal law draws a clear

the Work of its Forty-Eighth Session' UN Doc A/CN.4/L.528 (Commentary Draft Code of Offences Against the Peace and Security of Mankind) (1996) 23).

132 In an interview between the author and Professor Tomuschat of Humboldt University, Berlin (27 April 2009).

133 An overview of negotiations was given in M. Bazyler, 'The Holocaust Restitution Movement in Comparative Perspective' (2002) *Berkeley Journal of International Law* 11, 38.

134 J. Borneman, 'Public Apologies as Performative Redress' (2005) 25 *Johns Hopkins SAIS Review of International Affairs* 53.

distinction between the accountability of the individual and the state.[135] An early example of this was the 1937 Convention for the Prevention and Punishment of Terrorism that dealt with the accountability of individuals while at the same time noting in Article 1 that states were under a duty not to 'encourage terrorist activities' by groups or individuals – a phrase that succinctly captures the separate role – and thus breach – of the state. The third point is that the more fundamental the norm is perceived to be (as with international crimes) the greater the scope of cooperation between members of the international community to ensure the breaching party is held accountable, albeit that these developments all relate to individual accountability. In accordance with this view, the International Criminal Tribunal for the Former Yugoslavia (ICTY) noted in *Prosecutor v Furundzija* that the breach 'of an international obligation of essential importance for safeguarding the human being', which was the prohibition on torture and arguably a *jus cogens* norm, required redress from the individual pursuant to international criminal law and in addition redress from the state.[136]

Although the contemplation of state crimes and criminal state responsibility in the 20th century gives credence to the argument that the international community views some form of answerability beyond civil liability as desirable, there is insufficient evidence to argue that state accountability, as an evolving norm of international relations, is criminal in nature. However, evaluative criteria are still required in order to analyse state practice. At this point, the approach is therefore to refer directly to state practice for the purpose of identifying what associations exist in terms of making states answer for breaching public international law. This chapter cites only a few isolated incidents so as to establish some evaluative criteria, rather than seeking to paint a comprehensive picture of state accountability in practice. Thus, the caveat is again repeated that any criteria adopted at this time may subsequently be altered or displaced as the analysis continues to unfold and develop.

2.2.2 Is state accountability associated with state responsibility?

The most logical assumption is that state accountability is associated in some way with the doctrine of state responsibility. However, the growth of human rights

135 The definition of respective international crimes confirms that the breach by an individual is a separate matter to breach by the state. For example, the Appeals Chamber for the *ad hoc* Tribunals have ruled that the legal elements of crimes against humanity do not require a policy or plan, which would then imply involvement by the state (*Prosecutor v Kunarac* (Appeal) IT-96-23-A (2002) para 98). The *Kunarac* judgment followed the drafting of the Rome Statute of the ICC where Article 7 requires a 'State or organizational policy'. However, the Preparatory Commission considered that such 'a policy may in exceptional circumstances be implemented by a deliberate failure to take action' (Preparatory Commission for the International Criminal Court 'Elements of the Crimes' UN Doc PCNICC/2000/INF3/Add.2 (2000) Article 7, footnote 6). Therefore, while there will often be state participation, this is not an essential ingredient in order to hold the individual accountable for the crime.

136 *Prosecutor v Furundzija* (Judgment) IT-95-17/1-T (1998) para 142.

courts and tribunals shows that states are increasingly made to answer for breaches of international law in other forums. Where, then, would a norm of state accountability, if found to exist, fit into this framework? An entire chapter will be taken to analyse the relationship between state accountability and state responsibility; in the meantime the conclusions of that investigation are pre-empted here by clearly stating that the two concepts are different and that the doctrine of state responsibility only plays a discrete role in terms of making states answer for breaches of public international law.

To illustrate that state responsibility is not the sole means of getting states to answer for breaching international law it is best to refer to practice. As of 2010 there were no claims of state responsibility pending on the docket of the ICJ against the US or the UK as a result of the invasion of Iraq in 2003. Of course, it makes sense that no application has been brought before the ICJ if the states in question had not breached their obligations under international law; however, two factors suggest otherwise. First, both the US and the UK attempted to show that their actions had Security Council authorisation and that Iraq had breached its legal obligations pursuant to Security Council Resolution 1441 to warrant invasion. Similarly, states that provided assistance to the US and the UK, such as Germany, sought to justify their involvement by relying on the NATO treaty arrangement.[137] Secondly, there was widespread condemnation of the invasion. The presence of the US and the UK on the Security Council guaranteed that there would never be a resolution passed to condemn their actions but this did not stop individual members opposing the invasion on the basis that there was insufficient evidence to establish an imminent threat of nuclear attack to justify the use of force. Non-Security Council member states likewise expressed the view that peaceful means should have been exhausted before resorting to what was described as the 'rush to war', with the implication – in describing the use of force as war – being to reject any claim of self-defence.[138] Even former UN Secretary General Kofi Annan expressly stated that the invasion was illegal.[139] Thus, the lack of an express claim for state responsibility did not mean that there was no breach of international law. Rather, the lack of a formal application to the ICJ combined with the debate and criticism noted above illustrated that a determination of and response to breaches of international law was not limited to the state responsibility framework, which is only one of the responses taken when states breach international law. The first evaluative criterion is therefore to question whether the response to a breach of international law occurred beyond the state responsibility framework – in other words, state accountability is associated with seeking more in terms of answerability than merely engaging the state's responsibility.

137 Speech of Bundeskanzler Schroeder at Bundestag (19 March 2003).

138 Security Council Press Release 'Iraq, Middle East, Afghanistan, Africa Key Issues Before Security Council In 2003' UN Doc SC/7982 (2004).

139 E. MacAskill and J. Borger, 'Iraq War was Illegal and Breached UN Charter, Says Annan' *The Guardian* (2004) available at http://www.guardian.co.uk/world/2004/sep/16/iraq.iraq.

2.2.3 *Is state accountability associated with the particular law breached?*

The state responsibility doctrine is only one of many responses when states breach public international law that is currently tolerated in international relations, which is a reasonable observation given the diverse circumstances and range of breaches that occur in state practice and that necessitate a response. The underlying argument in this book is that the framework of international law and relations is evolving to ensure states are made to answer for all violations of public international law, not just those breaches within the scope of the state responsibility doctrine. It is submitted here that effective state accountability ensures redress because the specific norm was breached and regardless of the process in obtaining that objective; hence, the doctrine of state responsibility may still be a contributing means in holding states accountable. Thus, it is logical that the response to a grievous violation of the law will be seen as holding the breaching state accountable if the response in question reflected both the context of the breach and the specific norm that was breached.

The relevance of the context and the norm in determining that a state has been held accountable is illustrated by considering the response of the international community to Israel's use of force in the Gaza Strip in 2008/2009. States and human rights organisations contended that the bombing campaign by Israel could not be justified as an act of self-defence, was disproportionate even if the bombings did amount to self-defence and thus breached international law. At the time, the UN General Assembly expressed concern about the deterioration in the humanitarian and security situation 'resulting from the Israeli military actions against civilian areas',[140] while Secretary General Ban-Ki Moon noted that the attacks – including destruction of UN facilities – were unacceptable and called on the responsible parties to be 'held accountable for their actions'.[141] Because the parties directly affected were individuals (so, for example, Israel was considered to have breached its obligations under the 2005 Agreement on Movement and Access between the Palestinian Authority and Israel), the prolonged process of bringing a claim of state responsibility before the ICJ would have been ineffectual. Instead, General Assembly Resolution 63/98 on 'Israeli Practices Affecting the Human Rights of the Palestinian People in the Occupied Palestinian Territory, Including East Jerusalem' demanded that Israel 'comply with its legal obligations under international law, as mentioned in the Advisory Opinion rendered on 9 July 2004 by the International Court of Justice'. In 2009 the Security Council adopted Resolution 1860 to 'condemn all violence and hostilities directed against civilians and all acts of terrorism' including a school for displaced children that the Palestinian Ministry

140 'Israeli Practices Affecting the Human Rights of the Palestinian People in the Occupied Palestinian Territory, Including East Jerusalem' UN General Assembly Resolution 63/98 (2008).

141 Secretary General Ban-Ki Moon 'Remarks at the Opening of the 2009 Session' of the Committee on the Exercise of the Inalienable Rights of the Palestinian People' UN Doc SG/SM/12097 GA/PAL/1112 (2009).

of Health claimed resulted in over 1300 deaths.[142] Resolution 1860 is remarkable not so much for what it expressly said, which was to condemn the violence and call on member states to intensify efforts to sustain a durable ceasefire; rather, it was the fact that the resolution was even adopted and not vetoed by the US that indicated the gravity with which Israel's actions were viewed. The historical support that the US has given to Israel means that the implied criticism in permitting Resolution 1860 to be passed affords it significant weight in terms of political accountability.

It is apparent that the grievous nature of the alleged breaches was likewise influential, in terms of seeking legal accountability. The findings of the fact-finding body established under Human Rights Council Resolution S-9/1 to investigate violations of international human rights law and international humanitarian law by Israel as the occupying power in the Gaza Strip were released in 2009 and are colloquially known as the Goldstone Report, after the principal investigator, Richard Goldstone. It is submitted here that the report prescribes to the two-step approach to accountability set out in the earlier discussion, as well as highlighting that state accountability is context specific in terms of both process and outcome. On the basis of the fact-finding mission, conclusions were reached that war crimes and breaches of humanitarian and international law were perpetrated by Israel. The report identified that the State played an instrumental role, for example by 'taking into account the ability to plan, the means to execute plans … and statements by the Israeli military that almost no errors occurred' and the Commission determined 'that the incidents and patterns of events considered in the Report [we]re the result of deliberate planning and policy decisions'.[143] Furthermore, 'Israel violated its duty to respect the right of the Gaza population to an adequate standard of living'[144] and in respect of the approximately 700,000 Palestinians 'detained by Israel' the report held that Israel's actions 'resulted in violations of international human rights and humanitarian law'.[145] Having determined Israel's liability, the section of the report entitled 'Accountability' then concluded that because 'the Israeli system overall present[ed] inherently discriminatory features that make the pursuit of justice … very difficult',[146] the preferred means of redress from Israel was recourse to both universal jurisdiction and reparations. It is even more convincing to argue that the Goldstone Report is an example of state accountability in practice, given the follow-up in February 2010. The General Assembly adopted Resolution 64/253 (by 98 votes to 7),[147] which called on Israel to undertake credible investigations in conformity with international standards

142 T. El-Khodary and S. Tavernise, 'In the Fog of Urban War, Crimes and Ethics Blur' *New York Times* (25 January 2009).

143 'Report of the United Nations Fact-Finding Mission on the Gaza Conflict' UN Doc A/HRC/12/48 (2009) para 61.

144 Ibid, para 73.

145 Ibid, paras 86 and 91.

146 Ibid, para 122.

147 'Follow-up to the Report of the United Nations Fact-Finding Mission on the Gaza Conflict' General Assembly Resolution 64/253 (2010).

into the serious violations of international humanitarian and international human rights law reported by the fact-finding mission as steps 'towards ensuring accountability and justice'. Indeed, when the representative for Qatar introduced the resolution it was noted that the objective was to promote accountability and justice. The express wording of Resolution 64/253 and the earlier related Resolution 64/10 adopted in November 2009, first, reiterated that Israel had breached international law and, secondly, called on Israel to take steps to ensure redress as a result – stating that both elements were necessary for accountability.

The context and nature of the breach are fundamental to why the response to the bombings in 2008/2009 can be interpreted as the wider international community seeking to hold Israel accountable. As already noted, the Goldstone Report concluded that Israel had committed breaches of human rights and humanitarian law – in particular civilians were targeted, residents from the Gaza had been used to form human shields in violation of Article 31 of the Fourth Geneva Convention and Israel breached its prior legal undertakings including the 2005 Agreement on Movement. The response to the bombings utilised a range of measures from condemnation to collective action and sanction, which cumulatively were more severe than simply engaging Israel's responsibility under the state responsibility doctrine and which indicated the universal interest in seeking accountability owing to the grievous nature of the breach. There was also a marked difference in the tone used to condemn the violence in 2008/2009 compared, for example, with the response in 2006 following the 34 day conflict between Israel and Lebanon, when the closest that Security Council Resolution 1701 came to condemning Israel's actions was to imply that the State had breached Lebanon's sovereignty. The Security Council reiterated the support it had expressed in all its previous relevant resolutions 'for the territorial integrity, sovereignty and political independence of Lebanon within its internationally recognised borders', rather than directly stating that Israel had attacked Lebanon. The calls in 2006 to protect state sovereignty and enter into a ceasefire appear to have been motivated by the maintenance of international peace and security, in comparison with 2009 when the violence against civilians was directly condemned. Likewise, in Resolution 63/98 the UN General Assembly responded as a result of the grievous nature of the breach, identifying 'the continuing systematic violation of the human rights of the Palestinian people by Israel' and stating that 'all measures and actions taken by Israel … in violation of the relevant provisions of the Geneva Conventions and contrary to the relevant resolutions of the Security Council, are illegal and have no validity.'

The shift from noting that Lebanon's territorial integrity had been compromised by Israel to severely condemning Israel for its systematic violation of human rights in the Gaza Strip implied that the breach of certain norms (in this case norms of humanitarian protection), or at least a breach with particularly grievous consequences, inspired a harsher response from states. Indeed, the interest in holding Israel accountable for breaching humanitarian and human rights protections did not only arouse a response from the Security Council and the General Assembly. In its 2008 'Resolution on the Situation in the Gaza Strip' the Council of Europe's Parliamentary Assembly adopted a similar tone to that of the UN bodies, calling upon 'Israel to fulfil its international obligations' and bring an 'end to all acts of violence'. As the only directly-elected body of the EU, any criticism levelled by the 736 strong representatives makes a significant impact in terms of reflecting popular consensus, compared with the condemnation of bodies comprised of, and influenced by, political appointments. The point being made here is that the circumstances of the breach and the particular law that is breached have a direct bearing on the nature of the response (for example, the means to hold Israel accountable were necessarily limited to political criticism given the likelihood that the US would veto any action by the Security Council, but in addition means beyond the state responsibility doctrine were employed), the scope of the response (for example, the fact that the gravity of the breaches meant that the US did not block Security Council Resolution 1860 which condemned the violence by Israel and that condemnation was largely universal) and whether the response can be taken to have held the state accountable (for example, the Goldstone Report specifically condemned Israel for war crimes and breaches of humanitarian law rather than direct obligations owed to a specific party). The second evaluative criterion is therefore that state accountability will be a response commensurate to the specific law breached and the context of that breach, rather than a formulaic response to a breach of international law such as the state responsibility doctrine, which orders reparation on the basis that a state has breached its primary obligations to another state.

2.2.4 *Is state accountability solely associated with legal accountability?*

It was argued earlier that quasi-legal responses to the breach of public international law cannot be precluded, in terms of being seen as a means to hold states accountable. A completely separate consideration is whether state accountability is ever associated in international relations with measures that are expressly illegal. To answer this question regard is given to the mechanisms used in response to the practice of EU member states assisting extraordinary rendition that violates a cornucopia of human rights and international obligations.

In 2006 the Venice Commission was established, comprising independent experts from member and eventually non-member states, to draft an opinion on the consequences if states actively participated or passively acquiesced in the practice of extraordinary rendition. The 'Draft Opinion on the International Legal Obligations of Council of Europe Member States in Respect of Secret Detention Facilities and Inter-State Transport of Detainees' was adopted under Resolution 1562, entitled 'Secret Detentions and Illegal Transfers of Detainees Involving Council of Europe Member States'. The Commission found certain Council of Europe states had been involved in 'a "spider's web" of illegal transfers of detainees woven by the Central Intelligence Agency'[148] and considered there was no defence,

148 By 2009, the European Parliament amassed evidence – including findings by the Polish Public Prosecutor and admissions by the UK and Spanish Foreign Ministers – showing that member

regardless of whether the state was complying with its treaty obligations, given that the fulfilment of a state's treaty obligations must be 'in a manner compatible with their human rights obligations', including the European Convention on Human Rights and the ICCPR. Furthermore, the Commission presumed that the reason for extraordinary rendition is to interrogate individuals using techniques that may otherwise be seen as torture, in which case states that acquiesced or assisted rendition were breaching a non-derogable 'peremptory norm (*jus cogens*)'.

Having noted the gravity of the alleged offending, the report outlined a variety of responses that neither necessitated the adoption of a formal response mechanism nor the law to be violated – but all of which required the breaching states to account for their actions. Two examples are representative. First, even though permission is needed to search foreign military bases on a state's territory, a host state is still 'obliged to prevent, and react to such abuse of its territory'. In such cases, the Commission concluded that the host state could 'exercise powers in respect of registration and control of aliens, and demand identification and movement orders of those present on the military base in question'[149] in order to ensure agents of the foreign state were not committing offences on the host state's territory. Indeed, 'all possible measures',[150] including diplomatic channels were to be used to protest where the practice was occurring. Secondly, if a member state had cause to suspect that individuals were being transferred by air for the purposes of interrogation, two possible responses were envisaged. If the aircraft falsely claimed civilian status in breach of the 1944 Chicago Convention on Civil Aviation, then the member state had the right to search the plane and 'take all necessary measures to secure human rights'. Alternatively, if there was a link between the aircraft and the flag state, then the immunity of the flag state under international law prevented seizure of the aircraft, in which case the member state could refuse flight clearance for the aircraft or make use of the airspace conditional on consent to search the aircraft.[151] Thus, irrespective that the Commission considered that there was no defence for extraordinary rendition and that the assistance given by member states to the US arguably breached the *jus cogens* prohibition of torture, the 'possible measures' that could be taken to hold the allegedly recalcitrant states accountable for their actions had to be within the bounds of international law. On that basis, the third evaluative criterion is that any response to a breach

states had permitted the US to land extraordinary rendition flights within their respective territories and had therefore breached Article 3 of the European Convention on Human Rights and the United Nations Convention against Torture and Other Cruel, Inhuman or Degrading Treatment or Punishment (European Parliament Resolution on the Alleged Use of European Countries by the CIA for the Transportation and Illegal Detention of Prisoners' Doc 0045 (2009) para B).

149 'Draft Opinion on the International Legal Obligations of Council of Europe Member States in Respect of Secret Detention Facilities and Inter-State Transport of Detainees' European Council Opinion No 363/2005 EC Doc No CDL-DI 001 Rev (2006) para 134.

150 Ibid, para 147.

151 Ibid, paras 149–51.

that is illegal cannot be interpreted as a means of holding the breaching state accountable – at least in terms of being a credible indicator that the concept is evolving as a norm of international relations.

2.2.5 Is state accountability associated with political or moral accountability?

In addition to being either legal or quasi-legal, the means of redress in the few practical examples cited thus far have been political rather than legal in nature, including criticism by the UN bodies, sanctions imposed by states and condemnation by human rights monitoring bodies. Thus, the fourth proposed evaluative criterion is that in practice state accountability may be more than merely legal in nature. Political accountability would relate to both the determination of liability, for example the findings of the Goldstone Report or declaration by a majority of states in the General Assembly, and the nature of the redress, as in the examples highlighted above. Furthermore, forms of moral accountability are not excluded from the analysis. Thus, the determination of liability and equating redress could be moral in nature, for example where a state identifies its own wrongdoing and then establishes some form of public commemoration, as was the case in both Chile and Argentina in the years following their respective dictatorships.[152]

Pragmatically, and as already discussed, state accountability is likely to be achieved through a combination of measures. Indeed, the argument that there is an evolving norm of state accountability can only be made at this time if accountability is interpreted as being more than simply legal in nature. However, there are certain benefits, highlighted by Balint, in terms of holding states legally accountable that must be recognised.[153] First, a legal determination of liability provides an official acknowledgement of the role played by the state and undermines any denial of the breach. Secondly, on the basis of that determination an objective history is established that delineates the transition from before and after the breach as well as what the breach entailed. This set of legal facts can also be used to hold individuals accountable and be employed in terms of other transitional and rehabilitative measures. Thirdly, although states cannot be imprisoned there is still the scope for legal forms of punishment such as punitive compensation, conditional on prior determination of legal liability. The perception that the state has been punished is more likely to benefit the direct stakeholders in accountability, such as victims of human rights breaches, in terms of a personal belief that justice has been done. Finally, forms of redress that are legally sanctioned are more likely to address some of the systemic causes of the breach, for example by leading to a change in the law. To highlight further why legal accountability is preferable, a comparison with forms of moral accountability such as public

152 E. Jelin, *State Repression and the Labours of Memory* (Minneapolis: University of Minnesota Press, 2003).

153 Note 96 above, 125.

commemoration is useful. On the one hand, memorials and apologies appear to be a state acknowledging and providing redress for the breach yet, on the other hand, a state's moral accountability is as likely to be influenced by the same subjective influences that affect the moral accountability of individuals. For example, an act of public commemoration legitimises the state's perception of the wrongdoing and gives credence to the state's interpretation of events, while legal accountability depends upon an objective determination of liability and redress that then theoretically creates an unbiased record of events. To the extent that the state is able to own and construct the official memory of the breach there is legitimate doubt as to whether it can truly be said that the state has been held accountable.

At this time, practice suggests that forms of state accountability are predominantly political in nature. The uncomfortable international pressure on the US as a result of the detention centre in Guantánamo Bay, Cuba and the subsequent questioning before the UN Human Rights Committee (UNHRC) illustrated the overlap between legal and political redress that in turn can be interpreted as state accountability. It is submitted that the UNHRC is part of a broader development that includes the Human Rights Council and introduction of the Universal Peer Review mechanism, as effective sources of monitoring state power in a public forum. The UNHRC is comprised of 18 human rights panellists, appointed on the basis of their expertise and because they are not affiliated with a certain state. The potential impact of the UNHRC was seen in the 2006 questioning of the US when specific answers, rather than generalised responses, were sought to justify the treatment of prisoners in the US detention facility in Guantánamo Bay. In challenging the US on its report submitted under Article 40 ICCPR, the UNHRC asked questions relating to the implementation of relevant US domestic law, such as Section 1005 of the Detainee Treatment Act 2005, the independence of review boards, whether the US could explain 'restrictions on the rights of all detainees to have access to all proceedings' and 'the reasons justifying force-feeding'.[154] In its Concluding Observations, the UNHRC criticised the US for failing to include information relating to how rights under the ICCPR were being protected in relation to individuals outside the State's territory. The Committee noted 'shortcomings concerning the independence, impartiality and effectiveness of investigations into allegations of torture and cruel, inhuman or degrading treatment or punishment inflicted by United States military and non-military personnel or contract employees, in detention facilities in Guantánamo Bay' and expressed concern that 'Section 1005(e) of the Detainee Treatment Act bars detainees in Guantánamo Bay from seeking review in case of allegations of ill-treatment or poor conditions of detention'.[155]

154 'Concluding Observations of the Human Rights Committee: Consideration of Reports Submitted by States Parties Under Article 40 of the Covenant, United States of America' UN Doc CCPR/C/USA/CO/3 (2006).

155 Ibid, paras 14 and 15.

There was no attempt – or ability on the part of the Committee – to seek legal accountability from the US in relation to Guantánamo but the State was required to explain its actions within a public forum. In addition, there were political consequences, beyond the criticism levelled by the UNHRC, notably with the closure of the detention facility at Guantánamo being a campaign issue in the 2008 US Presidential elections. In 2009, an Executive Order was issued that noted 'the significant concerns raised … both within the United States and *internationally*'[156] and which led the new government administration to pledge, first, that 'no individual currently detained at Guantánamo shall be held in the custody … except in conformity with all applicable laws governing the conditions of such confinement, including Common Article 3 of the Geneva Conventions' and, secondly, that 'the detention facilities at Guantánamo … shall be closed as soon as practicable'.[157] A change in state policy that can be expressly linked with international concern expressed as to the respective state's policy is a strong case for state accountability in practice, and an indicator of the association between state accountability and political accountability.

2.3 Conclusion

This chapter has sought to construct an interpretive framework that may be used to examine state practice and assess the extent to which states are held accountable under international law for breaching *jus cogens* norms and the extent to which state accountability is evolving as a principle of international law.

The first step was to canvass the debate on the role of legitimacy versus legality in international relations – notably the argument that state intervention is permissible for humanitarian reasons – and the way that state practice emphasises compliance with the law. Based on this discussion, parameters were set as to the scope of responses when states breach international law that could be analysed as mechanisms for holding the state accountable. The conclusion was that while an extra-legal response could be interpreted as a means of seeking accountability, an illegal response could not. A useful metaphor here is to envisage a continuum of responses when states breach international law. On this continuum, illegal responses sit at one end (the use of force, military overthrow of the government), responses that are set down in black letter international law are located at the other end (the doctrine of state responsibility, loss of immunity) and responses that are not prohibited, but neither are they expressly condoned, lie in the middle (sanctions, censure). State accountability has the potential to cover the whole spectrum up to the point that the response is illegal – indeed, the most likely scenario is that accountability will be achieved as a result of a combination of permissible responses.

156 'Executive Order: Review and Disposition of Individuals Detained at the Guantánamo Bay Naval Base and Closure of Detention Facilities' Section 2. Emphasis added.

157 Ibid, Sections 3 and 6.

The second step in constructing the analytical framework and viewing the concept as a whole was to identify a set of evaluative associations, which will subsequently be tested for robustness when looking for evidence of state accountability in practice. In particular, it is assumed, first, that if the response exceeds the scope of the state responsibility doctrine, then something more is sought than merely reparation because the state breached its legal obligations to another state; secondly, it is assumed that any response capable of holding states accountable for breaching public international law would not be illegal; thirdly, it is assumed that in order for the state to be held accountable the response must reflect both the context and specific law breached; and, finally, it is assumed that state accountability will not be solely legal in nature but also moral and, in all likelihood, political.

3 The relationship between state accountability and *jus cogens* norms

Chapter 3 explores the debate surrounding *jus cogens* to determine the legal status of these norms. *Jus cogens* are pivotal because they provide the link between conceptual state accountability and established public international law. Because the focus here is on accountability for the breach of the norm rather than its legal development, no single definition of *jus cogens* endorsed, nor the argument made that certain norms are or are not *jus cogens*. Instead, clarity is given as to the unique properties of *jus cogens* that are instrumental to, and indicative of, the evolution of state accountability.

3.1 *Jus cogens* as the link between conceptual state accountability and established international law

The debate relating to the origin and content of *jus cogens* norms suggests the term is more an academic convenience than a legal reality. An alternative perspective is to blend both views and recognise that the academic reality of these so-called non-derogable norms (that in fact are often derogated from) means that it is more accurate to describe *jus cogens* as a legal convenience. This is because the *jus cogens* doctrine gives form to an indeterminate body of substantive law by reconciling the otherwise uncertain relationship between fundamental principles and other rules of public international law. In other words, and the approach taken here, *jus cogens* can be seen as a vehicle, first, to articulate that certain fundamental rules of public international law are increasingly recognised as requiring protection and, secondly, to illustrate that in practice there is political and moral will in favour of protecting such norms. On that basis, there is no need to resolve the debate surrounding *jus cogens* or to adopt a normative conception of *jus cogens* in the scope of this work.

Certainly, the term is used more in the context of academic debate surrounding these mythical-like norms than it is given practical effect in terms of state practice, as recognised by the ECtHR in the *Al-Adsani* case.[158] The Court considered that isolated developments in relation to the application of the immunity doctrine could be linked with the increased acceptance and recognition of *jus cogens* by states.

158 *Al Adsani v United Kingdom* 123 ILR (2003).

However, the Court then noted that because the immunity is an established doctrine of international law, it has primacy over emerging and indeterminate principles including *jus cogens*. This is not to say that the failure expressly to identify which norms are *jus cogens* automatically hinders recognition that certain norms are fundamental and worthy of international protection. For example, General Assembly Resolution 3314, which defined aggression, and the 1973 Convention on the Suppression and Punishment of the Crime of Apartheid do not use the terms 'peremptory' or *jus cogens*; yet the prohibitions of apartheid and aggression are arguably two of the most widely acknowledged norms in that category. Furthermore, if the analysis were limited here to instances where the breach was of a norm expressly stated to be *jus cogens*, then there would likely be little evidence from which to identify a typology of accountability in practice. This is because there are certain implications in recognising a definitive normative as *jus cogens*, notably that there can be no derogation or exception to the principle, which undoubtedly discourage express recognition.

To the extent that states accept that *jus cogens* are non-derogable, it would be reasonable to expect there would be some sort of response when these norms were breached – the argument here being that such responses would indicate an evolving principle of state accountability. Therefore, it is not sufficient for the purposes of this analysis merely to claim that certain norms are recognised by the majority of states as *jus cogens* – there must be reasons why *jus cogens* are considered to be non-derogable and therefore why the international community is theoretically inspired to seek accountability when these norms are breached. This is not to say that an unequivocal determination of the existence and content of *jus cogens*, or a novel normative construction will be reached in the limited space available. Instead, a working definition can be adopted and then proven or disproven with the subsequent analysis of state practice; indeed, the conclusion may be that currently there is very little evidence that states give any practical recognition to *jus cogens* in terms of seeking accountability. The objective of this chapter is therefore to identify what norms are recognised as *jus cogens* and why, by looking for any state and juridical consensus as to *jus cogens* as a concept, providing an overview of the controversy as to definition and by considering the norms' source and substance.

3.2 The debate and attempting to define *jus cogens*

Theorists such as Grotius, in his work *De Inis et de Iure Belli Reflectiones*, have long been interested in the degree of symbiosis between legal norms and the moral interests of the broader community, while cultures and philosophies dating from the Stoics in the classic tradition are underpinned by associations with natural law. Lao Tzu referred to 'a universal governing principle' in the *Tao-Te Ching*; Islam recognises the divine Shar'ia in the Qur'an; Jewish faith takes direction from the Torah; and Canon law is based on the Christian faith. It was not until the 19th and 20th centuries that the view that a body of norms exists protecting the interests of the entire international community and not just states, was expressed as a matter of international law. The prohibition on slavery, the emergence of international humanitarian law that was subsequently codified in the Hague and Geneva Conventions, the progression in international criminal law at Nuremberg and judicial references to fundamental norms[159] have all contributed to the move away from a purely state-centric conception of international law and acted as a precondition for the broad acceptance of *jus cogens*. As Brownlie noted, however, 'more authority exists for the category of *jus cogens* than exists for its particular content'.[160]

3.2.1 Distinguishing jus cogens *norms from standard norms*

Supporters of *jus cogens* contend that there is a body of norms under international law that are universally binding and that are different to standard norms of international law.[161] In its 2006 Report on the Fragmentation of International Law, the ILC agreed that certain 'elementary considerations' enjoy a 'special status in the international legal system',[162] including *erga omnes* obligations and aspects of the UN Charter. The ILC then drew a distinction between the wider category of 'intransgressible principles of international law' and *jus cogens* by referring to Article 53 of the 1969 Vienna Convention Law on Treaties (VCLT) and noting that the non-derogability from and 'universal acceptance' of the 'superiority' of the content distinguished *jus cogens* from other fundamental principles of international law.[163] Whether these elements are to be taken together (so that the reason why *jus cogens* norms are non-derogable is their content) or read separately (so that the

159 *Oscar Chinn Case* (Merits) PCIJ Series A/B No 63 (1934); the 1928 French-Mexican Claims Commission in *Pablo Najera* French-Mexican Claims Commission 5 RIAA (1928) 472; *Case Concerning the Application of the Convention of 1902 Governing the Guardianship of Infants* ICJ Reports (1958) Quintana J at 106–107; *Case Concerning the Right of Passage over Indian Territory* ICJ Reports (1960) Fernandes J at 135; *South West Africa Cases (Ethiopia v South Africa; Liberia v South Africa)* (Second Phase 1966) ICJ Reports 1960, Tanaka J at 298; *North Sea Continental Cases (Federal Republic of Germany v Denmark; Federal Republic of Germany v Netherlands)* (Merits 1969) ICJ Reports 1967 Nervo, J. at 97.

160 I. Brownlie, *Principles of Public International Law* (Oxford: Oxford University Press, 1979) 515.

161 For examples of *jus cogens* supporters see Christenson, who describes *jus cogens* as 'a legal system of entirely distinctive norms guarding fundamental interests of international society' (G. Christenson, 'Jus Cogens: Guarding Interests Fundamental to International Society' (1988) 28 *Virginia Journal of International Law* 585, 587). See also the distinction drawn between *jus cogens* and *jus dispositivum* by A. Verdross, '*Jus Dispositivum* and *Jus Cogens* in International Law' (1966) 60 *American Journal of International Law* 55, 58. Other advocates include G. Fitzmaurice, 'The General Principles of International Law Considered from the Standpoint of the Rule of Law' (1957) 92 *Recueil des Cours de L'Académie de Droit International de La Hague* 1, 125–26; K. Parker, and L. Neylon, 'Jus Cogens: Compelling the Law of Human Rights' (1989) 12 *Hastings International and Comparative Law Review* 411, 422; E. Schwelb, 'Some Aspects of International *Jus Cogens* as Formulated by the International Law Commission' (1967) 61 *American Journal of International Law* 946; G. Tunkin, 'International Law in the International System' (1975) 147 *Recueil des Cours de L'Académie de Droit International de La Hague* 1, 98.

162 'Conclusions of the Work of the Study Group on the Fragmentation of International Law: Difficulties Arising from the Diversification and Expansion of International Law' UN Doc A/61/10 (2006).

163 Ibid, paras 32 and 33.

reason why *jus cogens* norms are non-derogable is that they are universally accepted as such) is at the heart of the *jus cogens* debate.

There are certainly issues in relying on the VCLT as definitive in elucidating upon the concept of *jus cogens*. First, Article 53, which defines *jus cogens* as 'accepted and recognized by the international community of states as a whole as a norm from which no derogation is permitted', must be interpreted in accordance with the objective of the VCLT to manage treaty relations between states. Unless Article 53 is adopted more broadly, for example as a principle of customary international law or incorporated into domestic law, then strictly speaking the VCLT definition is limited to the context of treaties. Secondly, only states have the right to invoke Article 53 when a treaty breaches *jus cogens*; thus, if the VCLT is definitive there would be a discrepancy between having fundamental norms on the one hand and a limited capacity to protect those norms on the other. States such as Chile and Israel recognised this gap in protection but were unsuccessful in seeking to introduce into the Convention a broader right to invoke Article 53.[164] Thirdly, the VCLT was drafted at a time when states dominated international law and relations, which is apparent as Article 53 expressly refers to the 'international community *of states* as a whole', although the ILC did note that the wording was selected 'to stress the paramountcy that states have over the making of international law',[165] rather than deny that parties other than states may have an interest in *jus cogens* norms. Undoubtedly, the pragmatic reason why states play a central role in identifying *jus cogens* is because states are the dominant actors in the international framework and any form of international accountability largely depends on state participation. In addition, states play a central role in the recognition of *jus cogens* as a matter of legal rationality. Article 38 of the ICJ Statute is the accepted statement of traditional sources of international law, using similar language to Article 53 VCLT in referring to principles of law 'recognised by civilised nations', conventions and principles of law that are 'recognised' by states and custom that is 'accepted' by states. Of course, if both *jus cogens* and non-*jus cogens* principles depend upon state recognition then the distinction between them must relate to the second characteristic set down in Article 53, being the non-derogability of *jus cogens*.

What it means to say that *jus cogens* are non-derogable is uncertain because Article 53 does not clarify whether the norm is non-derogable owing to the fact

164 Czalinski argues that there is the potential for third parties to claim a treaty is void in accordance with Draft Article 48 of the 'Draft Articles on the Responsibility of States for Internationally Wrongful Acts' UN Doc A/Res/56/83 (2001) (W. Czalinski, '*Jus Cogens* and the Law of Treaties' in C. Tomuschat, and J.-M. Thouvenin (eds), *The Fundamental Rules of the International Legal Order* (Boston: Martinus Nijhoff Publishers, 2006) 83, 89). The clear wording of Draft Article 48, which refers to states, would mean that the limit of that potential would be to include third party states but the point is that there are issues associated with the Vienna Convention that make the definition of *jus cogens* under Article 53 authoritative rather than definitive.

165 'Draft Articles on the Responsibility of States for Internationally Wrongful Acts' UN Doc A/Res/56/83 (2001) and 'Report of the International Law Commission on the Work of its Fifty-Third Session' UN Doc A/56/10 (2001) Commentary on Article 25 para 18.

that the international community of states has recognised it as such or alternatively the norm was always non-derogable and now the international community of states has recognised this fact. The easiest way to approach this conundrum is to consider the meaning of the word derogation. The Oxford Law Dictionary defines derogation as a 'lessening of the authority, strength or power of a law, right or obligation', thus different from a dispensation, which is only granted to a specific party bound by the law. Derogation underlies the legal framework of human rights protection; for example, both Article 15 of the European Convention on Human Rights and Article 4 of the ICCPR provide that the respective Convention or Covenant may only be derogated from in times of public emergency and even then the derogating state must take steps to inform other states, illustrating that the specific protection cannot be easily displaced. By comparison, there is no stated exception that permits derogation from a *jus cogens* norm set down in the VCLT. Any treaty that is incompatible with a *jus cogens* norm is void and, pursuant to Article 71, the parties to that treaty must eliminate the consequences of the breach and bring their actions into conformity with the norm. Clearly, derogation is not taken to have any exceptional meaning within the context of the VCLT, and simply means a deviation from the law in question.

The second approach in determining what it means to say that *jus cogens* are non-derogable, as discussed below, is to consider juridical indicators and evidence of state opinion as to whether *jus cogens* are non-derogable because of the substantive content of the norm or because of its source (ie the community of states recognises that certain norms are non-derogable and therefore *jus cogens*; rather than the community of states recognising that certain norms are *jus cogens* and therefore non-derogable, in which case there would appear to be no distinction with standard norms that are legally constructed on the basis of state recognition as noted earlier).

3.2.2 *The source and substance of* jus cogens

Jus cogens have been given near-mythical characteristics by advocates; for example, the Mexican delegate in negotiations for the VCLT claimed that *jus cogens* 'derive from principles that the legal conscience of mankind deem absolutely essential to coexistence in the international community'.[166] An association between *jus cogens* and higher law has led supporters of this view to conclude, as Verdross did, that *jus cogens* norms provide an 'ethical minimum'[167] that bind states regardless of whether or not they consent and comply. This does not mean that Article 53 is superfluous – indeed, state recognition is still essential for identifying which norms are or are not non-derogable from *jus cogens*. Furthermore, Article 64 VCLT

166 'Conference on the Law of Treaties' UN Doc A/CONF/39/11/Add.2 (1968) Statement of Mexican Delegate 294.

167 A. Verdross, 'Forbidden Treaties in International Law' (1937) 31 *American Journal of International Law* 571, 574.

supports this approach because it provides that a new *jus cogens* norm 'emerges' so that its substance is recognised as already having been non-derogable, rather than the new norm being recognised and only then becoming non-derogable (in which case an adjective such as 'formed' would be more appropriate). Indeed, critics of *jus cogens* do not tend to dispute the existence of *jus cogens* per se. For example, the French delegate to the Vienna Convention claimed that 'France would have had no problems in subscribing to a concept of *jus cogens* restricted to certain basic human values shared by all States but did have problems accepting an ill-defined concept of *jus cogens*'.[168] Instead, the reason that states such as France elected not to adopt the Convention in 1969 was owing to the lack of clarity about the content of *jus cogens* (speculating that the norms would magically be distinguished from the general corpus of international law on the basis of substantive content) and the contention that *jus cogens* could ever come into existence without state consent.

It is worthwhile noting that initially Article 53 VCLT made no reference to recognition by the community of states so that the later inclusion of this factor suggests it was the substance of the norm that was considered definitive.[169] The subsequent addition of state recognition suggests either an emerging or dominant positivist association between *jus cogens* and custom that meant some form of state acceptance was considered an integral component of the definition. Prosper Weil, who is one such positivist and critic of the concept, cited 'the difficulty, even the impossibility of identifying the substance of rules of *jus cogens*; the risk presented to the stability of treaties; and its underlying incompatibility with the structure of the international system'[170] if *jus cogens* emerged as an alternative source of international law irrespective of state consent. Weil warned that placing *jus cogens* beyond the accepted sources of law listed in Article 38 of the ICJ Statute in order to overcome a lack of definitional consensus would only serve to undermine the established framework of international law. Given that supporters perceive *jus cogens* as fundamental to this framework and should Weil's prediction be correct, it is unlikely that *jus cogens* could exist completely independent of state input. Certainly the ICJ believed, albeit in the context of its 1995 *Advisory Opinion on the Legality of the Threat or Use of Nuclear Weapons* limiting the legal weight of the statement, that the 'question whether a norm is part of *jus cogens* relates to the legal character of the norm',[171] rather than its substance.

168 Note 166 above, Statement of French Delegate.

169 International Law Commission Yearbook of the International Law Commission (1966) Volume II 183.

170 P. Weil, 'Le Droit International en Quête de Son Identité' (1992) 237 *Recueil des Cours de L'Académie de Droit International de La Hague* 269. This was translated by the author from the French original: 'la difficulté, confinant à l'impossibilité, d'identifier les règles de *jus cogens*; le risque qu'elle comporte pour la stabilité des traités; son incompatibilité essentielle, viscérale presque, avec la structure du système international'. Weil's views reflect the position taken by the French Government in electing not to ratify the Vienna Convention.

171 *Advisory Opinion in the Case of the Legality of the Threat or Use of Nuclear Weapons* ICJ Reports (1995) para 83.

What is clear is that both supporters and critics recognise that in theory *jus cogens* norms seek to protect the fundamental interests of the entire international community or, as described by the German Federal Constitution Court, *jus cogens* norms 'are indispensable to the existence of the law of nations as an international legal order and the observance of which can be required by all members of the international community'.[172] It would seem reasonable to expect that a shared interest in *jus cogens*, which could inspire the designation of certain norms as non-derogable, would also give rise to an obligation on states to comply and ensure compliance with those norms. Accordingly, the third perspective taken here in unpacking *jus cogens* and understanding why these norms are recognised as non-derogable is to consider whether the consequences of derogation are solely negative (states must not derogate from the norm and to do so would make the instrument or action void) or whether states are also under an obligation to take positive steps to ensure compliance with the norm.

3.2.3 Are states under a positive duty to comply and ensure compliance with jus cogens *norms?*

If a boundary treaty was inconsistent with the right to self-determination (assuming the right to self-determination is recognised as *jus cogens*), would states only be obligated to declare that the treaty was invalid or would they be required to take measures to protect the self-determination of those individuals affected? Furthermore, do these obligations extend to all states or just those directly responsible for the breach?[173] On the one hand, if *jus cogens* are non-derogable owing to their substantive content then rationally every state must be under a legal obligation to ensure maintenance. On the other hand, if *jus cogens* are non-derogable on the basis of being recognised as such by the community of states, then there would need to be some form of recognition that all states were obligated to comply and, in addition, to ensure compliance. Irrespective of the view taken, the lack of evidence that any such duty is upheld in practice suggests that there is in fact no such obligation at this time, that there is universal state practice contrary to that obligation, or that there are difficulties in terms of implementing such an obligation.

One fundamental difficulty is determining what the consequences are if states fail to satisfy any obligation to maintain *jus cogens*. Rationally, if such an obligation does exist then it must be owed *erga omnes* to the international community as a whole so that another state could bring a claim of state responsibility. However, the lack of a legal alternative to engaging state responsibility highlights the book's

172 Judgment of 7 April 1965, Bundesverfassungsgericht, BverfGE.

173 There has yet actually to be a judicial declaration that a treaty is void for conflicting with a *jus cogens* norm, but Czalinski cites several examples of treaties that arguably could have invoked Article 53 but did not, including the Western Sahara Treaty (1975) which Algeria claimed was invalid on the basis that it undermined the principle of self-determination but which other states claimed was invalid owing to the lack of capacity to conclude the treaty in the first place (n 164 above, 83, 88–89, 94–95).

underlying thesis whereby there are limited means of redress available when states breach their obligations in the current international law framework, regardless of the underlying norm on which the obligation is based. One option might be a claim similar to that of an *actio popularis* but the ICJ rejected the concept in the *South West Africa Cases*. In the First Phase, the Court dismissed South Africa's preliminary objections as to jurisdiction because Ethiopia and Liberia lacked a direct interest and held that all states had 'a legal right or interest in observance of [South Africa's] obligations'[174] as Mandatory of the territory. By the Second Phase the Court changed its mind and considered there was no 'legal right or interest' in general observance of South Africa's Mandate, which it stated would be the same as a 'right resident in any member of a community to take legal action in vindication of a public interest'. In other words, it would amount to an *actio popularis*, which 'is not known to international law as it stands'.[175] The ICJ's view that *actio popularis* is not recognised under international law did not alter even after its infamous *Barcelona Traction* dicta, where the Court observed that certain obligations are owed *erga omnes* by states to the international community as a whole (which, if found to exist, would include any obligation to ensure compliance with *jus cogens*)[176].

Logically, the answer to whether an obligation exists must remain unanswered at this time regardless of the issues noted above in relation to identification and implementation. This is because the argument made here, that there is an evolving norm of state accountability, is premised on an emerging (rather than established) consensus that states are under a positive obligation to respond to breaches of *jus cogens*.

3.2.4 Which norms are jus cogens *norms?*

It is unsurprising that there is no consensus as to the scope of any duty on states to comply and ensure compliance with *jus cogens* when there is little agreement as to which norms are in fact recognised as *jus cogens* – which in turn is understandable given the continuing debate in identifying what it is that distinguishes this body of norms. One example of the impact that a lack of clarity has had in terms of hindering a consistent juridical treatment of *jus cogens* was the startling view of the German Constitutional Court in 2003 that even 'basic rules for the protection of the environment' are *jus cogens*.[177] By 2004 the court adopted a more temperate stance in the *German Expropriations* case to link *jus cogens* with accepted consitutional

174 *South West Africa Cases (Ethiopia v South Africa; Liberia v South Africa)* ICJ Reports (1960) 343.

175 Ibid (Second Phase 1966) ICJ Reports (1960) 47. In this case, the general interest being referred to was not all states, merely states in the League of Nations. The rationale remains the same, however, given that it is the public interest factor that is said to give rise to the legal interest in observance.

176 Confirmed in *Nuclear Tests Case (Australia v France; New Zealand v France)* ICJ Reports (1974); *East Timor (Portugal v Australia)* ICJ Reports (1991).

177 *Order of the Second Senate the German Federal Constitutional Court* BVerfG, 2 BvR 685/03 24/06 (2003) para 67.

principles in Articles 1.2 and 25 of the Basic Law, and describe *jus cogens* as 'indispensable to the existence of public international law, the compliance with which all members of the community of States may require'[178] – this time giving self-determination as an example. Even the small body of norms that is widely cited as *jus cogens*, and canvassed below, is controversial owing to notable gaps in protection including the failure to take gender into account as identified by Charlesworth and Chinkin who argued that, as the list of widely accepted *jus cogens* norms currently stands, 'women are peripheral to the understanding of fundamental community values'.[179] In the same vein, Simma and Alston considered that the fact that there are no economic or social rights recognised as *jus cogens* illustrates the extent to which any so-called consensus is subject to political factors and the influence of a few powerful states.[180]

In 1968, at the time of drafting the VCLT, the ILC considered there was insufficient consensus amongst states to identify which norms were recognised as *jus cogens*. To avoid becoming 'engaged in a prolonged study of matters which fall outside the scope of present [international law]',[181] the Commission preferred that the content of *jus cogens* 'be worked out in State practice and in the jurisprudence of international tribunals'[182] so that, by 2001, the ILC perceived there was sufficient agreement between states to be able to identify the minimum in *jus cogens* norms. Evidence of consensus amongst states was drawn, first, from international instruments that did not permit derogation in certain circumstances such as the view expressed by the Human Rights Committee in General Comment No 24 that particular 'provisions in the Covenant [on Civil and Political Rights] that represent customary international law (and *a fortiori* when they have the character of peremptory norms) may not be the subject of reservations';[183] secondly, from the inability to waive certain standards under the Geneva Conventions;[184] and, thirdly, from jurisprudence of both domestic and international courts.[185] Ultimately, the

178 *East German Expropriation Case (Order of the Second Senate of the German Federal Constitutional Court)* BVerfG 955/00 (2004) paras 97–98.

179 H. Charlesworth and C. Chinkin, *The Boundaries of International Law* (Manchester: Manchester University Press, 2000) 120.

180 B. Simma and P. Alston, 'The Sources of Human Rights Law: Custom, Jus Cogens and General Principles' (1988) 12 *Australian Yearbook of International Law* 82, 94.

181 Note 166 above.

182 Note 169 above at 25.

183 It must be noted, however, that the reaction of states to the stance taken by the Human Rights Committee was not necessarily favourable with the USA and UK arguing that the Committee had exceeded its authority (C. Doebbler, *International Human Rights Law: Cases and Materials* (Washington: CD Publishing, 2004) 281).

184 Articles 7, 10, 11 and 55 Geneva Convention for the Amelioration of the Condition of the Wounded and Sick in Armed Forces in the Field (First Geneva Convention) (1949), Article 6 Geneva Convention Relative to the Treatment of Prisoners of War (Third Geneva Convention) (1949), Articles 7, 8 and 11 Geneva Convention Relative to the Protection of Civilian Persons in Times of War (Fourth Geneva Convention) (1949).

185 Citing the ICTY in *Prosecutor v Furundzija* (Judgment) IT-95-17/1-T (1998) and *R v Bow Street Magistrates' Court Ex Parte Pinochet (No 1)* [1999] 1 AC 61, 897.

ILC concluded that 'clearly accepted and recognised' *jus cogens* norms 'include the prohibitions of aggression, genocide, slavery, racial discrimination, crimes against humanity and torture, and the right to self-determination'.[186]

Common amongst all the norms the ILC claim are recognised by the community of states as *jus cogens* is that they 'arise from those substantive rules of conduct that prohibit what has come to be seen as intolerable because of the threat it presents to the survival of States and their peoples'.[187] This quote from the Commission captured two salient points being, first, that states are acknowledging that their fundamental interests are tied to the welfare of peoples in recognising that this specific body of *jus cogens* norms exists. Secondly, mere recognition of a norm as *jus cogens* does not automatically make the substantive content of the norm more important and has certainly not prevented the daily reality whereby the survival of peoples continues to be at risk. Thus, based on the discussion above that has identified that *jus cogens* remain a highly contentious topic and the inescapable fact that any academic progress in terms of recognition has had little impact in protecting the fundamental interests of the international community, the utility in considering *jus cogens* in the context of this work is that it establishes a conceptual link between state accountability and public international law. The tone of scepticism that permeates the discussion would make it hypocritical to adopt anything other than a working definition of *jus cogens* for the balance of the analysis.

3.3 A working definition of *jus cogens*

De Hoogh captured it best when he said that 'the essence of *jus cogens* lies not in the impossibility of derogation, but in the impossibility of eluding the application of norms of *jus cogens*'.[188] In other words, the interests of states and their peoples must be protected regardless of how the imperative is expressed in legal, normative terms. The overview given here of the debate surrounding the content and existence of *jus cogens* was less about resolving the controversy, and more about substantiating the argument that international law is evolving in order to ensure the fundamental interests of the entire international community are protected. Recognising the most fundamental interests as *jus cogens* is one adaptation and, if identified, the normative evolution of state accountability would be another. *Jus cogens* provide a link between the concept of holding states accountable for threatening the interests of states and their peoples, on the one hand, and public international law, on the other.

There may not be any consensus as to the source or substantive content of *jus cogens* but there is recognition of the concept in terms of all four sources of public

186 Note 165 above, Commentary to Article 26 para 5.
187 Note 165 above, Commentary to Article 40 para 3.
188 A. de Hoogh, 'The Relationship Between *Jus Cogens*, Obligations *Erga Omnes* and International Crimes: *Jus Cogens* Norms in Perspective' (1991) 42 *Austrian Journal of Public and International Law* 183, 186.

international law listed in Article 38 of the ICJ Statute. Many pertinent judicial decisions and academic writings have been cited above, and to this can be added the Draft Articles on State Responsibility, which make separate provision for the breach of an obligation based on a *jus cogens* norm. The VCLT expressly refers to the existence of *jus cogens*; other treaties give implicit recognition, for example the Rome Statute of the ICC lists genocide as an international crime; and in both 2006 and 2007 the ICJ stated that 'the norm prohibiting genocide was assuredly a *jus cogens* norm of international law'.[189] The exercise of universal jurisdiction in state practice can be linked with the recognition of *jus cogens* norms, as it is the threat to fundamental community interests that is thought to justify the assumption of jurisdiction, as in *Demjanjuk v Petrovsky* when the US Federal Courts assumed jurisdiction over a defendant for alleged crimes against humanity committed under the Nazi regime on the basis of 'the universal character of the crimes in question'.[190] In addition, in the *Eichmann* case, the Israeli Supreme Court considered whether it had jurisdiction on the basis that the norm in question arose from 'a universal source pertaining to the whole of mankind'.[191] In fact the circumstances of the case show that Israel was more than simply exercising universal jurisdiction because Eichmann was a Nazi war criminal seized by Israeli agents in Argentina and taken to Israel for trial, thus Israel exercised jurisdiction in violation of Argentina's sovereignty. The Israeli Supreme Court considered that if the alleged crimes 'shocked the conscience of nations' the 'judicial and legislative authorities of every country' could 'bring [the] criminals to trial'.[192] Given that Israel was not required to return Eichmann or allow another state to exercise jurisdiction and the only response by the Security Council was to 'request' that Israel issue an apology and pay reparations to Argentina, it seems that the Court's opinion was viewed with sympathy by other states[193]. Implicit recognition of *jus cogens* is further complemented by express juridical statements, including the US Third Restatement of the Law which noted that 'norms that create "international crimes" … are also *jus cogens*'[194] and the decision by the ECtHR in *K-H W v Germany* that recognition of a norm as *jus cogens* must lead to criminalisation of the act when the perpetrator was an individual in order to prevent impunity for its breach.[195]

189 *Application of the Convention on the Prevention and Punishment of the Crime of Genocide (Bosnia and Herzegovina v Yugoslavia (Serbia and Montenegro))* (Preliminary Objections 1996) ICJ Reports (1993) para 161 and *Case Concerning Armed Activities on the Territory of the Congo (New Application 2002) (Democratic Republic of the Congo v Rwanda)* (Jurisdiction of the Court and Admissibility of Application 2006) ICJ Reports (2002) para 64.

190 *Demjanjuk v Petrovsky* 776F.2d (6th Circuit) (1985) 571, 582.

191 *Attorney General of Israel v Eichmann* 36 ILR (1968) para 30.

192 Ibid, para 26.

193 Security Council Resolution 138 (1960).

194 Revised Third Restatement of the Foreign Relations Law (1987) Reporter's Notes para 6.

195 *K-H W v Germany* (2001) European Court of Human Rights 463. Although, as Kadelbach notes, the Court's statement is misleading because the breach must still be expressly criminalised under international criminal law, regardless of the status of the norm (S. Kadelbach, '*Jus Cogens*, Obligations *Erga Omnes* and Other Rules – The Identification of Fundamental Norms' in C.

These few examples of recognition exist within a broader framework whereby it cannot be denied that the concept of *jus cogens* is controversial in terms of both existence and content. Therefore, and in order to construct a working definition that can transcend the debate and be applied for the purpose of the analysis here, two questions must be answered. First, how can *jus cogens* be the link between state accountability and public international law when the very notion is controversial? In response, it is submitted that there is evidence that *jus cogens* exists if these norms are understood as one component, albeit at this time relatively theoretical, in a wider movement to protect the fundamental interests of more than simply states. The development of international criminal law, humanitarian law and human rights law can all be seen as part of this project and the indeterminacy of, for example, human rights has not prevented the evolution of regional and international frameworks for human rights protection. Accordingly, a lack of conceptual specificity does not frustrate the adoption of a working definition here and the first limb of that definition is that *jus cogens* norms seek to protect the interests of the international community as a whole and can be distinguished because they have the additional characteristic of being non-derogable.

The second question follows on from the first to ask how specific norms can be identified for the purpose of analysing their breach, when the concept of *jus cogens* has been defined above in such a way that recognises it is currently indeterminate. Quite simply, because the list of norms that the ILC considers to be recognised as *jus cogens* was taken from an overview of state practice and opinion it is appropriate that the same list be used here. The second limb of the working definition is therefore that 'the prohibitions of aggression, genocide, slavery, racial discrimination, crimes against humanity and torture, and the right to self-determination'[196] are all *jus cogens* norms.

A final point to note in terms of the working definition adopted is that the link made between *jus cogens* and the fundamental interests of peoples pre-empts the issue of inter-temporal application from arising in the subsequent case studies. The inter-temporal principle in the context of international law means that 'it is not permissible to import into the legal evaluation of a previously existing situation … doctrines of modern law that did not exist or were not accepted at the time'.[197] Therefore, any evaluation of state practice would arguably need to be restricted to case studies after 1969 when the term *jus cogens* was first adopted by states in the VCLT. However, evidence that the inter-temporal principle is subject to qualification can be found in the 1971 *Advisory Opinion on the Legal Consequences for States of the Continued Presence of South Africa in Namibia* when the ICJ stated that 'an international instrument has to be interpreted and applied within the framework of the

Tomuschat and J.-M. Thouvenin (eds), *The Fundamental Rules of the International Legal Order* (Boston: Martinus Nijhoff Publishers, 2006) 21, 40).

196 Note 165 above, Commentary to Article 26 para 5.

197 G. Fitzmaurice, 'The Law and Procedure of the International Court of Justice' (1953) *British Yearbook of International Law* 1, 5.

entire legal system prevailing at the time of interpretation'.[198] Centuries of contemplation and implied legal acknowledgement that certain norms protect more than just the interests of states and are fundamental to the framework of international law preceded the express legal recognition of *jus cogens*. The term *jus cogens* thus describes norms that have arguably existed for centuries and is simply a legal convenience to interpret those norms within 'the entire legal system prevailing' today. On that basis, it is justified to analyse alleged breaches of norms that were *ex post facto* listed by the ILC as having *jus cogens* status.

3.4 Conclusion

This chapter has sought to clarify what consensus exists, if any, in relation to how *jus cogens* norms are defined and identified. Two conclusions were reached. First, the list of norms identified by the ILC remains authoritative and provides an appropriate reference point in assessing the responses to breaches of *jus cogens*, rather than non-*jus cogens* norms. Secondly, because *jus cogens* norms seek to protect the interests of the international community as a whole, and not merely those of states, the interest in holding states accountable for breaching *jus cogens* norms is likewise expected to be held by the international community as a whole, and not only by states. The discussion thus far has progressed toward tracing the normative evolution of state accountability and, crucially, it has shown that there is a link between established international law and a concept of state accountability, which is the protection of *jus cogens* norms. It is the recognition of *jus cogens* by states, as well as the fact that these norms relate to the interests of the international community as a whole, that has already affected entrenched legal doctrines such as state sovereignty and is arguably influencing the evolution of state accountability. Using *jus cogens* to evaluate state conduct provides a measuring stick for assessing practice and provides a legal language by which to describe that a principle of state accountability has juridical support and is legally possible.

Arguably, the benefits are reciprocal because examining state accountability in practice applies a second, quasi-legal language – or at least an extension of the interpretive framework – to *jus cogens*. Thus, the subsequent analysis will still be of benefit even if the reader continues to dispute the existence of *jus cogens*. For the sake of clarity, if there is a clear practice of holding states accountable for breaching *jus cogens* norms, then there will be greater evidence of what states consider those norms to be and if there is no practice, then cynics have a stronger argument as it is illogical that a body of norms could be defined on the basis that they are non-derogable if there was no reaction when breached. Accordingly, the discussion can now narrow to focus on the juridical feasibility and practical state support for the concept of state accountability from the specific perspective of breaches of *jus cogens* norms.

198 *Advisory Opinion on the Legal Consequences for States of the Continued Presence of South Africa in Namibia (SW Africa) Notwithstanding Security Council Resolution 276* ICJ Reports (1971) 3.

4 The relationship between conceptual state accountability and doctrinal state responsibility

Chapter 4 illustrates that state responsibility and state accountability are not incompatible; they merely serve separate functions. Particular limitations of the doctrine are shown to be that the right to invoke state responsibility is limited to states and that there is no guarantee of redress for the underlying norm. However, it is argued that attempts to expand the doctrine of state responsibility, within the discrete legal space it currently occupies so as to facilitate a more comprehensive framework of answerability, give juridical support to the concept of state accountability.

4.1 An introduction to the doctrine of state responsibility

This chapter considers if and why there would be state or juridical support for state accountability evolving as a legal norm, when an established principle of state responsibility already exists in public international law. There are two objectives here, the first of which is to identify the differences and points of convergence between the doctrine of state responsibility and the concept of state accountability. This task is necessary because at first glance the *Chorzów Factory* principle that underpins the state responsibility doctrine, whereby a 'breach of an engagement involves an obligation to make reparation in an adequate form', already appears to capture the essence of state accountability. The discussion here aims to show that the distinction between the doctrine and a broader concept of state accountability relates to the separate role played by each, in terms of what aspect of international law the state is being made to answer for and the manner in which it is being made to answer. The second objective of this chapter is to determine whether, despite the difference in function, indicators can be identified from within the legal space inhabited by state responsibility that a broader approach to seeking redress from states is juridically viable.

A note relating to terminology must be made at this point. The Draft Articles refer to 'peremptory' norms but, for the purposes of continuity this chapter will continue to refer to '*jus cogens*' norms. In addition, it has already been noted that 'responsibility' has a different meaning from 'accountability', which requires the discharge of responsibility through both a determination of liability and redress as a result. Readers with a cursory knowledge of the state responsibility doctrine will recall that a state must provide reparation when found to have breached its international obligations, suggesting that the doctrine has the same conceptual elements as state accountability. However, this assumes that reparation – when the state's responsibility is engaged – and redress – for the purpose of holding the state accountable – are the same thing. This chapter will provide clarification on that point but, until that time, readers should note that all subsequent references to 'responsibility' are to be understood within the context of discussing state responsibility.

An example of the doctrine in practice sets the scene for a textual analysis of the Draft Articles, by illustrating the relationship between state responsibility, which is an established tenant of public international law, and state accountability, which is evolving in normative terms as a response by the international community to ensure states are made to answer for breaching the fundamental values protected by public international law. The *Genocide Convention* case is particularly appropriate because the obligations breached by Serbia arose from the prohibition of genocide, which was included on the ILC's list of *jus cogens* norms that are generally recognised by states.

The ICJ's 2007 judgment in the *Genocide Convention* case was criticised on the basis that it failed to identify and communicate the gravity of Serbia's actions;[199] however, the Court's role was only to resolve Serbia's responsibility 'for genocide or for any of the other acts enumerated in Article III' of the 1948 Genocide Convention, arguably rendering such criticism unjustified.[200] The focus was on determining Serbia's responsibility for failing to punish and prevent genocide and for the commission of genocide pursuant to the Convention – and therefore irrespective of the fact that the alleged breaches were also 'of obligations under peremptory norms'.[201] For that reason, the judgment was unlikely to result in Serbia being comprehensively made to answer for all its culpable acts and omissions during the entirety of the conflict in the former Yugoslavia. This does not mean that the findings of state responsibility could not also have contributed in terms of holding Serbia accountable, and closer examination of the case seeks to highlight the extent to which state responsibility is and is not, in addition to its discrete function, an effective tool to hold states accountable in the broader sense and as conceptualised here.

In light of the definition of 'state accountability' reached earlier, the extent to which engaging Serbia's responsibility could also be seen as holding the state accountable requires that the ICJ determined that Serbia breached its legal obligations in an individual capacity, rather than simply as a manifestation of its

199 For a high profile example of the criticism see A. Cassese, 'A Judicial Massacre' (2007) available at http://www.guardian.co.uk/commentisfree/2007/feb/27/thejudicialmassacreofsrebr.

200 *Application of the Convention on the Prevention and Punishment of the Crime of Genocide (Bosnia and Herzegovina v Yugoslavia (Serbia and Montenegro))* (Judgment 2007) ICJ Reports (1993) para 147.

201 Ibid.

organs and agents. The ICTY has found many Serbian government officials guilty of genocide but in this case the ICJ concluded that Serbia was not responsible for committing genocide because the level of 'political, military and logistical relations between the federal authorities'[202] did not show that Serbia had exercised effective control over those officials.[203] Responsibility could only be engaged where there was a clear link between Serbia exercising its 'influence'[204] and the illegal acts and omissions of the individual perpetrators, which in this case occurred when the structural support provided by Serbia meant that the culpable individuals, state leaders and military groups were not prevented from carrying out the genocide. The ICJ considered that Serbia's 'position of influence, over the Bosnian Serbs who devised and implemented the genocide in Srebrenica … owing to the strength of the political, military and financial links'[205] was sufficient to engage Serbia's responsibility, but only for failing to prevent genocide and not the direct commission of genocide. Based on the evidence, Serbia 'could hardly have been unaware of the serious risk'[206] that genocide would occur and the Court found that Serbia 'refrained from using'[207] its power in order to prevent the genocide at Srebrenica. However, the same factors that engaged Serbia's responsibility for failing to prevent genocide were the same systemic preconditions that allowed the genocide to occur and it is argued here that ultimately the higher threshold for attribution under the state responsibility doctrine led to a gap in Serbia's answerability.

The second observation in terms of examining the utility of the state responsibility doctrine as a means for holding states accountable, within the context of discussing the *Genocide Convention* case, relates to the potential scope and effectiveness of redress. State accountability is associated with redress that reflects both the context and the specific law breached; however, the state responsibility doctrine restricts the forms of reparation available and dictates that reparation is only granted to the holder of the primary obligation, which in this case was Bosnia and Herzegovina. Within those constraints the ICJ considered that Serbia was not responsible for any damage arising from the genocide because it was not responsible for the genocide itself and, rather than award compensation for harm done to the victims of the genocide, the Court made a declaration of the breach and ordered Serbia to cooperate with the ICTY.[208] In terms of holding Serbia responsible, the reparation was appropriate as it sought to 'wipe out the consequences of the breach' and, as far as possible, 're-establish the situation which would …

202 Ibid, para 413.

203 Even the fact that the Serbian Government was paying the salaries of Bosnian Serb leaders, such as Generals Mladić and Karadžić who were charged at the ICTY with the Srebrenica genocide, was insufficient to establish a link (*Prosecutor v Karadžić and Mladić* (Indictment) IT-95-18-1 (2002)).

204 Note 200 above, para 430.

205 Ibid, para 434.

206 Ibid, para 436.

207 Ibid, para 438.

208 Ibid, para 461.

have existed if that act had not been committed'.[209] In terms of holding Serbia accountable, as opposed to responsible, the reparation was arguably less effective because the declarations failed to amount to more than a determination of Serbia's liability. An alternative perspective is that the political instability in the region (relating to Kosovo's independence and government elections) meant that any form of redress beyond condemnation could have seen tensions spill over and affect other states. Thus, the judgment could be viewed as 'an opportunity for the direct reconciliation of people in the former Yugoslavia'.[210] By the same token, the continued failure to comply with the ICJ's orders and ensure the arrest of wanted suspects such as Ratko Mladić,[211] suggests that Serbia has not truly atoned for its failure to prevent the genocide at Srebrenica. That there was a lack of Serbian accountability can also be implied, for example, from the former chief prosecutor at the ICTY, Carla Del Ponte, calling for the negotiations for a 'Stabilization and Association Agreement' between the EU and Serbia to be suspended until Mladić was arrested – having described Serbia's cooperation with the ICTY as ordered by the ICJ, as merely 'adequate'.[212]

The *Genocide Convention* case illustrates that there are points of compatibility between state responsibility and the concept of state accountability being mooted here, but also highlights some of the doctrinal limitations that mean the two are separate concerns. A textual analysis of the Draft Articles seeks to confirm that the function of state responsibility is not comprehensive from the perspective of making states answer for breaching public international law. In addition, an analysis of the Draft Articles, which states including Germany and Jordan consider reflect the doctrine under customary international law,[213] will help to provide further evidence that states recognise the existence of *jus cogens*. Draft Article 40 expressly refers to 'peremptory norms' and there is implicit recognition through the inclusion of *erga omnes* obligations and Draft Article 50, which makes the use of counter-measures conditional on ensuring 'the protection of human rights' to invoke a parallel with the fundamental interests of more than just states – and thus *jus cogens*. However, mere reference to 'peremptory' norms is an insufficient basis to argue that the Draft Articles provide redress for breaching *jus cogens*, to the extent required to meet the threshold of also holding the state accountable. Thus, the question here is whether any indication exists that the state responsibility doctrine pursuant to the Draft Articles was ever intended, or could implicitly be used, as a means to hold states accountable for breaching *jus cogens* norms.

209 Quoting the *Chorzów Factory* case in the *Application of the Convention on the Prevention and Punishment of the Crime of Genocide* (n 200 above, para 460.

210 D. Charter, 'Serbia Cleared of Genocide Charge Over Killing of 8,000 at Srebrenica' (2007) *The Times* (2009) available at http://www.timesonline.co.uk/tol/news/world/europe/article1444140.ece.

211 'Bosnian TV Airs "Mladić Pictures"' (2009) available at http://www.news.bbc.co.uk/1/hi/world/europe/8094664.stm.

212 'Annual Report of the ICTY' (2008) UN Doc A/63/210-S/2008/515.

213 J. Crawford and S. Olleson, 'The Continuing Debate on a UN Convention on State Responsibility' (2005) 54(4) *International and Comparative Law Quarterly* 959, 963.

4.2 State responsibility under the ILC's Draft Articles

The work of the ILC in codifying the state responsibility doctrine culminated in the 2001 Draft Articles, although the project's origins can be traced back to work by the League of Nations in seeking a means to ensure redress from states for grievous breach of international law, culminating in the 1930 Codification Conference in The Hague. In 1947 the UN formally requested the ILC to 'undertake the codification of the principles of international law governing state responsibility',[214] as 'desirable for the maintenance and development of peaceful relations between States'.[215] An extensive historical overview of the drafting process is beyond the scope of the discussion here, although some reference is required to highlight the consistent theme throughout the Commission's work that something more than standard state responsibility was needed to respond to breaches of international law that were particularly grievous and that affected the interests of the wider international community.

Progress by the ILC was slow, the reasons for which included the lingering debate as to whether a principle of criminal state responsibility should be adopted. State criminality had been rejected at Nuremberg but an appropriate form of redress for the sort of atrocities witnessed during the Second World War was yet to be agreed on, and thus 'the question of the criminal responsibility of States' remained on the ILC's agenda – at least initially.[216] By the 1960s, the Sub-Committee on State Responsibility concluded that the bifurcated focus on both primary and secondary obligations was slowing progress so that the ILC was forced to make a 'strategic retreat'[217] and remove the question of criminal state responsibility from its agenda.[218] The project shifted to deal solely with the secondary consequences when states breach their primary obligations, which was justified given that any inquiry into which primary obligations or norms bind states encroached on the prerogative of states to determine the content of international law. By the 1970s, the ICJ had given its famous dictum in the *Barcelona Traction* case, which highlighted that certain international obligations are owed by states to the international community as a whole, and the VCLT had expressly referred to *jus cogens* norms from which no derogation was permitted. The scope of obligations and norms for which state responsibility could potentially be engaged had thus expanded beyond bilateral obligations incurred in treaties and under

214 In accordance with its general mandate under Article 1, Statute of the International Law Commission (1947) (adopted under UN General Assembly Resolution 174 (II)).

215 'Request for the Codification of Principles of International Law Governing State Responsibility' General Assembly Resolution 799 (VIII) (1953).

216 'Survey of International Law in Relation to the Work of Codification of the ILC' A/CN.4/1/Rev.1 (1949) 57.

217 J. Crawford, 'The ILC's Articles on Responsibility of States for Internationally Wrongful Acts: A Retrospect (Symposium: The ILC's State Responsibility Articles) (Response to Articles in this Issue)' (2002) 96(4) *The American Journal of International Law* 874, 877.

218 'Report of the Chairman on the Sub-Committee on State Responsibility' International Law Commission Yearbook of the International Law Commission (1963) 227.

customary international law to include obligations owed universally and based on norms that sought to protect the interests of more than just states. In order to reflect these developments the Commission again reverted back to the idea of state criminal responsibility in its 1976 Draft.

The now infamous former Draft Article 19 stated that any breach of norms, such as 'self-determination' and 'respect for human rights and fundamental freedoms', considered 'essential by the international community as a whole', would be 'an international crime'. Distinguishing between state crimes and state delicts illustrated that obligations based on 'essential' norms were different from obligations that were not, and that redress for both was, at that time, thought to come within the scope of the state responsibility doctrine. By the final draft in 2001, however, the crime/delict distinction was removed and the only direct reference to *jus cogens* was in Draft Article 40. Sztucki argued that the 2001 Draft ultimately kept the question of redress for a breach of *jus cogens* norms 'independent of the problem of legal responsibility',[219] which if true has the potential to leave a gap in accountability relating to *jus cogens*. Greater consideration of the specific provisions of the 2001 Draft is needed in order to confirm this proposition.

4.2.1 Can the international community as a whole invoke state responsibility?

The focus on *jus cogens* that is taken in this book is because a breach of those norms is perceived, by supporters of the concept, to affect the interests of more than just states, which in turn provides the greatest impetus and justification for adopting a broader conception of what is needed to hold states accountable. In determining whether state responsibility plays a role within this accountability matrix it is therefore rational to consider if the doctrine can be engaged by all members of the international community, as otherwise its utility in the context of state accountability is limited. Under the Draft Articles, responsibility may be invoked by an injured and a non-injured state. A state is injured if it is directly owed the obligation and is affected by the breach or, pursuant to Draft Article 42, the obligation is owed to the 'international community as a whole'. In comparison, pursuant to Draft Article 48, a non-injured state is entitled to invoke responsibility where the breached obligation is owed to a group of states including that state or likewise the obligation is owed to the international community as a whole. Thus, even if the obligation is owed to the international community as a whole, only states can invoke the doctrine. The Draft Articles therefore recognise that the international community as a whole may have a legal interest in compliance without providing a reciprocal procedural right to seek redress when the obligation is breached.

219 J. Sztucki, *Jus Cogens and the Vienna Convention on the International Law of Treaties* (Vienna: Springer-Verlag, 1974) 6.

An alternative view, as argued by Vermeer-Kunzli,[220] is to interpret the phrase 'international community' to mean those parties that are able and willing to respond to a breach of the obligation, which would accord with the focus of the doctrine on inter-state relations and reflect that only states have judicial standing before the ICJ and the physical resources to implement a judgment. Whatever interpretation is adopted it is apparent that the phrase 'international community' does not expand the scope of parties entitled to invoke responsibility; it only expands the category of obligations for which state responsibility can be engaged.

States may seek to engage the responsibility of another state where the effects of that breach were primarily felt by non-state actors, namely individuals; however, this does not lead to a blurring of the doctrine's conceptual lines as the right to invoke is still linked to the obligation being owed to the invoking state. For example, diplomatic protection is based on obligations owed pursuant to the Vienna Convention on Diplomatic Relations 1961, and even though the individuals in question are directly affected by the breach, state responsibility is only engaged in relation to violation of the particular Convention obligation. This position reflects the traditional view of the international courts from the 1924 *Mavrommatis Palestine Concessions* case, where the Permanent Court of International Justice found that in taking up the case of one of its citizens, the state was in reality asserting its own rights. Furthermore, Draft Article 33 provides that engaging a state's responsibility is 'without any prejudice to any right arising from the international responsibility of a State which may accrue directly to any person or entity other than a State', albeit that non-state actors must seek redress in a different forum. Thus, even though Draft Article 40 expressly refers to obligations based on 'peremptory' norms, there is no provision that expands the category of parties entitled to invoke responsibility for such obligations. Of course, the logistical issues arising from a universal right to bring a claim before the ICJ would be prohibitive and, in that sense, it is rational that only states have capacity to invoke the doctrine. In fact, the risk of a gap in accountability only arises if there are no additional means by which states and non-state actors can seek redress beyond the state responsibility doctrine.

Indeed, accountability might be the cumulative impact of engaging the state's responsibility in addition to other means of redress, as was arguably the case in relation to Iran's liability arising from the 1979 Tehran Hostages Crisis. In *United States Diplomatic and Consular Staff in Tehran* (*Tehran Hostages* case), the ICJ held that Iran had breached, and was continuing to breach, the obligations it owed directly to the US pursuant to, amongst others, the Vienna Convention on Diplomatic Relations of 1961. Having made its findings on the question of state responsibility, the Court also drew 'the attention of the entire international community to the irreparable harm' caused by the breach because the obligations in question were

220 A. Vermeer-Kunzli, 'A Matter of Interest: Diplomatic Protection and State Responsibility *Erga Omnes*' (2007) *International and Comparative Law Quarterly* 553, 578.

'vital for the security and well-being of the complex international community'.[221] Iran's actions could not 'fail to undermine the edifice of law carefully constructed by mankind' and the 'rules developed to ensure the ordered progress of relations';[222] not that the Court had any jurisdiction to order redress on such grounds. The response by other members of the international community shows that there was sympathy with the Court's view and that something more than engaging Iran's responsibility was desired. The Security Council criticised and then called upon the Iranian Government to 'release immediately the [Embassy] personnel',[223] which showed that Council Members implicated the state in the hostage crisis, even if only because the Iranian Government had the ability to effect a release of the hostages. In addition, the US introduced a resolution for economic sanctions before the Security Council, which unsurprisingly was blocked by the USSR given the Cold War context. The US then resorted to unilateral sanctions and measures, including travel restrictions to Iran and reparations, before being joined in these sanctions by member states of the European Community.[224] Even if the extra sanctions imposed by the US did have less than altruistic, arguably even retributive, motives it does not prevent the fact that the additional measures were largely tolerated, and even supported, by other states. It is acknowledged that this will be owing to the political power of the US but it is argued here that acquiescence was also because a finding of state responsibility was an insufficient means to hold Iran accountable given the perception that Iran's acts and omissions posed a threat to more than just the US's interests.

Draft Article 48, which permits any state to bring a claim if the obligation was owed to the entire international community, both provides non-injured states with standing to invoke the doctrine and prima facie compensates for the lack of standing given to non-state parties. The ILC considered that Draft Article 48 'involves a measure of progressive development, which is justified since it provides a means of protecting the community or collective interest at stake'.[225] Yet the Commission also acknowledged that the effect might be more theoretical than practical as a state invoking responsibility under Draft Article 48 'may be called on to establish that it is acting in the interest of the injured party'.[226] The Commission reached this conclusion by noting that 'various human rights treaties allow invocation of responsibility by any state party' but in such cases 'a clear distinction has been drawn between the capacity of the applicant state to raise the matter and the interests of the beneficiaries of the obligation'.[227] If a non-injured state sought to bring a claim under Draft Article 48 and the injured party was not a state, the

221 *United States Diplomatic and Consular Staff in Tehran* ICJ Reports (1979) para 92.

222 Ibid.

223 Paragraph 1 of both Security Council Resolutions 457 and 461 (1979).

224 'Bulletin of the European Communities' (1980) 13(4) 20.

225 'Report of the International Law Commission on the Work of its Fifty-Third Session' UN Doc A/56/10 (2001) Commentary Article 48 para 12.

226 Ibid.

227 Ibid.

Commission foresaw even 'greater difficulties, which the present Articles cannot solve'.[228]

Additional limitations relating to Draft Article 48 as a means to broaden the accountability impact of state responsibility include the fact that the remedies are limited to requesting cessation, non-repetition and performance of the obligation. Furthermore, Draft Articles 43, 44 and 45 continue to apply when responsibility is invoked on behalf of another party so that the invoking state is still required to establish the nationality of claims and the exhaustion of local remedies which, as Evans points out, is incongruous with Draft Article 48 being used to seek redress where the interests of the entire international community are at stake – if that was the intention.[229] Ultimately, the lack of claims brought on the basis of Draft Article 48 is testimony to its minimal impact. Indeed, even where Israel's actions in constructing the wall around East Jerusalem were recognised by the ICJ as contravening international law, in breach of *erga omnes* obligations owed by Israel and undermining what are arguably considered to be *jus cogens* norms, no state has sought to invoke the state responsibility doctrine[230].

4.2.2 Is state responsibility for violating an erga omnes *obligation effectual in terms of holding states accountable for breaching the underlying* jus cogens *norm?*

Draft Articles 33 and 48 state that responsibility may be engaged for breaches of obligations owed to the 'international community as a whole', which includes obligations *erga omnes* that arise from *jus cogens* norms. However, to the extent that there is a difference in content between the obligation and norm then state responsibility is only engaged insofar as the norm is the mirror image of the obligation and any gap between them is to the prejudice of making states answer for breaching the norm. A practical illustration is the obligations that derive from the prohibition on genocide that are expressed under the 1948 Genocide Convention and range from punishing perpetrators to not conspiring with perpetrators, yet it is the cumulative effect of these obligations that represent the totality of the norm.

Bassiouni described the relationship in terms of obligations pertaining to 'legal implications' and norms relating to 'legal status',[231] Austin identified the difference in terms of an obligation being 'a duty' and a norm being 'a command',[232] while Kelsen

228 Ibid.

229 M. Evans, 'State Responsibility and the ECHR' 139, 149 in M. Fitzmaurice, *Issues of State Responsibility before International Judicial Institutions* (Oregon: Hart Publishing, 2004).

230 *Advisory Opinion Concerning the Legal Consequences on Construction of a Wall in the Occupied Palestinian Territory* ICJ Reports (2004) para 155.

231 C. Bassiouni, 'Searching for Peace and Achieving Justice: The Need for Accountability' (1996) 59 *Law and Contemporary Problems* 9, 63.

232 J. Austin, 'Lectures on Jurisprudence' (1832) cited in H. Kelsen, (trans J. Trevino), *General Theory of Law and State* (Cambridge: Harvard University Press, 2005) 71.

considered that 'the content of legal norms' is comprised of 'legally established obligation[s]'.[233] Thus, the link between norms and obligations is derivative – norms derive their legal expression from obligations in the form of treaties and custom while obligations derive their rank from norms that mean the obligation is then legally binding. However, while the existence of obligations is dependent on the existence of norms, the recognition of norms is frustrated if legal obligations are not sufficiently comprehensive. Charlesworth and Chinkin gave the example of domestic violence, which is not 'regarded as an international legal issue' so that there are no legal obligations that could give rise to a claim of state responsibility. This is despite the fact that a state may be culpable because 'the violence is tolerated by a legal and political system that provides inadequate remedies to the victims of violence'.[234]

The highly academic distinction between norms and obligations is only relevant for these purposes if there is also a practical difference in the legal content of each, which is then borne out in terms of the scope of redress when breached. For example, in its 2003 Opinion in *Beazley v USA* the Inter-American Commission on Human Rights concluded that the actions of the US in sentencing and executing the youth petitioner were 'contrary to an international *norm* of *jus cogens*'[235] but the US was liable because, in breaching a precautionary measure issued under Article 25 of the Rules of Procedure, it 'failed to act in accordance with its fundamental human rights *obligations* as a Member of the Organization of American States'.[236] As a result of violating Article 25, the Commission 'recommended' that compensation be given to the petitioner's family.[237] In terms of holding the US accountable, because it breached what the Commission considered was a *jus cogens* norm, compensation of itself does not dismantle the structural component within the state that allowed the breach to occur. However, the Commission also ordered a review of the USA's law on capital punishment and immediate publication of its Opinion. These additional measures highlighted, and required the state to address, the legal framework that meant officials were able to violate fundamental human rights.

Redress for breaching an obligation is not the same as redress for breaching the underlying norm at a theoretical level, although the two can overlap in practice as the *Beazley* case shows. Any risk of a gap in redress because state responsibility is only engaged under the Draft Articles to the extent that a norm 'is captured by a legal obligation'[238] is therefore overly simplistic. The reality is far more complicated

233 H. Kelsen, (trans M. Knight), *Pure Theory of Law* (New Jersey: Law Book Exchange Ltd, 2002) 169.

234 H. Charlesworth and C. Chinkin, *The Boundaries of International Law* (Manchester: Manchester University Press, 2000) 148.

235 *Beazley v USA* Inter-American Commission on Human Rights (2003) paras 2, 48, 51 and 55. Emphasis added.

236 Ibid, paras 4–5. Emphasis added.

237 Ibid, paras 60–61.

238 Note 225 above, Commentary Article 22 para 13.

and requires an understanding of whether reparation in the context of the state responsibility doctrine overlaps with redress in the context of state accountability.

4.2.3 How effective is reparation under the Draft Articles in holding states accountable?

It has been argued here that no one modality of redress exists in order to hold states accountable and that state accountability for the breach of a *jus cogens* norm depends upon recognition that the breach had the potential to affect the interests of the international community as a whole. Given that in 2001 the ILC noted that the 'basic legal consequences' set out in the Draft Articles did not 'preclude the future development of a more elaborate regime of consequences'[239] for breaches of obligations arising from *jus cogens* norms, the assumption from the outset is that reparation under the doctrine is somehow insufficient. Tomuschat is just one commentator who agrees and has noted that, although Draft Articles 40 and 48 are 'in consonance with the growing trend'[240] that recognises that state responsibility 'is not only due to the "injured State" but to the community of Nations',[241] it is unlikely that there can be any relief under the Draft Articles insofar as reparation is only granted for the breach of an obligation owed between states.[242] This point has already been conceded, but it does not preclude finding that a remedy granted in the context of holding a state responsible cannot be taken in conjunction with other remedies to ensure the state is held accountable – unless there are inherent limitations in the form of reparation itself.

Reparation takes three forms under the Draft Articles, namely restitution, compensation and satisfaction. If, for example, the primary obligation no longer existed or there was nothing left to restore, as in the context of the obligation to prevent genocide in the *Genocide Convention* case, then compensation and satisfaction is ordered instead. Before analysing each modality separately, several issues will be noted relating to all forms of reparation. First, the breach of an obligation may result in that obligation being brought to an end as in the *Genocide Convention* case as just noted. However, the breach of a norm does not alter the status or existence of the norm, in which case the most appropriate form of reparation

239 Ibid, Commentary Article 41 para 14.

240 C. Tomuschat, 'Individual Reparation Claims in Instances of Grave Human Rights Violations: The Position Under General International Law' 1, 4 in A. Randelzhofer. and C. Tomuschat (eds), *State Responsibility and the Individual* (Great Britain: Kluwer Law International, 1999).

241 'Study Concerning the Right to Restitution, Reparation and Rehabilitation for Victims of Gross Violations of Human Rights and Fundamental Freedoms' UN Doc E/CN.4/Sub.2/1993/8 (1993) para 44.

242 Note 240 above; see also M. Kaplan, 'Using Collective Interests to Ensure Human Rights: An Analysis of the Articles of State Responsibility' (2004) 79(5) *New York University Law Review* 1902, 1927.

may differ for the norm vis-à-vis the obligation.[243] Secondly, reparation for breach of the primary obligation might not necessarily reflect the underlying norm that was also breached; for example, if a state violated its treaty obligations and invaded another state then restitution could reinstate the treaty but this would have no direct bearing on redress for having also breached the normative prohibition on using force. Thirdly, in the context of state responsibility, reparation is only ordered to the extent necessary to 'wipe out all the consequences of the illegal act'.[244] That may be minimal in terms of actual damage, in which case it is unlikely that reparation would be sufficient to communicate that the breach had the potential to affect the interests of the international community as a whole. Fourthly, reparation cannot be 'out of all proportion'[245] to the breach and must be assessed against a standard of 'equity and reasonableness'.[246] Yet it is difficult to see how the same proportionality threshold could apply in terms of remedying the breach of an obligation owed to an invoking state and the breach of a *jus cogens* norm that seeks to protect the interests of the international community as a whole, whereby it is axiomatic that the consequences are significant. Finally, there is no penal function associated with reparation under the doctrine, which could have the effect of distinguishing between the breach of an obligation based on a *jus cogens* as opposed to a standard norm of international law. The ILC stated unequivocally that 'the award of punitive damages is not recognised in international law even in relation to serious breaches of obligations arising under *jus cogens* norms',[247] although the Commission acknowledged that without a penal quality the function of reparation is considerably narrowed. This point was also noted by former US President Johnson while seeking assurances and guarantees of cessation and non-repetition from the USSR for breaching obligations relating to diplomatic protection when he stated that 'regret and compensation are no substitute for adequate protection'.[248]

In terms of the specific forms of reparation, restitution is any step necessary to return to the '*status quo ante*' and to 're-establish the situation which existed before the wrongful act was committed',[249] including the release of nationals illegally held in the 1979 *Tehran Hostages* case and the return of Cambodia's national treasures that were wrongfully taken by Thailand in the 1959 *Temple of Preah Vihear* case.

243 A. de Hoogh, 'The Relationship between *Jus Cogens*, Obligations *Erga Omnes* and International Crimes: Peremptory Norms in Perspective' (1991) 42 *Austrian Journal of Public and International Law* 183, 186.

244 *Factory at Chorzów (Germany v Poland)* (Merits) PCIJ Series A No 17 (1928).

245 Draft Articles 35 and 37 use this express wording in relation to restitution and satisfaction respectively and Draft Article 36, which relates to compensation, provides that the extent of compensation is limited to proven loss for which restitution had failed to remedy the damage.

246 Note 225 above, Commentary Article 35 para 11.

247 Ibid, Commentary Part II Chapter 3 para 5. The Commentary to Draft Article 36 specifically provides that reparation 'is not concerned to punish the responsible State, nor does reparation have an expressive or exemplary character' (see n 225 above, Commentary Article 36 para 4).

248 Ibid, Commentary Article 30 para 9.

249 Ibid, Commentary Article 35 paras 2 and 5.

The ILC considered restitution was 'of particular importance'[250] where the obligation is based on a *jus cogens* norm as the breaching state is required to comply with the primary obligation, yet – pragmatically – reversing the consequences when *jus cogens* norms are breached is often impossible. This is not only because the interests of the international community as a whole may potentially be affected but also because these breaches tend to be catastrophic in terms of the results. For example, if in the *Genocide Convention* case Serbia was found responsible for the commission of genocide and thus in contravention of the normative prohibition of genocide, restitution could not have been granted because there was literally nothing to restore. In the 1996 Draft the ILC did not even include restitution as a form of reparation when the breached obligation was based on a *jus cogens* norm, although delegates considered the move unnecessary because, as the French representative noted, 'it is providing for possibilities that do not seem to have arisen in the past and do not seem likely to arise in the future'.[251] Similarly, certain members of the ILC have labelled restitution as a 'trivial' response when an obligation based on a *jus cogens* norm is breached,[252] which is apt because it acknowledges that restitution cannot convey the potential enormity when *jus cogens*, or obligations based on such norms, are breached and to suggest otherwise runs the risk of trivialising the norm.

To the extent that restitution cannot provide redress, then compensation is granted pursuant to Draft Article 36, with the primary limitation on its broader effectiveness being that compensation is only ordered 'in so far as damage would not be made good by restitution'. Furthermore, compensation is only awarded to the state that invokes responsibility and decisions by the ICJ in the 1986 *Nicaragua* case, the 1949 *Corfu Channel* case and the 1979 *Tehran Hostages* case all confirm that the state is the beneficiary, regardless that the loss was incurred by its nationals and that states have seldom sought compensation on behalf of third parties.[253] Finally, compensation is only awarded where damage can be quantified in financial terms and is excluded for 'the affront or injury caused by a violation of rights not associated with actual damage',[254] which in theory does not allow for recognition of the breach per se but which bypasses the issue of assessing damage incurred through the breach of an obligation *erga omnes*.

There are, however, examples where the level of compensation implies a punitive characteristic to suggest that reparation is for the damage caused; in addition

250 Ibid, Commentary Article 35 para 6.

251 C. Grey, 'The Choice Between Restitution and Reparation (1999) 10 *European Journal of International Law* 413, 421.

252 International Law Commission Yearbook of the International Law Commission (1998) Volume II para 298.

253 Tomuschat highlighted that, in certain circumstances, it may be against the interests of the state to seek compensation on behalf of its citizens and notes the example of the Korean and Philippine comfort women whose right to compensation was waived by their respective governments in the context of managing their international relations with Japan (see n 240 above).

254 Note 225 above, Commentary Article 36 para 1.

there is condemnation for breaching the primary obligation in question. In such cases, it seems logical to link the implicit penal element with recognition that the interests of more than merely the state in question are potentially affected by the breach, as illustrated in the 1920s *Mexican Claims Commission* cases. Mexico was found to be in breach of its obligations to ensure that the perpetrators of crimes committed against US nationals were punished. Compensation was ordered both on the basis of attributing the acts of the individual perpetrators to the state and because Mexico had failed to 'take proper steps to apprehend and punish' the responsible parties.[255] The punitive level of compensation (for example US$12,000 in the *Janes Claim*, which was a significant sum in 1926) can be linked to Mexico's failure to punish the perpetrators of crimes, which is – and was at the time – a fundamental pillar of human rights and customary international law.[256]

In contrast, the decision not to award compensation in the *Genocide Convention* case on the basis that full reparation was otherwise guaranteed through the Court's declarations, highlights the fact that the ICJ currently views compensation as having a limited, non-penal role in the context of reparation when state responsibility is engaged. However, it is worth noting that when the Genocide Convention was drafted in 1948, the majority of parties considered that state responsibility for breaching the Convention could include payment of damages and that 'the question of States having to compensate their own nationals ... also caused some interest'.[257] Thus, states did not consider it unthinkable that compensation could be a suitable means of redress were a state to commit genocide.

The function of compensation within the state responsibility framework is primarily 'to address the actual losses incurred as a result of the internationally wrongful act', while satisfaction 'is concerned with non-material injury'.[258] Draft Article 37 provides that satisfaction is any 'appropriate modality' that satisfies the gap in reparation insofar as the injury 'cannot be made good by restitution or compensation', which gives the term its 'legal character' because there is no limit on the form that satisfaction may take but there is a limit on the scope of its application in the context of the state responsibility doctrine. Its function as a sort of last resort remedy implies flexibility; indeed, Draft Article 37 is not exhaustive and can include an 'acknowledgement of the breach, an expression of regret [or] a formal apology'. Satisfaction is therefore more likely to ensure redress when the obligation is *erga omnes* because it will remedy injuries that are of a 'symbolic character, arising from the very fact of the breach of the obligation [and] irrespective of its material consequences'.[259] Satisfaction can be tailored to the particular facts and nature of the breach so there is a greater chance of states being held accountable

255 *Janes Claim (USA v Mexico)* 4 RIAA (1926) 82, 86.

256 L. Oppenheim and R. Roxburgh (eds), *International Law – A Treatise* (3rd edn London: Longmans, 1920).

257 M. Shaw, 'Genocide and International Law' in Y. Dinstein (ed), *International Law at a Time of Perplexity – Essays in Honour of Shabtai Rosenne* (Dordrecht: Martinus Nijhoff Publishers, 1989) 818.

258 Note 225 above, Commentary Article 36 para 4.

259 Ibid, Commentary Article 37 para 3.

at the same time as being held responsible – albeit that accountability would not have been the primary objective.

However, practice dispels the illusion of utility because the hierarchy in the forms of reparation under the Draft Articles means that satisfaction is still only relied on insofar as is necessary to ensure full reparation. The *Rainbow Warrior Arbitration* illustrates the point.[260] France breached the terms of a settlement treaty concluded with New Zealand after France admitted its liability in relation to the bombing of a Greenpeace vessel in New Zealand waters. The treaty breach occurred when France repatriated the responsible French agents from exile and the form of reparation ordered was satisfaction, on the basis that the breach of the treaty did not give rise to any damage for which compensation could be provided. There can be no criticism in terms of a true application of the state responsibility doctrine, and the declarations by the Arbitration Tribunal were effective in redressing the breach of France's treaty obligations, although they were ineffective in relation to the norms that were also breached. The Tribunal noted that breach of the treaty settlement between France and New Zealand was grievous because it was in response to breaches of what is arguably the *jus cogens* prohibition on using force against the territorial integrity of another state. Despite this, the Tribunal considered that a declaration of French responsibility was still the most appropriate form of redress as it could 'put an end to the present unhappy affair to promote close and friendly relations'.[261]

The doctrine of state responsibility, as it is expressed under the Draft Articles and more broadly captured as a general principle of law in the *Chorzów Factory* case, is clearly not the same thing as a broader concept of state accountability. The Draft Articles are progressive in terms of recognising the existence of *jus cogens* norms and the effect that *erga omnes* obligations have had on the law on state responsibility, but the idiosyncratic characteristics of the doctrine that have been noted here illustrate that state responsibility has not substantively adapted to take these developments in international law into account. Instead, the doctrine continues to fulfil a specific function and occupy a discrete legal space. This is not to say that a finding of state responsibility will never lead to state accountability – instead the doctrine should be viewed as one of the many mechanisms that form part of the accountability matrix, just not the only mechanism. Having concluded that the doctrine is different to the concept under discussion, on the one hand, but noting that state responsibility remains the only formal framework in terms of requiring states to answer for breaching international law, on the other, it is pertinent to also consider whether the doctrine itself offers any juridical indicators that a separate principle of state accountability is evolving beyond the parameters of state responsibility.

260 *Rainbow Warrior Affair* 20 RIAA 217 (1990).
261 Ibid.

4.3 Juridical support for state accountability in the context of the state responsibility doctrine

State responsibility cannot possibly be the sole means for holding states accountable for all breaches of public international law owing to the unassailable tension between the doctrine of state responsibility, which is based on state sovereignty and equality, and the concept of state accountability, which is based on the assumption that protecting the interests of the international community as a whole is key to the future development of public international law. A hypothetical example of how this tension could manifest is that, although 'charges of exceptional gravity' may arouse both a moral and legal imperative that a culpable state is made to answer for its acts, the state responsibility doctrine can only be engaged (and therefore have the potential to fulfil that objective) when there is 'fully conclusive' evidence to implicate the state.[262] Solely relying on the doctrine to ensure states are required to answer for their actions would therefore seem to lead to the risk of impunity owing, for example, to the high evidentiary standard required in terms of engaging the responsibility of one state towards another. This book argues that no such risk exists because the state responsibility doctrine is not the only means of responding when states breach international law. However, even if the state responsibility doctrine did give rise to a risk of impunity due to doctrinal limits on the scope of its application, this section seeks to show that the attempts to expand the doctrine, considered below, indicate that a more comprehensive approach to ensuring states are held accountable has juridical support.

State responsibility is not the sole means for seeking redress from states but, out of necessity and given the lack of an alternative institutionalised framework, it remains a conduit for that purpose. 'State responsibility in the layman's sense'[263] is applied in a variety of forums, including the ECtHR that seeks to uphold the principles in the European Convention on Human Rights by using 'the language of State responsibility … to broaden the scope of substantive legal obligations'[264] for which redress can be sought. Another means by which the doctrine has been manipulated, albeit impliedly, in order to seek greater accountability for breaches of international law is the adoption and adaptation of the attribution principle by various international courts, and for which each approach is jurisdiction specific. The ICJ used a test of effective control in the *Genocide Convention* case to determine Serbia's responsibility for acts of secessionist entities. In contrast, an overall control test was used by the ICTY Appeals Chamber in *Tadic*, to determine whether the conflict was international in nature so that the individuals could be tried for breaches of the Geneva Conventions – liability that, in theory, could be attributed to the relevant state.[265] Finally, an effective overall control test was applied by the

262 Note 200 above, para 209.
263 Note 229 above.
264 Ibid.
265 *Prosecutor v Tadic* (Appeal Judgment) IT-94-1-AR7 (1999).

ECtHR in *Cyprus v Turkey* in order to attribute the acts and omissions of the Turkish Republic of Northern Cyprus to Turkey and prevent a 'regrettable vacuum in the system of human rights protection'.[266] If the ECtHR had employed the standard of effective control, required to engage state responsibility in the doctrinal sense, then there was a risk Turkey could escape liability, suggesting that the Court's approach was influenced by moral compulsion rather than dictated by strict legal tests. Underlying the mandate of all these courts is that culpable parties must be made to answer for breaching international law and, where a court's inherent limitations prevent it from being comprehensive in the scope of accountability that may be imposed, then theoretically the jurisdiction exercised by the other international courts should meet this gap in answerability. It is because redress is sought beyond the state responsibility framework that a broader conceptualisation of state accountability has juridical viability.

In addition, moves to ensure state responsibility reflects 20th century developments in public international law suggests that a more comprehensive approach to holding states accountable is evolving. Attempts to give legal recognition to the fact that certain norms and obligations relate to the interests of more than just states, indicates that a more comprehensive framework of accountability is sought than was traditionally available under the state responsibility doctrine. The first attempt was the short-lived inclusion of criminal state responsibility in the Draft Articles. Draft Article 19 sought to overcome what the ILC saw as a contradiction 'if the same consequences continued to be applied to the breach of obligations arising out of the rules defined as *jus cogens*',[267] by distinguishing between delicts and crimes. However, the views expressed by states in relation to Draft Article 19 show that there was in fact no consensus that criminal state responsibility existed *lex lata*. The US had 'fundamental concerns about the very concept of State crimes',[268] the UK expressed reservations that state crimes had 'an adequate juridical basis'[269] and Austria argued that the evidence established that state crimes had 'not been accepted in State practice'.[270] There was, however, some support for recognising that not all obligations should be treated the same, including the USSR, which considered it of 'fundamental importance' and Kenya who stated that it was of 'the greatest importance'[271] that a distinction be drawn. Even states, such as the UK that disputed the existence of state crimes, noted 'growing evidence of the existence of a distinction between civil and criminal responsibility

266 *Cyprus v Turkey* (2001) European Court of Human Rights, para 78.

267 International Law Commission Yearbook of the International Law Commission (1976) Volume II 102.

268 Remarks of J. Crook, Office of the Legal Advisor US Department of State, Sixth Committee (1996) in N. Jorgensen, *The Responsibility of States for International Crimes* (Oxford: Oxford University Press 2003) 256.

269 Statement to the Sixth Committee by I. Brownlie, Representative of the UK on Item 146 (1996) in Jorgensen (n 268 above) 257.

270 'Comments by Austria under Article 19' UN Doc A/CN.4/488.

271 'Progress Report' UN Doc A/C.6/31/SR (1976) 22.

based on the importance attached by the international community as a whole to certain obligations of a fundamental nature'.[272] Acknowledgement that a distinction should be drawn did not solve the issue of how a distinction could be drawn, which at that time was considered by the Czech representative to be 'in a relatively fragmentary, unsystematic or indirect form'.[273] The ILC envisaged that the Security Council would play a significant role, but even this suggestion may have contributed to the unpopularity of criminal state responsibility, given the potential power this could divest to the Security Council.[274]

By 1998, the ILC had 'failed entirely to provide defined procedures and to attach distinctive consequences to crimes'[275] and Draft Article 19 was ultimately removed. The ILC clearly intended to deal with the anomaly that while states recognise that certain norms have a higher status, international law has yet to acknowledge the fundamental nature of those norms by providing suitable redress when those norms are breached, making any designation of status a misnomer. The second attempt to give effect to this distinction and to indicate that more was sought in terms of making states answer for breaching both standard and fundamental obligations, was the introduction of the 'serious breach' regime in the 2001 Draft, which sought to link the breach of an obligation based on a *jus cogens* norm to 'a stricter regime of responsibility than that applied to other internationally wrongful acts'.[276]

The combined effect of Draft Articles 40 and 41 is that a serious breach of an obligation arising from a 'peremptory norm' attracts 'particular consequences' that do not apply when the obligation is not based on a *jus cogens* norm, but it is argued here that the practical effect of the serious breach regime in terms of broadening the scope of the doctrine is limited. First, the ILC confirmed that responsibility is still only engaged for breach of the obligation and not the 'peremptory' norm on which it is based.[277] Secondly, 'less serious' breaches do not give rise to the stricter form of responsibility envisaged and thus the benefit of the distinction drawn in Draft Article 40 is that it acknowledges that certain breaches are more grave than others, while the utility in referring to the underlying *jus cogens* norm appears merely to be as an indicator that breaches of obligations arising from those norms are more likely to be serious – but there is no guarantee that this will always be the case.

272 Ibid, 18.

273 'Comments by the Czech Republic under Article 19' UN Doc A/CN.4/488.

274 International Law Commission Yearbook of the International Law Commission 1983 Volume II 11. For further discussion on this see B. Graefrath, 'International Crimes and Collective Security' 237 in K. Wellens, (ed), *International Law: Theory and Practice — Essays in Honour of Eric Suy* (The Hague, Martinus Nijhoff, 1998).

275 International Law Commission Yearbook of the International Law Commission 1998 Volume II 65 paras 243–45.

276 Note 225 above, Commentary Article 40 para 7.

277 Ibid, Commentary Article 40 para 7.

Thirdly, Draft Article 41 does not impose any additional consequences on the state that commits a serious breach beyond what is already provided for in the Draft Articles. The designated consequences of a serious breach are instead imposed against the international community of states as a whole and the first consequence is that all states are under a positive duty to cooperate in order to bring an end to serious breaches.[278] Arguably, this duty arises because of the normative origins of the obligation but, certainly, it highlights that the ILC was aware of the practical limitations of the doctrine given its view that international cooperation 'in response to the gravest breaches of international law' was 'often the only way of providing an effective remedy'.[279] In turn, the call for international cooperation is a strong indicator that the ILC considered that certain breaches affect the interests of more than just the invoking party to justify the international community of states responding as a result. The second additional consequence in Draft Article 41 is non-recognition of the breach and non-assistance to facilitate its continuation. There are, however, political and legal implications that may dissuade states from an act of non-recognition (which necessarily involves an act of recognition that the state in question also breached the underlying norm) – to undermine its effectiveness as a means of redress. For example, the delay by the US Government in recognising that the atrocities in Rwanda in 1994 were genocide was arguably because the US sought to avoid its pre-existing legal obligations under the Genocide Convention.[280] Furthermore, non-recognition has little impact in terms of providing redress, albeit indirectly, for breaching the *jus cogens* norm underlying the obligation because *jus cogens* are non-derogable and therefore any act of recognition that purported to legalise the breach would be invalid.

The mere existence of Draft Articles 19 and 40 'reflect that there are certain consequences flowing from the basic concepts of *jus cogens* norms'[281] that have affected the development of public international law, but this discussion has illustrated that there has been limited success in effectively expanding the state responsibility doctrine to accommodate the changes. The lack of practical recognition in the context of the state responsibility doctrine does not displace the fact that, as Lauterpacht described it, 'international delinquency ranges from ordinary breaches of treaty obligations involving no more than pecuniary reparation to violations of international law amounting to a criminal act in the generally accepted meaning of the term'.[282] For example, the fact that there has been no

278 Ibid, Commentary Article 41 para 3.

279 Ibid, Commentary Article 41 para 3.

280 President Clinton specifically noted the responsibility of the entire international community on a visit to Kigali airport in 1998 where he said: 'the international community, together with nations in Africa, must bear its share of responsibility for this tragedy, as well. We did not act quickly enough after the killing began … We did not immediately call these crimes by their rightful name: genocide'. (M. Gibney and E Roxstrom, 'The Status of State Apologies' (2001) 23 *Human Rights Quarterly* 911, 923).

281 Note 225 above, Commentary Part II para 7.

282 L. Oppenheim, *International Law: A Treatise:* (8th edn London: Longmans, 1955) 339.

finding of state responsibility against Germany following the Second World War has not prevented a combination of apologies made, reparations under the Potsdam Agreement and compensation paid to victims being used to hold Germany accountable for grievous breaches of international law including what has been recognised, ex post facto, as *jus cogens* prohibitions on genocide and crimes against humanity. Ultimately, attempts to expand the doctrine have not been successful because state responsibility has a specific and discrete objective; which is not concerned with seeking accountability from states in the more comprehensive form conceptualised here. What these attempts do show us is that there is juridical and state support for a more comprehensive approach to making states answer for breaching international law – and what is now required in order to determine where on the spectrum from *lex fernada* to *lex lata* such a concept sits, is evidence that state accountability occurs in practice.

4.4 Conclusion

The doctrine of state responsibility is a separate legal question to the quasi-legal, sometimes moral and usually political nature of what it means to hold a state accountable. The right to invoke state responsibility is limited to states, there is no guarantee in providing reparation for the obligation that was breached that there will be redress for the norm (although sensibly the two will usually overlap) and reparation under the doctrine is applied only insofar as necessary to wipe out the consequences of the breach and restore the relationship between the breaching and invoking states. Thus, state responsibility and state accountability are not incompatible; they merely serve separate functions. Indeed, there is nothing to preclude a finding of state responsibility comprising part of the matrix of responses that lead to a state being held accountable – or, to coin a phrase, 'layman's State responsibility'.[283] Furthermore, attempts to expand the doctrine of state responsibility, within the discrete legal space it currently occupies, so as to facilitate a more comprehensive framework of accountability were noted here as giving juridical support to state accountability.

The term 'juridical support' means there is evidence that international law either expressly acknowledges, permits by implication or is evolving in such a way as to accommodate the concept in question. Having established that juridical support exists, the final, and most important, component of this academic inquiry is to search for evidence of conceptual state accountability in practice.

283 Note 229 above.

5 State accountability in state practice

Chapter 5 applies the interpretative framework to a series of representative case studies from state practice to determine whether the various responses (or lack thereof) by the international community when states breach *jus cogens* norms demonstrates there is, or is evolving, a norm of accountability. The case studies illustrate how the complexities in holding states accountable are (or are not) dealt with in practice; including what is an effective response, whether accountability is the prerogative of states or whether non-state actors are instrumental in the process, and how it is determined that the breach occurred in the first place.

5.1 Setting the scene to analyse state accountability in practice

Juridical indicators that state accountability is more than simply a political aspiration and has legal validity are of little utility without practical evidence that a global consensus can, and is, mobilised when states breach international law in such a way that threatens the interests of the international community as a whole. Therefore, this chapter applies the interpretative framework developed throughout the preceding discussion to state practice to determine whether the various responses (or lack thereof) by the international community when states breach *jus cogens* norms demonstrates there is, or is evolving, a norm of accountability. Protecting the interests of the global community, rather than states acting merely out of self-preservation, was the impetus for significant changes in international relations throughout the 20th century – notably seen with the establishment of the United Natious (UN). It is thus particularly appropriate to introduce the case studies and reiterate the argument that the protection of international interests is now inspiring an evolution in international law at the start of the 21st century, by referring to the largest meeting of states hosted by the US since the San Francisco Conference that established the UN in 1945. Central to the agenda of the April 2010 Nuclear Security Summit (attended by 47 states, the UN, the International Atomic Energy Agency and the European Council) was gaining a consensus amongst participants as to the establishment and maintenance of a legal structure capable of ensuring adequate regulatory supervision of states' nuclear holdings and industry. A peripheral goal to the summit's primary objective of non-proliferation

(NP) was 'the need to hold nations accountable when they do not live up to their NP obligations'[284] and it is argued here that Iran was the primary target of such accountability measures.

First, the failure to invite Iran to attend the summit was implicitly condoned by the very fact that other delegates did participate (including China, from whom Iran had been used to receiving diplomatic support in this matter). Secondly, a consensus and commitment was sought amongst delegates to impose Security Council sanctions on Iran for failing to comply with its NP obligations. It cannot be argued that the summit was completely apolitical, especially given Israel's refusal to attend owing to the risk that other states would use the opportunity to criticise Israel's nuclear stance. However, the fact that the proposed sanctions regime against Iran would effectively be global in scale created a distinction from sanctions typically imposed by only a few states, which in turn arguably meant that the measures taken by the summit delegates transcended politics and were evidence of state accountability in practice.

Five case studies have been selected from throughout the 20th century, the period in which states – and the development of international law – have afforded the greatest recognition of *jus cogens*. A representative overview of state practice cannot resolve every lingering issue as to the form and nature of state accountability and it is inevitable that the concept will remain somewhat indeterminate even after the analysis in this chapter. Particular attention will, however, be given, first, to testing the evaluative criteria adopted in Chapter 2 and, second, to three key issues that have emerged from the preceding discussion. Each problem is introduced here so that answers to the respective issue can be given following – and drawing on – the case studies.

5.1.1 *Who determines whether a state breached international law?*

The first issue when seeking to demonstrate state accountability in practice is identifying if and how it had been determined that the state violated the relevant norm – in order that the subsequent reaction can be interpreted as a response to the breach. Ideally, any determination that a state has breached international law will be impartial and unbiased – and therefore comparable to the findings of an international court.

The logical solution is thus to use an international court with the mandate to determine whether states have breached *jus cogens* norms or, more generally, public international law. There are many difficulties in using the ICJ for this purpose including, but not limited to, the fact the Court's jurisdiction is restricted to questions

284 White House Press Briefing 'Press Briefing to Preview the Nuclear Security Summit' (9 April 2010) available athttp://www.whitehouse.gov/the-press-office/press-briefing-preview-nuclear-security-summit-gary-samore-white-house-coordinator-.

of state responsibility, which is not the same as determining a breach of international law per se.

On the one hand, the Court's mandate is dependent on state consent, so the risk arises that states would not consent to jurisdiction and, on contentious issues only, applications by states can be heard so there is the potential that no application would ever be made. On the other hand, Kleffner argued that the ICC's jurisdiction over heads of state and international crimes that imply state participation, such as apartheid as a crime against humanity, already establishes jurisdiction over states – albeit that jurisdiction is indirect. However, given that not all states are party to the Court,[285] that Article 124 affords states 'seven years after the entry into force of this Statute' not to 'accept the jurisdiction of the Court' with respect to certain crimes alleged to have been committed by nationals or on the state's territory and that the preamble to the Rome Statute emphasises 'that nothing in this Statute shall be taken as authorizing any State Party to intervene' in the affairs of another state, it appears very unlikely that states would ever tolerate the ICC or a similar quasi-criminal court having the power to adjudicate over them directly.[286]

To the extent that at this time a judicial determination seems unlikely, the question is whether a political determination could be possible, by states either individually or in concert pursuant to a treaty-based relationship such as NATO, through regional forms of state organisation such as the EU, or through international organisations such as the UN. Article 35 of the UN Charter discourages unilateral action preferring states, whether or not they are UN members, to 'bring any dispute … to the attention of the Security Council or of the General Assembly', which is potentially broad enough in its wording to include questions of state accountability for grievous breaches. It is doubtful that the determination of a single state would ever be accepted and instead it is more likely that, in order for such a determination to be accepted, it would need to be made by a collective of states or an international organisation comprised of state members. The UN is the most viable candidate, given that it has the greatest number of state members of any other international organisation but there are issues in this scenario that serve

285 Notably, the US stated, through its representative Department of State Legal Advisor John Bellinger that 'our concerns about the ICC are well known … we share the goals of the ICC for international criminal justice and accountability. We have concerns only about how the Rome Statute was ultimately set up' and in particular, the perception that the Court divests the Security Council of power in favour of the Prosecutor at the ICC, and due to the risk that the Court might indict US citizens (AMICC Business Council for the UN 'Chronology of US Opposition to the ICC: From "Signature Suspension" to Immunity Agreements to Darfur' (2009)). See also D. Scheffer, Ambassador-at-Large for War Crimes Issues and Head of the US Delegation to the UN Diplomatic Conference on the Establishment of a Permanent ICC 'Testimony Before the Senate Foreign Relations Committee, Washington, DC' (1998) available from the website of the US Department of State http://www.state.gov/www/policy_remarks/1998/980723_scheffer_icc.html and W. Schabas, 'United States Hostility to the ICC: It's All About the Security Council' (2004) 15 *European Journal of International Law* 701.

286 J. Kleffner, *Complementarity in the Rome Statute and National Criminal Jurisdictions* (Oxford: Oxford University Press, 2008).

to undermine the credibility of using such a determination as the basis on which to seek redress from a rogue state.

The legal basis on which the UN could determine that a state should be held accountable is uncertain. Article 39 provides that 'the Security Council shall determine the existence of any threat to the peace, breach of the peace, or act of aggression' and 'make recommendations, or decide what measures shall be taken in accordance with Articles 41 and 42, to maintain or restore international peace and security'. To the extent that breaching *jus cogens* norms amounts to a threat to international peace and security, the Security Council thus has the indirect legal sanction to determine liability and impose measures, provided that such measures were also necessary for the purpose of maintaining or restoring peace and security. The range of permissible measures in Articles 41 and 42 is broad and includes non-aggressive means such as 'interruption of economic relations and of rail, sea, air, postal, telegraphic, radio, and other means of communication, and the severance of diplomatic relations'; as used in response to the illegal regime in Rhodesia after the Unilateral Declaration of Independence, when Security Council Resolutions 216 and 217 called upon member states not to recognise the regime, and were followed in 1966 and 1968 with Security Council Resolutions 232, 253 and 409 that imposed mandatory economic sanctions. The Security Council has a greater arsenal than merely using force. This in turn would be more likely to lead to accountability at the same time as protecting international peace and security; however, there are instances where breaches of *jus cogens* norms do not amount to a threat to international peace and security, thus apprearing to strip the Security Council of its legal authority to respond. Torture, for example, can be perpetrated as a crime against humanity, 'when committed as part of a widespread or systematic attack'[287] but can also involve a single perpetrator and victim,making it highly improbable that the Security Council could conclude there was a threat to international peace and security and act as a result.

At the time that the UN Charter was drafted, member states considered that the Security Council was the most appropriate body to determine what constituted a threat to peace and security and what the response should be. However, whether more than 60 years later that translates to the legal authority to determine breaches of international law for which the state in question should then be held accountable is dubious. Even if it does have legal authority, Article 27 provides that decisions by the Security Council need the agreement of nine states and thus cannot be seen as representative of a state consensus, which would add weight to the argument that the response was seeking accountability rather than responding to a security threat. There are also questions as to the legitimacy in allowing a few states to adopt a semi-judicial role when *jus cogens* seek to protect the interests of the entire international community – a function the Security Council

287 Rome Statute of the ICC Article 7(1) (1998).

has thus far disavowed in relation to the criminal liability of individuals by establishing, for example, the *ad hoc* international tribunals.[288]

In contrast, Article 18 provides that the General Assembly requires a two-thirds majority when voting on 'important matters', which undoubtedly includes breaches of *jus cogens* norms and certainly the more members that comprise a consensus the more likely it is that censure will have an effect on the state in breach. The UN was founded on the premise that individual states consider the opinion of the collective to be influential, which would suggest that the greater number of states in the General Assembly makes it a more credible body to determine when accountability can be sought from states. But, as with the Security Council, there are issues to be considered.

First of all, the powers of the General Assembly are not as clearly defined in the UN Charter as the affirmative legal authority expressly given to the Security Council. Chapter IV allows the General Assembly to 'consider', 'discuss' and 'make recommendations' without giving any further direction on how far these contemplations may be taken but, because Article 10 provides that Chapter IV relates to 'any questions or any matters within the scope of the present Charter', the scope of consideration is still wider than peace and security.

Secondly, Article 12 states that 'the General Assembly shall not make any recommendation with regard to that dispute or situation [regarding international peace and security] unless the Security Council so requests', seemingly preventing the General Assembly from making any determination if the Security Council was already exercising its jurisdiction in the matter. In its 2004 *Advisory Opinion Concerning the Legal Consequences on Construction of a Wall*, the ICJ did note, however, that the practice of the Security Council and the General Assembly had evolved and Article 12 was not so restrictively applied that both bodies could not simultaneously deal with the same issue. The Court noted that the General Assembly tended to deal with matters such as the disputes' 'humanitarian, social and economic aspects'[289] and that the competence of the Security Council pursuant to Article 24 to deal with issues relating to international peace and security was not 'exclusive'.[290]

The third issue is pragmatic in that the greater the number of states within a consensus, the more difficult it is for that consensus to be reached. Finally, the most significant obstacle in using either the General Assembly or the Security Council is the risk of powerful states exercising influence, forming voting blocs and voting in accordance with their own interests. In other words, a cynic could expect that the same political issues that affect the daily business of the UN will not be set aside simply because the question relates to a breach of *jus cogens* norms. The question for

288 N. Jorgensen, *The Responsibility of States for International Crimes* (Oxford: Oxford University Press 2003) 214.

289 *Advisory Opinion Concerning the Legal Consequences on Construction of a Wall in the Occupied Palestinian Territory* ICJ Reports (2004) para 27. The ICJ concluded that requesting an advisory opinion from the Court did not exceed the General Assembly's competence and was not *ultra vires* and in breach of Article 12.

290 Ibid, para 26.

the case studies is whether practice shows that the UN is primarily given the task of determining a breach of international law – despite or because of politics – or whether some third party, not yet considered in this discussion, has a role to play.

5.1.2 What forms of redress ensure the breaching state is held accountable?

The indeterminate and theoretical nature of the concept raises many issues in terms of deciding what form or forms of redress are effective in that the breaching state is held accountable. Just some of the problems are highlighted here.

First, is the form of effective redress always the same or does practice illustrate that some forms of redress are more effective than others, which would displace the earlier assumption that state accountability is contextual. For example, does an isolated act of torture by a group of rogue police officers warrant the same redress from the state compared to a sustained policy of kidnapping and torturing individuals? Secondly, is it possible to hold a state accountable without punishing the individuals within that state especially given that it is often the citizens of the rogue state who are the victims? Alternatively, is it possible to strike a balance between avoiding collective punishment and ensuring redress from the state and other culpable parties? Thirdly, when is redress effective in communicating the gravity of the breach, in particular when states have breached a *jus cogens* norm? This begs the question of whether there is a hierarchy amongst breaches of *jus cogens* and thus responses to genocide should perhaps be more severe than the response to an isolated act of torture. Fourthly, are there any limitations on the extent to which redress from individuals or organs of the state can be attributed to the state? For example, is a quantum assessment needed whereby only a certain percentage of the individual's accountability counts towards the state's accountability? Fifthly, can redress for the purposes of accountability be implied from or co-exist with other goals in responding to the breach? For example, would compensation for loss paid by the culpable state to survivors of genocide be seen as redress for breaching the actual prohibition on genocide? Alternatively, could the use of force in response to aggression also be a means of holding the aggressive state accountable, given that the primary goal would probably be either repulsion or self-defence (when initiated by the invaded state) or international peace and security (under a Security Council action)?

The case studies seek to identify what means are available to and are utilised by the international community when responding to breaches of *jus cogens* norms. In 'choosing and combining these mechanisms so as to advance the society's goals for accountability',[291] when is the outcome effective?

291 S. Ratner and J. Abrams, *Accountability for Human Rights Atrocities in International Law* (2nd edn Oxford: Oxford University Press, 2001) 159.

5.1.3 Is state accountability solely a state prerogative?

This book seeks to identify a paradigmatic shift in public international law whereby the protection of fundamental interests of the global community is influencing normative developments and, in particular, an evolving principle of state accountability. In order to identify the typology of such an accountability norm, which must logically mean that the concept is currently indeterminate, a great deal of emphasis is placed here on state practice. The need to do so is especially pertinent because while many states recognise that *jus cogens* are fundamental, there is sufficient debate as to the existence and content of this category of norms to frustrate a definitive conclusion that states are under a separate legal obligation to protect, maintain and ultimately respond when breached. If there is no legal obligation on states to respond to breaches of *jus cogens* norms, the question therefore arises whether the fact that fundamental norms represent the interests of the entire international community means that there is a global right to seek accountability that includes both state and non-state actors. In particular, and what can only be gleaned by referring to practice, is the extent to which any right, duty or obligation to hold a rogue state accountable equates with the desire or the logistical capability to do so. Rationally, the need for ability to coincide with willingness and the speculative nature of any right or obligation suggests that the dominant feature of state accountability will be collective action, and the question for the case studies is whether, in practice, state accountability is a collective prerogative.

5.2 Case studies

5.2.1 Armenian massacre 1915

The view taken here is that the widespread violence in Turkey between 1915 and 1923 that has controversially been stated by some commentators to be part of a government policy to destroy the Armenian population was not met with any effective response by states and Turkey has not been held accountable.[292] Turkey acknowledges that violence occurred during this period but has vehemently denied that there was a 'massacre',[293] let alone genocide or crimes against humanity, claiming instead that the Ottoman authorities authorised the use of force in response to insurgency by the minority Armenians. Realistically, Turkey could not dispute the violence and significant death toll, given that, first, the Ottoman

292 T. Akcan, '*A Shameful Act: The Armenian Genocide and Turkish Responsibility*' (Metropolitan Books, 2006); J. Balint, 'The Place of Addressing Internal Regime Conflicts' (1996) 59 *Law and Contemporary Problems* 103; M. Kielsgard, 'Restorative Justice for The Armenians, Resolved: It's The Least We Can Do' (2008) *Connecticut Journal of International Law* 1.

293 The current website for the Ministry of Culture and Tourism states clearly that 'there was no evidence at all to prove that such a crime as alleged Armenian massacre [was] ever committed in Turkey' (2009) available at http://www.kultur.gov.tr/EN/BelgeGoster.aspx?17A16AE30572D3136407999D5EC50F8959AD2977D8BAC059.

authorities were involved in a series of court martials conducted between 1919 and 1920 that partially related to the violence in 1915 and, secondly, that the Sultan, at the time of the trials, labelled the violence as *kanuni insaniyete … karsi ika edilen ceraim*, translated by the author as 'against the laws of humanity', to recognise the gravity of events.[294] Of course, Turkey had little option, following its defeat at the end of the First World War, but to participate in the war trials conducted after the Armistice. Thus, there is the implication that any admission by Turkey relating to the violence at that time was not freely given and certainly in the following years Turkey has sought to highlight the historic context in which the deaths occurred to displace any perception that the state's actions were anything other than justified.

At the end of the 19th and beginning of the 20th centuries violence escalated as the Ottoman Empire disintegrated, resulting in a reduction of territory and the emergence of a dominant Turkish culture and authority. This process led to conflict between the many ethnic groups, including earlier violence under Sultan Abdul Hamit (1894–1896) and continuing throughout the rule of the Turk Ittihads (1908–1918) but, although commentators such as Dadrian and Kielsgard can date the more generalised violence from as early as 1895, the historic record places the massacres as occurring from 1915, and resulting in the death or deportation of approximately 1.5 million Armenians.[295] As early as 1915 the notable historian and jurist Viscount Bryce, who at that time spoke on the matter in the House of Lords, presented evidence that the massacres were part of an official state policy to exterminate the Armenian population.[296] British historian Arthur Toynbee described the violence as carried out 'under the cloak of legality, by cold-blooded governmental action', arguing that the deaths 'were not mass murders committed spontaneously by mobs of private people'.[297] In its 1985 'Revised and Updated Report on the Question of the Prevention and Punishment of the Crime of Genocide', the UN Sub-Commission on Prevention of Discrimination and Protection of Minorities noted that reports in US, German and British archives and communiqués of diplomats in the Ottoman Empire corroborated the findings of Bryce and Toynbee. For example, even the German Ambassador, as a formal

294 V. Dadrian, 'The Turkish Military Tribunal's Prosecution of the Authors of the American Genocide: Four Major Courts-Martial Series' (1997) 11 *Holocaust and Genocide Studies* 28.

295 This statistic was given in US Senate Resolution 106 'Calling on the President to Ensure that the Foreign Policy of the United States Reflects Appropriate Understanding and Sensitivity Concerning Issues Related to Human Rights, Ethnic Cleansing, and Genocide Documented in the United States Record Relating to the Armenian Genocide' (2007) and in the UN Sub-Commission on Prevention of Discrimination and Protection of Minorities 'Revised and Updated Report on the Question of the Prevention and Punishment of the Crime of Genocide' UN Doc E/CN.4/Sub.2/1985/6 (1985).

296 Viscount Bryce's work was completed with the historian Arthur Toynbee and is a painstaking compilation of interviews, correspondence and government documents published by the British Government in 1916: Viscount J. Bryce and A. Toynbee, *The Treatment of Armenians in the Ottoman Empire* (London, HMSO, 1916 republished by Taderon Press: Reading, 2000).

297 Ibid.

ally of Turkey, was quoted as writing in July 1915 that 'the Government is indeed pursuing its goal of exterminating the Armenian race in the Ottoman Empire'.[298] The Commission felt that there was sufficient evidence to conclude that as a result of the Ittihad policies of deportation and discrimination, 'at least one million Armenians were killed or death marched'.[299]

Substantiating the argument that there was a preconceived strategy by the Ittihad Government was the fact that by 1915 a number of policies had been adopted in those parts of the Balkan region densely populated by the Armenian community such as Macedonia and Albania, of which three in particular discriminated against the Armenians. First, the large-scale deportation of Armenians, which reached in excess of 700,000 by 1917, was instituted pursuant to the 1915 Temporary Deportation Law.[300] Deportation of the male population began in 1914 before expanding in 1915 as a formal government policy to include all Armenian citizens in the area; so, for example, Armenians in the province of Erzurum were marched to camps all the way in the south of the Ottoman Empire, in what is now Syria.[301] The US ambassador Henry Morgenthau, who was in Turkey during the violence, considered that 'when the Turkish authorities gave the orders for these deportations, they were merely giving the death warrant to a whole race' and believed that government officials with whom he met 'made no particular attempt to conceal the fact'.[302]

The second discriminatory policy was property confiscation under the 1915 Temporary Law of Expropriation and Confiscation that applied to all Armenian land and property. This included any property that had been abandoned because the individual concerned had been deported, which likewise became the property of the state.

The third policy involved widespread arrests and executions on charges of terrorism that were pursued under the Turkish legal system with disregard for natural justice standards.[303]

Certainly, in the face of ongoing discrimination and without the protection of the law any population is vulnerable, as was shown subsequently in Nazi Germany where legalised persecution was the forerunner to the attempted physical destruction of the Jewish population. In such situations, the state is implicated

298 UN Sub-Commission on Prevention of Discrimination and Protection of Minorities 'Revised and Updated Report on the Question of the Prevention and Punishment of the Crime of Genocide' UN Doc E/CN.4/Sub.2/1985/6 (1985) footnote 13.

299 Ibid.

300 Report of the Ministry of Culture 'Armenian Allegations and the Facts' available at http://www.kultur.gov.tr/EN/BelgeGoster.aspx?17A16AE30572D3136407999D5EC50F8959AD2977D8BAC059.

301 V. Dadrian, 'The Historical and Legal Interconnections Between the Armenian Genocide and the Jewish Holocaust: From Impunity to Retributive Justice' (1998) 23 *Yale Journal of International Law* 503.

302 H. Morgenthau, *Ambassador Morgenthau's Story* (New York: Doubleday Page, 1919) 309.

303 Note 296 above, 629.

for having established the legal framework that prevents the population acting in its own defence, and therefore holding the state to account would be morally and politically – if not legally – justified. However, in this case, the relevant policies were instituted during the First World War and Turkey has argued that they were introduced because the Armenian population in the Balkans had strong links with the Armenian community in Russia, and was suspected of assisting the enemy.[304] In order to justify the claim that the international response to the massacres was seeking to hold Turkey accountable because the atrocities were part of the Ittihad Government's stated objective 'of Ottomanizing the Empire',[305] it therefore needs to be shown that those states that responded viewed the violence as more than the result of the Ottoman Government 'arrest[ing] the suspects of Armenian terrorism, violence and treachery'.[306]

In 1915, the Entente Powers of Britain, France and Russia jointly described the violence as 'crimes of Turkey against humanity and civilization', while the US referred to the atrocities as a campaign of racial extermination by the Ottoman Government.[307] The international community was clearly aware that the atrocities were occurring and the gravity thereof. Furthermore, the 'crimes' were associated with both state and government policy and there was recognition that the violence was directed at the Armenian population. Yet, because in 1915 the scope of recognised international crimes was limited to piracy and slavery, politically labelling the violence to be a crime was not the same as a legal determination from which then to seek redress. Crimes against humanity were later codified in Article 6(c) of the Charter of the International Military Tribunal, to include 'murder, extermination, enslavement, deportation, and other inhumane acts committed against any civilian population … or persecutions on political, racial, or religious grounds … whether or not in violation of the domestic law of the country where perpetrated' and from the evidence cited above, the violence against the Armenians would fall within this definition, directly implicating the state.[308] The view that the atrocities amounted to what would subsequently be a legal crime against humanity is strengthened given that, in the words of Schabas, 'the term "crimes against

304 Note 301 above, 503.

305 Speech of the Ittihad Minister of Interior Affairs Talat at a Turkish Congress meeting in 1910 and cited in Dadrian (n 294) at 180.

306 Turkish Ministry of Culture 'Armenian Allegations and the Facts'.

307 Joint Allied Declaration (28 May 1915). A copy of the Allied Declaration was sent to the US Department of State and was subsequently published in part in the *New York Times* (28 May 1915). It was later cited in the UN War Crimes Commission Report 'History of the United Nations War Crimes Commission and the Development of the Laws of War' (London: HMSO, 1948).

308 Dispute exists as to whether or not the acts need to be committed as part of a state plan under the legal definition of crimes against humanity but that discussion is beyond the scope of this discussion. What is apparent from amongst the varied expressions is that crimes against humanity are joined to 'the sphere of international criminalization' by some form of state involvement (Bassiouni in M. von Sternberg, 'A Comparison of the Yugoslavian and Rwandan War Crimes Tribunals: Universal Jurisdiction and the "Elementary Dictates of Humanity"' (1996) *Brooklyn Journal of International Law* 110, 138).

humanity" was itself coined to describe the massacres of the Armenians, in May 1915'[309] and use of the term by the Entente powers was hailed by Kielsgard as the first step in creating 'a new framework of international law'.[310]

More controversial is the allegation that Turkey committed what would become known after 1944 as genocide. In 1936, and therefore before the term was coined by Raphael Lemkin, American historian Langer considered that 'it was perfectly obvious that the Sultan was determined to end the Armenian question by exterminating the Armenians',[311] creating a parallel between the Sultan as an embodiment of the state seeking to destroy the Armenians and the definition of genocide, as the intended destruction of a national, ethnic, racial or religious group, in the 1948 Genocide Convention. Despite the apparent overlap between the violence in 1915 and the definition of genocide in the 1948 Convention, to which Turkey is a party, two points must be remembered.

First, the legal crime of genocide did not exist in 1915, which implies that pursuant to the principle *lex retro non agit* there could be no justification for seeking redress from the state on that basis (even as a form of delayed accountability). However, as argued in Chapter 3 in relation to *jus cogens* that were only formally recognised for the first time in the VCLT, there is juridical support that the principle of inter-temporality is qualified and that the prevailing framework of the entire legal system at the time should be taken into account. The ratification of the 1965 Convention on Non-Applicability of Statutory Limitations to War Crimes and Crimes Against Humanity by more than 50 states likewise indicates that impunity is not to be tolerated where the fundamental interests of the international community as a whole are affected; solely on the basis that international law does not make express provision for the breach at the date of commission. Thus, to the extent that in 1915 there was universal condemnation of the mass annihilation of groups of peoples, the failure legally to categorise such acts as a crime should not necessarily prevent accountability from being sought.[312] The second and more convincing problem in terms of determining that Turkey committed genocide is establishing that the Armenians were a distinct group that were intentionally singled out for destruction by the state, rather than generalised violence involving the Turkish population.

It is not only Turkey that claims that the violence in 1915 did not satisfy the definition of genocide subsequently set down in the 1948 Genocide Convention. In her capacity as the UK Spokesperson for Foreign and Commonwealth Affairs, Baroness Ramsay of Cartvale noted that 'in the absence of unequivocal evidence to show that the Ottoman administration took a specific decision to eliminate the

309 W. Schabas, 'Darfur and the "Odious Scourge": The Commission of Inquiry's Finding on Genocide' (2005) 27 *Leiden Journal of International Law* 871, 883.

310 Note 292 above, 20.

311 W. Langer, *The Diplomacy of Imperialism 1890–1902* (New York: Knopf, 1935) 203.

312 *Advisory Opinion on the Legal Consequences for States of the Continued Presence of South Africa in Namibia (SW Africa) Notwithstanding Security Council Resolution 276* ICJ Reports (1971) 3.

Armenians under their control at the time, British governments have not recognised the events of 1915 and 1916 as "genocide"'.[313] The UK's official position, as expressed in 1999, stands in contrast to that of former Prime Minister Winston Churchill, who was of the view that the violence was part of a government policy to wipe out the Armenian population in Turkey, and who stated there was 'no reason to doubt that this crime was planned and executed for political reasons [because] the opportunity presented itself for clearing Turkish soil of a Christian race opposed to all Turkish ambitions'.[314] The failure to label the violence as genocide in 1915 had little relevance as the term did not exist until 1944, while the fact that at the time the UK described the massacres as 'crimes of Turkey against humanity'[315] captured the perceived gravity of the violence. Furthermore, a closer inspection of the 1915 declaration by the Entente powers, including the UK, shows that the atrocities were described in such a way as to invoke the definition of genocide that was to come. The declaration highlighted that the victims comprised a single group, that the violence was facilitated by state authorities and included acts of murder, stating 'that for about a month the Kurd and Turkish population of Armenia has been massacring Armenians with the connivance and often assistance of Ottoman authorities'.[316] Irrespective of what contemporary official state position is taken on the massacres as satisfying the legal definition of genocide, it cannot be doubted that the UK has consistently viewed the violence as a crime against humanity by Turkey.

Indeed, the seemingly inconsistent views held by the UK reflect the status quo more generally as states prevaricate in determining whether the violence was genocide but are generally unequivocal in terms of finding that Turkey did perpetrate crimes against humanity. This case clearly highlights the significant political implications and pragmatic complexities, including identifying the legal breach to be overcome before even turning to the question of how to respond and hold the breaching state accountable, but given that both crimes against humanity and genocide are on the ILC's list of recognised *jus cogens* norms and that the Entente powers (who it would be accurate to describe as having significant power in international relations in 1915) determined that Turkey had committed what would formally become known as crimes against humanity, it is reasonable to proceed and consider whether redress was sought from Turkey and, if so, in what form. In the same way that future developments in international criminal law could not be anachronistically displaced and reflected in the established principles of public international law in 1915, there was little in the way of precedent for responding to grievous breaches of international law beyond the use of force.

313 Baroness Ramsay of Cartvale as Spokesperson for Foreign and Commonwealth Affairs (speaking on behalf of the British Government) House of Lords Hansard (14 April 1999) col 826.

314 W. Churchill, *The World Crisis 1911–1918* (London: Free Press, 2005) 157.

315 Note 307 above.

316 Ibid.

In addition, the principle of non-intervention was fundamental in governing inter-state relations, thereby restricting the potential responses that were available. A final contextual factor to be noted is that the violence occurred during the First World War, so that any response by the Entente powers (and subsequently the US) condemned Turkey not just for the violence against the Armenians but also as an enemy state. Bearing those points in mind, there were arguably several direct and indirect responses that can be seen as seeking some form of accountability from Turkey.

First, and as already discussed, there was widespread criticism of Turkey by states at the time of the violence. Tomuschat[317] has argued that, throughout the first half of the 20th century (until the Cold War, when criticism became a diplomatic tool with which to manage so-called East-West relations), states viewed criticism as a form of quasi-intervention, recalling the definition of intervention given in the *Nicaragua Case* and on the basis that one state is judging another state in relation to the exercise of its sovereign power.[318] Tomuschat expressed the opinion that states would only resort to criticism when the gravity of the situation was sufficient to warrant quasi-intervention; thus, the condemnation of Turkey in 1915 was not dissimilar to attempting to hold Turkey accountable because it was perceived by the criticising states as a justified response in light of the seriousness of the state's actions. The fact that Turkey was being criticised by its enemies may serve to link the denunciation to the broader defence of Europe by the Entente powers, making the argument less persuasive. On the other hand, there is nothing to preclude the criticism from achieving dual goals – both to condemn the enemy state and hold Turkey accountable for breaching international law.

The second response occurred at the end of the First World War when, pursuant to Article 230 of the 1920 Treaty of Sèvres,[319] the Entente powers required Turkey to surrender individuals 'responsible for the massacres committed during the continuance of the state of war on territory which formed part of the Ottoman Empire on August 1, 1914'. Although Article 230 provided for individual responsibility without referring to the state, this must be read in the broader context whereby the Entente powers had previously declared they would 'hold personally responsible … all members of the Ottoman government'[320] in response to 'crimes of Turkey against humanity and civilization'. Thus, Article 230 can be interpreted as a contributory means for seeking redress from the state. Of course, the Treaty of Sèvres was primarily drafted as a peace treaty and sought to impose consequences on Turkey as a vanquished party at the end of the First World War. Likewise, the 1919 Treaty of Versailles, Treaty of Neuilly, Treaty of Trianon and

317 This interpretation of criticism was raised in discussions between the author and Professor Tomuschat of Humboldt University, Berlin (27 April 2009).

318 Recalling the definition of intervention given in *Military v Paramilitary Activities In and Against Nicaragua* (Merits 1986) ICJ Reports (1984) paras 202–209.

319 Treaty of Sèvres 1919 (*The Treaties of Peace 1919–1923* (Carnegie Endowment for International Peace: New York, 1924)).

320 Note 307 above.

Treaty of Saint-Germain required each of the defeated states to give up territory, which could imply that Article 230 was solely seeking redress for Turkey's actions during the First World War. A detailed comparison of all these treaties is not required here but the point is that accountability for one breach may need to be inferred or may even be an unintended consequence of seeking accountability for an unrelated breach.

The third response also arose in the context of the Treaty of Sèvres but Article 88, which required Turkey to 'recognise Armenia as a free and independent State', was more persuasive than Article 230 in terms of arguing a direct attempt to seek accountability from Turkey for the Armenian massacre. Ultimately, the Treaty of Sèvres was superseded by the 1923 Treaty of Lausanne,[321] which made no reference to Armenia whatsoever; thus, the potential that a reduction of territory and recognition of the Armenian state may have provided an effective remedy to hold Turkey accountable, albeit in a political rather than a legal sense, was lost. The lingering impact of criticism levelled in 1915 and even the fact that the state is associated with the first quasi-legal use of the term crimes against humanity illustrates the gravity with which Turkey's acts and omissions were viewed by states. The argument that accountability was being sought from Turkey because the violence breached fundamental norms of international law is, however, somewhat undermined as these responses occurred in the context and aftermath of the First World War and were imposed by the Allied powers.

Since the initial acknowledgement and condemnation of Turkey for the violence in 1915, there has been little progress in terms of seeking accountability from the state for its role and the considerable lapse in time has only served to frustrate attempts to compile a strong evidentiary case to determine culpability one way or the other. The intervening decades have made it increasingly unlikely that formal accountability will ever be sought and the contextual factors that influenced the nature of the response in 1915 have simply been replaced by different political considerations. For example, the fact that a greater number of states now describe the violence as genocide, including 10 out of 28 NATO members,[322] could be interpreted as a form of redress owing to the stigma in being recognised as a state that committed genocide against its population – but this stigma is limited in scope to those states that share this opinion.

A second illustration of where political factors can be seen to have influenced the attainment (or not) of accountability from Turkey is in contrasting the response by the US at the time of the violence with the stance taken more recently. In 1915, the US condemned the massacres as a policy of racial discrimination and threats were conveyed through the US Ambassador at the time that diplomatic sanctions

321 Treaty of Lausanne 1923 (*The Treaties of Peace 1919–1923* (Carnegie Endowment for International Peace: New York, 1924)).

322 These are Belgium, Canada, France, Germany, Greece, Italy, Lithuania, the Netherlands, Poland and Slovakia: The Armenian Genocide Museum (2009) available at http://www.genocide-museum.am/eng/states.php.

would be imposed on Turkey. Steps were taken to support the victims, including Senate Resolution 12 (1916) that established a day of remembrance, the authorisation of funds by Congress to aid Armenian survivors, and Trask even argued that the US Senate's refusal to ratify the Treaty of Lausanne was linked to the removal of provisions from the treaty that referred to the Armenian issue.[323]

All these factors show that the initial reaction by the US was to condemn the violence as part of a state policy of racial discrimination. Yet in 2007, when US Senate Resolution 106 was introduced 'Calling On the President to Ensure that the Foreign Policy of the United States Reflects Appropriate Understanding and Sensitivity Concerning Issues Related to Human Rights, Ethnic Cleansing and Genocide Documented in the United States Record Relating to the Armenian Genocide' and the Government was requested to clarify 'the United States record relating to the Armenian genocide', former President Bush called for Congress 'to reject [the] Resolution'. The reason was not that there had been a change in the Government's perspective on Turkey's culpability but because the Resolution could 'do great harm to relations with a key ally in NATO and to the war on terror'.[324] In particular, the US wanted to maintain a positive relationship with Turkey, owing to the perceived risk of terrorism in the region and given the logistical support offered by Turkey including helping to combat Kurdish rebels in northern Iraq and allowing the US to use its airbases, which facilitated access into Iraq.[325] It appeared that, by 2007, the delay in seeking accountability had meant that contemporary political factors were prioritised over condemning Turkey for a genocide that occurred almost a century ago.

The extent of influence that political motivations have had on the official position of the US was made more apparent in 2010 when the Obama administration called for a resolution, similar to that unsuccessfully introduced in 2007, not to be passed by Congress – despite the President continuing to express the personal view that the violence had been an act of genocide. At the time Turkey was a revolving member of the Security Council and high on the US's foreign policy agenda was imposing Security Council sanctions on Iran for breaching its non-proliferation obligations, for which Turkey's support was needed.[326]

Turkey's pending application to join the EU also illustrates the extent to which the political considerations that influenced accountability in the past have been replaced by new political factors preventing a delayed form of accountability from being sought. In 1987, the European Parliament declared 'the refusal by the

323 The Senate rejected the Treaty by 50 votes to 34. The refusal has also been linked to the maintenance of oil concession contracts between American business and Turkey: R. Trask, *The United States Response to the Turkish Nationalism and Reform 1914–1939* (Minneapolis: University of Minnesota Press, 1971).

324 Knowlton 'Bush Warns Bill Would Irk Turkey – Armenian Resolution Calls Killings "Genocide"' *International Herald Tribune* (2007) cited in Kielsgard (n 292) 3.

325 Note 292 above, 3.

326 Fox News' White House View 'Turkey Troubles' (2010) abailable at http://www.whitehouse.blogs.foxnews.com/2010/03/05/turkey-troubles/.

present Turkish Government to acknowledge the genocide against the Armenian people … a[n] insurmountable obstacle to consideration of the possibility of Turkey's accession to the Community'.[327] Linking Turkey's membership with acknowledgment of the genocide appears significant – especially because it was described in terms of being 'a profoundly humane act of moral rehabilitation towards the Armenians'[328] and rehabilitation has strong associations with accountability. However, the European Parliament was clear to point out that seeking an acknowledgment that genocide occurred was not the same as Turkey being 'held responsible' for that genocide and it emphasised that no 'political nor legal or material claims against present-day Turkey can be derived from the recognition of this historical event as an act of genocide'.[329]

This is clearly an important distinction from the perspective of Turkey's accountability as it recognises that there was genocide per se without determining that Turkey was in any way a perpetrator of that genocide. This is the case even though Turkey's culpability is implicit owing to the level of organisation required to coordinate a policy of eradicating over one million Armenians across such a vast geographic area. Despite statements that Turkey should acknowledge the genocide, which the European Parliament noted in 2006 had still not occurred,[330] the intransigence of Turkey did not stop the EU from opening negotiations for accession in 2005. This *volte face* is less surprising if it is understood that Turkey's culpability for genocide was never in question – a point confirmed by the fact that in the 2007 Progress Report on Turkey's accession, recognition of the genocide was not even raised as an issue.[331]

Having applied the interpretive framework to analyse the possibility that practice-based evidence of state accountability could be identified from the responses to the Armenian massacre that occurred during the First World War, the conclusion is that there is little likelihood that Turkey was – or will be – held accountable given that even the matter of determining conclusively and consensually whether and for what breach the state was liable, has yet to be resolved. This verdict was reached despite noting, first, that there has been recognition by some states that Turkey breached what has subsequently been labelled the *jus cogens* prohibition on crimes against humanity and, secondly, the combination of condemnation and post First World War reparations that were to some extent linked with the violence toward the Armenians. This case implies that a temporal distance between the actual breach and the response to the breach makes it more likely that political

327 Then the European Economic Community. 'Resolution on a Political Solution to the Armenian Question' Council of Europe Parliamentary Assembly (1987) para 4.

328 'Resolution on a Political Solution to the Armenian Question' Council of Europe Parliamentary Assembly (1987) preamble.

329 Ibid, para 2.

330 'Report on Turkey's Progress Towards Accession' Council of Europe Parliament Doc No 2006/2118 (2006).

331 'Report on Turkey's Progress Towards Accession' Council of Europe Parliament Doc No 2006/1390 (2007).

factors are the dominant influence and motivation in how states react, rather than the gravity of the breach itself. A delay in seeking accountability may be contextually necessary, as here, where the violence occurred at the start of the First World War so that at a practical level the international community was otherwise engaged and at a political level any response was perceived as an attack on the enemy and not seeking to make Turkey account for its actions. The lesson, however, is that the severance in temporal proximity removes the imperative of responding to the seriousness of the breach per se and permits extraneous factors to influence the nature and motivation of the response, making it less likely that the outcome is to hold the breaching state accountable. Of course, the very foundation of this inquiry is that state accountability is a concept that started to evolve in the 20th century so it was unlikely that the response to the Armenian massacre, at the start of the 20th century, would provide a perfect precedent in terms of state practice. The logical expectation is that as the case studies progress there will be evidence that the limitations that frustrated accountability in this case were subsequently dealt with in order that states do not escape the consequences of such atrocities.

5.2.2 Crimes against humanity by the USSR – Holodomor famine 1933 and the Katyń Forest massacre 1940

The second case study considers allegations of crimes against humanity levelled at the USSR, which Jorgensen described in terms of 'international inaction in the face of criminal behaviour by a State'.[332] As with the case study of the Armenian massacre, various contextual historical and political factors justify a pre-emptive conclusion that the USSR was never held accountable for crimes against humanity. However, in contrast to the first case study, it can readily be shown that the international community has determined that the USSR did perpetrate the alleged crimes against humanity and the focus here is on whether the scale of the atrocities has motivated, or is currently inspiring, *ex post facto* attempts to seek accountability – from the Russian Federation (Russia) as the continuing or successor state of the USSR.

In 2006, the Parliamentary Assembly of the Council of Europe noted in Resolution 1481 on the 'Need For International Condemnation of Crimes of Totalitarian Communist Regimes' that 'the totalitarian communist regimes which ruled in central and eastern Europe in the last century, and which are still in power in several countries in the world, have been, *without exception*, characterised by massive violations of human rights'.[333] This claim is easily substantiated by

332 Note 288 above, 237.

333 Paragraph 2 listed the violations, which included 'individual and collective assassinations and executions, death in concentration camps, starvation, deportations, torture, slave labour and other forms of mass physical terror, persecution on ethnic or religious grounds, violation of freedom of conscience, thought and expression, of freedom of the press, and also lack of political pluralism'. Emphasis added.

referring to various incidents including 'extermination of 300,000 to 500,000 Cossacks between 1919 and 1920; 690,000 people arbitrarily sentenced to death and executed as a result of the "purge" in the communist party in 1937–1938; massive assassinations of approximately 30,000 "kulaks" (rich peasantry) during the forced collectivisation of 1929–1933 ... and assassinations and deportations of hundreds of thousands of Polish, Ukrainians, Lithuanians, Latvians, Estonians and Moldavians'.[334] These statistics are taken from the European Parliament's Report on the 'Need for International Condemnation of Crimes of Totalitarian Communist Regimes' that linked the USSR to 'the most violent crimes of the communist regimes like mass murder and genocide, torture, slave labour, and other forms of mass, physical terror', all of which are breaches of norms recognised by the ILC as *jus cogens*.[335]

The discussion here focuses on just two of the many atrocities alleged to have been perpetrated by the Soviet regime, being the Holodomor famine in Ukraine in 1933[336] and the massacre of Polish soldiers and elite in Katyń forest in 1940.

The Holodomor famine occurred after the Soviet Government confiscated the local harvest in response to rising Ukrainian nationalism resulting in estimates of between five and 10 million deaths.[337] In 1990, an International Commission of Inquiry into the Ukraine famine issued its final report detailing the Soviet Government's use of force, secret police and local members of the Communist party (the '25–thousanders') to confiscate and stockpile grain, decreeing that any attempt to take grain from storage facilities would result in death. The specific acts and omissions identified by the Commission included taking food from the population, state policies that prevented people from leaving famine afflicted areas and the failure to import rations during the famine. Based on 'all the available material, testimonies, documents, [and] studies',[338] the Commission 'attributed the key responsibility to Josef Stalin' and, rather than viewing the famine as arising from the acts of isolated or rogue authorities, it was linked to the head of state and therefore the state itself. High profile commentators such as the journalist

334 Report of the Political Affairs Committee Rapporteur Mr Göran Lindblad 'Need for International Condemnation of Crimes of Totalitarian Communist Regimes' European Parliament Doc 10765 (2005). In particular, the Report detailed the extent to which deportation was used by the USSR (para 38).

335 Ibid, para 40.

336 Holodomor means death by starvation in Ukrainian.

337 Y. Bilinsky, 'Was the Ukrainian Famine of 1932–1933 Genocide?' (1999) 1(2) *Journal of Genocide Research* 147–56. There are many wide-ranging estimates of the figures including five million in R. Conquest, *The Harvest of Sorrow: Soviet Collectivization and the Terror-Famine* (New York: Oxford University Press, 1986); 4.5 million by the International Commission of Inquiry 'Final Report into the 1932–33 Famine in the Ukraine' (1990) 3; and seven to 10 million by President Yushchenko of the Ukraine in 'Victor Yushchenko, President of Ukraine: Official Website' (2009) available at htp://www.president.gov.ua/en/news/8296.html.

338 International Commission of Inquiry 'Final Report into the 1932–33 Famine in the Ukraine' (1990) 28–54.

John Pilger and the genocide scholar Raphael Lemkin even go so far as to claim that the famine was 'not simply a case of mass murder' by the state but that it was 'a case of genocide'.[339] This position has also been adopted by certain states; for example, Australia's Senate Resolution No 680 (2002) and Resolution of the Senate of Argentina (No 1278-03) (2003) both refer to the Holodomor as 'genocide'.

However, the more generally accepted view by states, prominent individuals and international organisations is that the famine was a crime against humanity perpetrated by the USSR. The independent International Commission of Inquiry, which comprised legal scholars and jurists whose final report was then presented to the UN Under-Secretary for Human Rights and to the Council of Europe, concluded that there was insufficient evidence to show that the Soviet Government acted with the specific intent to destroy the Ukrainian population. Rezie is just one academic who adopted a similar position, citing correspondence between the Government of the Ukrainian People's Republic in exile and the League of Nations to argue that the Holodomor was a crime against humanity in the form of an 'engineered terror famine'[340] that aimed to force the collectivisation of Ukrainian farmers. In its 2008 Resolution on the 'Commemoration of the Holodomor, the Ukraine Artificial Famine (1932–1933)', the European Parliament stated that the famine 'was cynically and cruelly planned by Stalin's regime in order to force through the Soviet Union's policy of collectivisation of agriculture against the will of the rural population in Ukraine' and that the Holodomor amounted to 'crimes against humanity'. In 2003, 64 UN member states (including Russia) issued a Joint Statement at the 58th General Assembly declaring that 'in the former Soviet Union millions of men, women and children fell victim to the cruel actions and policies of the totalitarian regime', citing 'the Great Famine of 1932–1933 in Ukraine (Holodomor), which took from 7 million to 10 million innocent lives and became a national tragedy for the Ukrainian people'. Similarly, in 2007, UNESCO adopted its Resolution on 'Remembrance of Victims of the Great Famine (Holodomor) in Ukraine', stating that 'the tragedy of the Great Famine (Holodomor) was caused by the cruel actions and policies of the totalitarian Stalinist regime'. States have likewise used similarly unambiguous terms for condemning the USSR, typical of which was the Canadian Ukrainian Famine and Genocide Memorial Day Act 2008 that declared that the Holodomor was 'deliberately planned and executed by the Soviet regime', while influential individuals sharing the view that the famine was the result of Soviet Government policy included the late Pope John Paul II.[341] It would be difficult to gain a much

339 R. Lemkin, 'Soviet Genocide in Ukraine' (unpublished article and cited in R. Serbyn, 'Lemkin on Genocide of Nations' (2009) *Journal of International Criminal Justice* 123).

340 R. Rezie, 'The Ukrainian Constitution: Interpretation of the Citizens' Rights Provisions' (1999) 31 *Case Western Reserve Journal of International Law* 169, 176.

341 Pope John Paul II was speaking at an address on the 70th anniversary of the famine and stated: 'I speak of a horrendous crime that was committed in cold blood by the rulers of that period. The memories of this tragedy must guide the feelings and actions of Ukrainians' (address by Pope John

more comprehensive determination by the international community that the Holodomor famine was a crime against humanity and therefore that the USSR had breached a *jus cogens* norm.

All the statements cited above, however, were made after the Cold War and the collapse of the USSR. At the time of the famine in 1933, there was no formal condemnation of the USSR by states either individually or collectively as the League of Nations, while the fact that the USSR was admitted as a member of the League of Nations in 1934[342] and the rise in German nationalism that was distracting the attention of European states at the time offer just two speculative reasons for the apparent indifference to the Holodomor. It is almost trite to argue how influential the political environment was in terms of the scope and nature of international recognition that the famine occurred and the role played by the USSR; and for the purposes here it is sufficient to note that the USSR was clearly never required to account for its role in the Holodomor famine.

The relevance of historic context is equally apparent in relation to the second crime against humanity allegedly committed by the USSR, which was the massacre of more than 20,000[343] Polish soldiers and intelligentsia in the Katyń forest in 1940 by the NKVD (which was the secret service forerunner to the KGB).[344] The massacres have also been labelled as war crimes in breach of customary principles captured in the 1907 IV Hague Convention on the Law and Customs of Land Warfare and the 1929 Geneva Convention on the Treatment of Prisoners of War (given that the USSR was not a party to these instruments) and even as genocide on the basis that it was predominantly Polish intelligentsia and elite that were selected for execution. The order for execution of the prisoners was signed by Stalin and issued by the Politburo of the Central Committee of the All Union Communist Party (Bolsheviks) in Protocol 13 dated 5 March 1940, which instructed the NKVD to carry out the 'obligatory capital sentence of shooting' all 'incorrigible enemies of Soviet Authority',[345] so that the massacre was ordered pursuant to state policy and government directions and at a minimum constituted crimes against humanity.

Paul II to Ukrainians on 23 November 2003 on the 70th commemoration of the Holodomor) available at the website of the Association of Ukrainian citizens living in the UK (2009) http://www.augb.co.uk.

342 In comparison to the response when the USSR invaded Finland in 1939 and was expelled from the League (G. Scott, *The Rise and Fall of the League of Nations* (London: Hutchinson and Co Ltd, 1973)).

343 The Polish Institute of National Remembrance (established by the Polish Parliament in 1998) gives the figure as 21,768 taken from a report on the massacres by the Departmental Commission for the Prosecution of Crimes Against the Polish Nation (2010) availableathttp://www.ipn.gov.pl/portal/en/2/77/Decision_to_commence_investigation_into_Katyn_Massacre.htm.

344 G. Sanford, *Katyń and the Soviet Massacre of 1940: Truth, Justice and Memory* (London: Routledge, 2005).

345 Decision 5.III.1940 of the Politburo of the Central Committee of the All Union Communist Party (Bolsheviks) 'Protocol 13' (5 March 1940).

At the time there was little international response, which was unsurprising given that the graves at Katyń were not discovered until 1943, and even then the discovery was by Nazi forces. The Allies, who by 1943 were heavily reliant on the USSR to assist in fighting the Second World War, were reluctant either to pursue a thorough investigation or to condemn the shootings. Prime Minister Winston Churchill was quoted as saying that any investigation by the Germans could not be relied upon,[346] while President Roosevelt rejected a report by his special emissary to the Balkans, instead blaming the massacres on Germany.[347] In its 1952 report following investigations into Katyń, the position of the US House of Representatives could not have been more clear in regretting that 'in those fateful days nearing the end of the Second World War there unfortunately existed in high governmental and military circles a strange psychosis that military necessity required the sacrifice of loyal allies and our own principles in order to keep Soviet Russia from making a separate peace with Nazi Germany',[348] which was cited as the reason the US Government had earlier doubted that the USSR committed the massacres.

However, this report is not indicative that following the War the US then sought to lead the international community in addressing the massacres in an unbiased and impartial manner; despite the House requesting that the US Government present the case of Katyń to the UN General Assembly with the aim of establishing an 'international commission which would investigate … crimes against humanity'[349]. Rather, the fact that the report notes 'the striking similarity between crimes committed against the Poles at Katyń and those being inflicted on American and other UN troops' and states that the 'communist tactics being used in Korea are identical to those followed at Katyń'[350] to cloak the findings and recommendation in Cold War rhetoric undermines the prima facie assumption that accountability was being sought from the USSR. The more robust argument is that an international consensus recognising that the USSR was liable for the massacres could only truly be identified after the Cold War. At that time the Russian authorities, under President Gorbachev, issued a statement expressing regret at the massacres while describing the shootings as 'one of the serious crimes of Stalinism'.[351]

346 'Correspondence between the Chairman of the Council of Ministers of the USSR and the Presidents of the USA and the Prime Ministers of Great Britain during the Great Patriotic War of 1941–1945' Document No 151 (Moscow: Progress Publishers, 1953).

347 B. Fischer, 'The Katyń Controversy: Stalin's Killing Fields' (2007) Centre for the Study of Intelligence, Central Intelligence Agency Publication (2010) available at https://www.cia.gov/library/center-for-the-study-of-intelligence/csi-publications/csi-studies/studies/winter99-00/art6.html.

348 'Report No 2505 82nd Congress Concerning the Katyń Forest Massacre' Committee on House Administration US House of Representatives Document 100-183 (1952) (Washington: US Government Printing Office, 1988) Conclusions 11.

349 Ibid, Conclusions 13.

350 Ibid, Conclusions 12.

351 TASS Statement (14 April 1990).

As with the Holodomor famine, recognition of the massacre at Katyń and the role played by the USSR was significantly influenced by the historic and political context and in neither case can it be said that the state was held accountable. Thus, the focus taken here is on the potential, now that the Cold War has ended and the political context shifted, that some degree of accountability has been – or is currently being – sought from Russia, as the USSR's successor or as a continuing state. The Alma Alta Declaration provided that 'with the establishment of the Commonwealth of Independent States, the USSR ceases to exist' and the 1991 Minsk Agreement, which was signed at the same time, noted that the USSR 'as a subject of international law no longer exists', yet there are sufficient grounds to argue that both the Soviet and subsequent Russian Governments intended that Russia would be the continuing and successor state of the USSR after its dissolution and the establishment of the Commonwealth of Independent States.

Official declarations by the former Soviet, and subsequently Russian, Foreign Minister Andrei Kozyrev describe Russia as 'a continuing State of the USSR',[352] while at a practical level Russia assumed all the treaty obligations incurred by the USSR and agreed to be depositary for all multilateral agreements.[353] In a letter to the UN Secretary General dated 24 December 1991, then President Boris Yeltsin declared 'that membership of the USSR in the United Nations, including the Security Council, is being continued by the Russian Federation' to which there was no objection by any other state.[354] Russia was not required to apply for membership to the UN, unlike the other states that comprised the Soviet Union. There is a distinction between continuity and succession both generally and as it relates to membership of international organisations;[355] however, there seems to be a strong case for arguing both continuity and succession in this case. As Shaw noted, 'the nature and importance of the UN is such that the question of membership of that organisation is strong evidence of continuity',[356] while commentators including Mullerson, Cassese and Crawford[357] view the claim of succession as equally legitimate, for a number of reasons. First, the 1991 Treaty on Succession granted

352 A. Kozyrev, 'Russia: A Chance for Survival' (1992) 71 *Foreign Affairs* 11.

353 Russian Federation Ministry of Foreign Affairs Note 11 (13 January 1992).

354 31 ILM (1992) 138.

355 Article 2(1) of the Vienna Convention on the Succession of States to Treaties (1978) and the Vienna Convention on the Succession of States in Respect of State Property, Archives and Debts (1983) define the succession of states to mean 'the replacement of one State by another in the responsibility for the international relations of territory'. These Conventions state that the definition only applies for the purposes of the respective Convention and, suffice it to say that for the purposes of this discussion, state succession can be understood as 'a phenomenon occurring upon a factual change in sovereign authority over a particular territory' (M. Shaw, *International Law* (6th edn Cambridge: Cambridge University Press, 2008) 959). State continuity, on the other hand, can be understood as one discrete manifestation of this phenomenon whereby the emerging state is a continuation of the former state in an altered form.

356 Ibid 961.

357 A. Cassese, *International Law* (Oxford: Oxford University Press, 2005); J. Crawford, *The Creation of States* (Oxford: Oxford University Press, 2006); R. Mullerson, 'The Continuity and Succession of

Russia, as opposed to any of the other states that comprised the USSR, the greatest proportion of territory. Secondly, when the Communist Party established the Soviet Government in 1922, the scope of its original authority extended to Russia's territory before subsequently expanding to establish the larger Soviet territory. Thirdly, Russia assumed responsibility for the armed forces of the USSR and 61 per cent of the USSR's assets and liabilities, compared, for example, with the 16 per cent share taken by Ukraine.[358] Finally, there is evidence that succession has been accepted in state practice, including statements by the Secretary of State for Foreign and Commonwealth Affairs on behalf of the British Government[359] and by France.[360]

This discussion does not propose to resolve the question of Russia's status as a successor or continuing state to the USSR,[361], although it does highlight some of the complex issues in terms of holding states accountable where the relevant breach occurs in the context of conflict so that there is a high chance of a change in government and even a shift of state borders. The resulting state is bound not only by principles of customary law but also by any obligation arising from a *jus cogens* norm. In order for those obligations to remain effectual it seems rational that a successive state may be required to answer for the breach committed by its predecessor.[362] Arguing that continuity and/or succession alone are a sufficient basis on which to seek accountability from Russia for crimes against humanity perpetrated by the USSR is not purely academic speculation. Precedent exists with the *Genocide Convention* case, when the ICJ concluded that Serbia could be held responsible after the Federal Republic of Yugoslavia (FRY) had breached its legal obligations. The Court reached its conclusion having noted that the chief prosecutors of both Serbia and Montenegro recognised that Serbia was a successor state of the FRY, that Serbia had assumed the FRY's international treaty obligations and that Serbia had accepted continuing status, while Montenegro had not.[363] There is no reason to suppose that if a successor state can be held responsible for the acts and omissions of its predecessor that it cannot also be held accountable.

A second precedent is the apology made in 1990 by the Federal Republic of Germany (FRG) for atrocities perpetrated by Nazi Germany. In 1955 France, the US and the UK ended their occupation of the FRG pursuant to the Potsdam Declaration but continued to 'retain the rights and the responsibilities, heretofore

States, by Reference to the Former USSR and Yugoslavia' (1993) 42 *International and Comparative Law Quarterly* 473, 477.

358 Mullerson (n 357) 477.

359 Cited in 'UK Materials on International Law' (1993) 63 *British Yearbook of International Law* 636.

360 Note 356 above, 961.

361 Continuity between Russia and the USSR is strongly disputed in M. Akehurst, *Akehurst's Modern Introduction to International Law* (7th edn London: Routledge, 1997) 166.

362 Note 357 above, 477.

363 *Application of the Convention on the Prevention and Punishment of the Crime of Genocide (Bosnia and Herzegovina v Yugoslavia (Serbia and Montenegro))* (Judgment 2007) ICJ Reports (1993) paras 70–75.

exercised or held by them, relating to Berlin and to Germany as a whole',[364] thus purporting to retain rights and responsibilities in relation to the German Democratic Republic (GDR)[365] and implying that the three Allied powers perceived that Germany continued to be a unified state.[366] The FRG in fact claimed it was the successor state of Nazi Germany.[367] It can be noted in support that on formal reunification the GDR was absorbed into the FRG by virtue of the 1990 Monetary, Economic and Social Union,[368] the accession of the GDR under Article 23 of the Basic Law of the Federal Republic (as set down in Article 1 of the Treaty of 31 August 1990 Between the Federal Republic of Germany and the German Democratic Republic) and that no state challenged the accession of the GDR to the FRG.[369] Irrespective of whether the FDR was a continuation of Germany in 1945 or a successor state, it is clear that the state's 1990 apology was on behalf of Nazi Germany and, it is argued here, was redress for the atrocities by the German state. It is submitted that this example of delayed accountability provides a permissive precedent in terms of holding Russia accountable for the acts and omissions of the USSR.

There have been no formal attempts to hold Russia accountable for crimes perpetrated by the USSR, which may mean that in reality there is insufficient legal overlap between Russia and the USSR to consider them the same state for accountability purposes. However, isolated examples do exist to show that Russia has provided, to a more limited extent, redress on behalf of the USSR, even if it cannot be said that Russia has been held accountable on behalf of the USSR. In its 2003 decision in *Timofeyev v Russia*, the European Court of Human Rights found that Russia had breached Article 6 of the 1950 European Convention on Human Rights because it failed to execute a 1992 judgment by the domestic courts in which the applicant was awarded compensation from the state for unlawful persecution by the Soviet authorities.[370] A similar issue arose in the Court's 2008 decision in *Matveyev v Russia*, where the applicant had been wrongly convicted and imprisoned in 1981 and whose original award of compensation by the Russian courts was then dismissed, which the applicant alleged was in breach of Article 3 of the European Convention on Human Rights. The substantive application was dismissed on the grounds that the Court did not have jurisdiction *ratione materiae*

364 Article 3 Convention on Relations Between the Three Powers and the Federal Republic of Germany 1954. In relation to the GDR this continued until reunification in 1990.

365 House of Commons Foreign Affairs Committee 'Fourth Report (from the) Foreign Affairs Committee: Session 1989–90: German Unification: Some Immediate Issues' (HMSO: London, 1990) 2.

366 Ibid, 3.

367 *Re Treaty on the Basis of Relations Between the Federal Republic of Germany and the German Democratic Republic* BVerfG 78 ILR (1972) 149.

368 Monetary, Economic and Social Union 29 ILM (1990).

369 S. Blay, *The Unification of Germany in International and Domestic Law* (Atlanta: Rodopi, 1997).

370 *Timofeyve v Russia* European Court of Human Rights (2003) para 11.

but what is remarkable in both these cases is that the need to account for the erroneous acts and omissions of the USSR did not end simply because the state no longer existed.

The lack of formal attempts to seek accountability from Russia does not preclude the use of indirect and informal means, which can range from an apology to compensation for surviving victims, monuments and memorials for the dead and even property restitution where appropriate. In addition, criticism is especially effective as a means of redress when the state that is criticised wishes to maintain its international relations, which was less likely to be the case with the USSR owing to the gulf in political ideology. In contrast, when Russia was asked by the UN Human Rights Committee to 'clarify the legal and practical consequences of the dissolution of the Soviet Union and the establishment of the Russian Federation as an independent state on the procedure for the implementation in that country of the rights set forth in the Covenant',[371] the Russian representative assured the committee that 'for the first time in the history of Russian legislation, the precedence of international law was acknowledged and that the basic rights and freedoms in conformity with the commonly recognised principles and norms of international law were recognised and guaranteed'.[372] Similarly, and this time before the Committee on Racial Discrimination, Russia has commented that 'the errors made as well as the frankly illegal acts that were countenanced and directed against national groups during the existence of the USSR are now being recognised and punished'.[373] Express statements such as these that Russia would make 'every effort to do historical justice to illegally repressed national groups … as well as in connection with the other forms of repression that took place when the Soviet Union held sway'[374] indicates a severance from the Soviet ideology that did not recognise the primacy of public international law. Further, such statements create a standard against which Russia's acts and omissions may be measured and criticised against in the future, showing a willingness by Russia to assist in atonement for victims of the Soviet regime. Thus, in certain circumstances, it appears that a delay may even be beneficial in seeking some form of accountability.

Certainly Russia has not proceeded, after the dissolution of the USSR, with complete disregard for the wrongful activities of the Soviet authorities and has sought to make amends of its own accord. An example of this is the Act of the Russian Federation on the Rehabilitation of Victims of Political Repression 1994 that concerned the rehabilitation and compensation of persons recognised as having been subject to political repression, which was defined in Article 1 as 'various measures

371 'Fourth Periodic of the Russian Federation Report' UN Doc CCPR/C/SR.1426 (1995) para 26.

372 Ibid.

373 'Thirteenth Periodic Report Under Article 9 Submitted by the Russian Federation Addendum' UN Doc CERD/C/263/Add.9 (1995) 3.

374 Ibid.

of coercion which were employed by the State for political reasons, in the form of deprivation of life or liberty' and included victims of repression from the years of Soviet rule. Non-compliance with the Act, as it relates to persecution by the Soviet authorities, exposes Russia to criticism both for failing to comply with its direct legal obligations and indirectly failing to ensure redress for past wrongs by the USSR. In the past, where Russia has failed to satisfy its undertakings pursuant to the 1994 Act, an explanation has been sought. However, criticism for failing to implement the Act was tempered owing to 'the economic and financial difficulties that the Russian Federation is experiencing at the present stage [which] do not always allow this Act, which is of the very greatest importance for the country, to be implemented in full'.[375] As with the breach itself, the context in which accountability is sought is clearly influential, particularly when the nature of redress is political as with criticism.

There is, however, the potential for legal redress where Russia has failed to satisfy its obligations under the 1994 Act, as seen with the pending applications before the European Court of Human Rights by descendants of victims of the Katyń massacre. The applicants claimed that the Russian courts refused them wronged-party status in the course of an investigation carried out by the Russian military prosecutor's office, which was discontinued in 2004 as falling within the relevant statute of limitations so there was no right to appeal and which was allegedly in breach of Russia's obligations under the 1994 Act.[376] On the one hand, the Court is only charged with determining Russia's liability for breaching its obligations under the 1994 Act and thus the historical background and context of the substantive application are irrelevant. On the other hand, in a situation such as this where the issue underlying the case relates to Russia's failure to ensure justice for the Katyń massacre committed by the USSR, as its predecessor state, the ensuing publicity and criticism of Russia may still hold weight in terms of accountability. This interpretation is more likely to be accurate given that in 2010 Russian President Putin attended a memorial of the Katyń massacre, providing a further indication that Russia acknowledged the USSR's culpability. Furthermore, the poignant death of Polish President Kaczynski, together with the majority of the Polish cabinet in a plane crash as they attended the 2010 commemorations for the massacre, makes it increasingly difficult for Russia to avoid its obligations to ensure justice for victims of the Soviet regime pursuant to the 1994 Act, without significant political recriminations – illustrating that the factual context can not only hinder but in cases such as these assist in holding states accountable.

The second case study confirms the finding in relation to the aftermath of the Armenian massacre, that the pervasive influence of the political and historic context in frustrating accountability is inescapable. Initially, it was the status of the USSR as a crucial war ally that shielded the State from accusations relating to

375 'Second Report by the Russian Federation' UN Doc CAT/C/17/Add.15 (1996) para 92.

376 E. Siedlecka, 'Ombudsman to Join Katyń Claims in Strasbourg Court' *Gazeta Wyborcza* (25 November 2008).

Katyń and Holodomor. Subsequently, its communist ideology politically isolated the USSR from the majority of states, which meant it was oblivious to attempts by the international community to make the USSR answer allegations of crimes against humanity. While it is unlikely after such a long time that there would ever be any comprehensive finding of accountability, the gravity of both incidents has led to growing awareness of the atrocities and Russia – either as successor or a continuing state – being encouraged, if not politically compelled, to compensate morally for the breaches by the USSR. While limitations that have historically undermined attempts at holding states accountable also frustrated the potential of holding the USSR accountable, the fact that the breaches were particularly grievous and threatened fundamental community interests – known as *jus cogens* norms – has encouraged the international community to respond, albeit that the reaction was delayed.

Thus, the third case study seeks evidence that the international community has reacted contemporaneously where states have breached *jus cogens* norms and in so doing ensured that the breaching state was made to answer for its acts and omissions.

5.2.3 Apartheid in South Africa

In contrast to the limited success in seeking accountability for the crimes against humanity committed by the USSR, the third case study seeks to illustrate a scenario where state accountability has been achieved in practice. The response by the international community to the policy of apartheid in South Africa led to the practice being abandoned, to South Africa bringing its domestic laws into conformity with international standards and, it will be argued, to the state being held accountable in accordance with how the term is conceptualised here. In order to prove the point, it is necessary to determine, first, that the practice of apartheid, which was legally sanctioned in South Africa, violated public international law; secondly, that the various reactions of states and other members of the international community led to the end of apartheid; and, thirdly, that a link exists between the end of apartheid and South Africa being made to answer for the establishment and maintenance of a legal framework that allowed the practice to continue for decades in defiance of global opinion.

Apartheid violates two separate *jus cogens* norms on the ILC's list, namely racial discrimination and crimes against humanity. Article 1 of the 1973 Convention on the Suppression and Punishment of the Crime of Apartheid (the Apartheid Convention), which has 31 state signatories and 107 parties and thus is recognised by a large number of states, defined apartheid as 'a crime against humanity … violating the principles of international law', as did Article 7 of the Rome Statute of the ICC and Article 18(f) of the 1996 Draft Code of Crimes against the Peace and Security of Mankind, while Article 1 of the Convention on the Elimination of All Forms of Racial Discrimination stated that 'inhumane acts resulting from the policies and practices of apartheid ... are crimes'. In addition, the prohibition is viewed as a *jus cogens* norm in its own right. The ILC listed apartheid as a 'peremptory norm'[377] in the Commentary to Article 53 VCLT and as an international crime that would have come within the now defunct Draft Article 19. South Africa's 'persistent intransigence and defiance of the international community'[378] in sustaining a policy of apartheid for over 40 years, has led scholars such as Charney to question whether the state was a persistent objector and thus not bound by the prohibition.[379] Were this to be answered in the affirmative then the *jus cogens* status of the prohibition is also brought into question as Article 53 VCLT provides that the non-derogability of the norm is premised on the community of states recognising this characteristic. However, little juridical support exists for the persistent objector rule, which only applies to customary international law and there is no consensus that *jus cogens* norms are necessarily customary norms; indeed, even when the ICJ referred to the principle in the 1950 *Asylum Case* and the 1974 *Fisheries Jurisdiction* case it was by way of obiter dicta.

Instead, apartheid is as close to being a state crime as the indeterminate nature of that term allows. The drafters of the Apartheid Convention envisaged a prosecuting authority with international criminal jurisdiction to hear charges and in 1980 the Commission on Human Rights circulated a draft statute for an international criminal court specifically to prosecute apartheid,[380] albeit limited to individuals and organisations. Article 22 of the Draft International Penal Tribunal for the Suppression and Punishment of the Crime of Apartheid and Other International Crimes envisaged that state responsibility would be engaged where apartheid was committed on its behalf but the nature of the state's responsibility was deemed to be quasi-criminal.[381] A criminal court to try offences of apartheid never came into existence but the fact it was even contemplated confirms the seriousness with which the prohibition of apartheid was viewed by state parties to the Apartheid Convention. Of particular concern to the international community was the entrenched policies and practices of apartheid ingrained within South Africa's legal framework, to the extent that Article 2 of the Apartheid Convention even defined apartheid as including 'similar policies and practices of racial segregation and discrimination as practised in southern Africa'.[382] After the National Party coalition assumed power following the general elections in 1948, it began a slow implementation of legislation that would envelope the country's entire constitutional framework and, ultimately, the entire state was governed by, and thus

377 'Conference on the Law of Treaties, 1st and 2nd Session, Vienna, 26 March—24 May 1968' UN Doc A/CONF/39/11/Add.2 (1968).

378 'Policies of Apartheid of the Government of South Africa' General Assembly Resolution 37/69 (1982).

379 J, Charney, 'Universal International Law' (1993) 87 *American Journal of International Law* 529.

380 'Report of M.C. Bassiouni to the Ad Hoc Working Group of Experts for the Commission on Human Rights' UN Doc E/CN.4/1426 (1981).

381 M. Bassiouni and D. Derby, 'Final Report on the Establishment of and ICC for the Implementation of the Apartheid Convention and Other Relevant International Instruments' (1981) 9 *Hofstra Law Review* 523, 540.

382 Apartheid Convention Article 2.

compelled to participate in, the policy of apartheid. For accountability purposes, however, it would be inaccurate to view the state as comprising all individuals within it, given that the majority of the population was adversely affected by apartheid. It is more accurate to describe 'South Africa' as the institutional structure that was active in the systematic legalising of racial discrimination – including the Senate, the House of Assembly of the Union of South Africa and the judiciary.[383]

There were two main categories of discriminatory legislation. First, segregation included the forced physical separation of races in different residential and business areas under the 1950 Group Areas Act and 1952 Native Laws Amendment Act; the establishment of black homelands and regional authorities under the 1951 Bantu Authorities Act;[384] the creation of a national register in which every person's race was recorded under the 1950 Population Registration Act; making it a criminal offence if a black person did not carry the designated identification under the 1952 Natives (Abolition of Passes and Co-ordination of Documents) Act; and forced segregation in all public amenities, public buildings and public transport, with the aim of eliminating contact between whites and other races pursuant to the 1953 Reservation of Separate Amenities Act. Secondly, disenfranchisement was legalised under the 1951 Separate Representation of Voters Act, which removed all black people from the common voters' roll. In addition to policies that were expressly discriminatory, there were laws that breached a range of international human rights. These included the 1949 Prohibition of Mixed Marriages Act that prohibited mixed racial marriage in contravention of Article 23 of the Universal Declaration of Human Rights;[385]; the 1950 Suppression of Communism Act that outlawed communism but defined the term so broadly that it covered other forms of political opposition in breach of Article 2 of the Universal Declaration of Human Rights; the 1951 Prevention of Illegal Squatting Act that gave the Minister of Native Affairs the power to remove blacks from public or privately owned land in breach of Article 17 of the Universal Declaration of Human Rights; and the 1953 Bantu Education Act establishing a Black Education Department to compile a separate curriculum, which then Minister of Native Affairs and later Prime Minister Dr Verwoerd stated was to prevent black Africans

383 Coverage of the steps taken by the National Party government to reconstitute the court system to pass the relevant apartheid legislation is given by du Pré; R.H. du Pré, *Separate but Unequal – The 'Coloured' People of South Africa – A Political History* (Johannesburg: Jonathan Ball Publishers, 1994) 134–39.

384 For discussion on the policy seeking to break the state into smaller states based on racial lines see J. Western, '*A Divided City: Cape Town*' (2002) (21)5 *Political Geography* 711.

385 South Africa in fact abstained from voting when the Universal Declaration of Human Rights was adopted by the UN General Assembly in 1948 but even though the Declaration is not legally binding it has been recognised by states as representative of customary international law; for example, the 'Final Act of the International Conference of Human Rights' in 1968 stated that the Declaration amounted to 'an obligation' for states UN Doc E/68/XIV.2 (1968). The human rights breaches noted here also contravene the ICCPR but South Africa did not the sign the Covenant until 1994 or ratify the Covenant until 1998: Status of Ratifications (ICCPR) (2009) available at http;//www2.ohchr.org/english/law/ccpr-ratify.htm.

receiving an education that would encourage them to seek employment beyond necessary labouring skills.[386]

Taken in combination, these Acts and Regulations establish that South Africa breached the prohibition of apartheid through state policies. Furthermore, the fact that disenfranchisement was a key characteristic of the apartheid confirms that for accountability purposes South Africa cannot simply be viewed as the state as a whole because any part of the population prevented from exercising the right to remove the offending government must necessarily be exempt from being made to account for the violations by that government. The range of reaction and criticism to apartheid from both state and non-state actors likewise drew a distinction between the population as a whole and South Africa as the culpable party. Che Guevara, in his capacity as the Cuban representative to the UN and in a speech before the General Assembly, stated that 'the brutal policy of apartheid is applied before the eyes of the nations of the world' and that 'we speak out to put the world on guard against what is happening in South Africa',[387] thus linking the oppression in South Africa with state policy. Guevara's words echoed the speech made by former UK Prime Minister Harold MacMillan to the South African Parliament in 1960, in which he noted 'the wind of change is blowing' in relation to historic tolerance by the international community of the apartheid. The Winds of Change speech, as it is known, effectively marked a shift in what, relatively, had been state inaction to the consolidation of South Africa's apartheid policies. MacMillan described the 'growth of national consciousness' as 'a political fact'[388] and the early 1960s marked a significant change in the response to apartheid.

While the 1960s would mark a notable shift in international tolerance, the earliest indications of unease dated from 1944 when India raised the question of discrimination of the Indian minority in South Africa, which was the first time that human rights concerns in a particular state were raised before the General Assembly.[389] By 1952, and after the repression and imprisonment of thousands of anti-apartheid protestors from the African National Congress and South African Indian Congress during the Defiance Campaign, the General Assembly adopted Resolution 616 on the 'Treatment of People of Indian Origin in the Union of South Africa' that called on South Africa to suspend implementation of the Group Areas Act and established a Good Offices Commission to investigate discriminatory policies, although only as these policies applied against the Indian population. Thus, the reality of the Commission was as a means to resolve the inter-state dispute between South Africa on the one hand and India and Pakistan on the other for alleged breaches of the Universal Declaration of Human Rights against the Indian population.

386 Note 383 above, 134–39.

387 C. Guevara, (Cuban representative to UN) 'Colonialism is Doomed' speech to the 19th General Assembly of the United Nations in New York City (11 December 1964).

388 F. Myers, 'Harold MacMillan's "Winds of Change" Speech: A Case Study in the Rhetoric of Policy Change' (2000) 3 *Rhetoric & Public Affairs* 555.

389 General Assembly Resolution 44/1 'Treatment of Indians in the Union of South Africa' (1944).

It was not until 1953 and Resolution 721 on the 'Question of Race Conflict in South Africa Resulting From Policies of Apartheid of the Government of the Union of South Africa' that the General Assembly specifically referred to the 'policies of apartheid of the Government of the Union of South Africa' as they affected all parties, not only the Indian population, and as contrary to the UN Charter and Universal Declaration of Human Rights. From then on, each year there was a similarly worded resolution in which the General Assembly would invite consultation with South Africa,[390] express its concern at the ongoing breaches of the UN Charter,[391] regret the lack of response by the government[392] and, finally, call upon South Africa to bring its policies and conduct into line with international law.[393] Eventually, in 1962, after police killed black protestors in the Sharpeville massacre and at the time of the Winds of Change speech, there was a change in the nature of the response made by the General Assembly. General Assembly Resolution 1761 on the 'Policies of Apartheid of the Government of South Africa' had four aspects that signalled a shift to what was a more assertive response than the UN had previously taken in condemning South Africa in the past.

First, while previous resolutions had condemned the 'policies of apartheid of the Government of South Africa', Resolution 1761 noted that South Africa continued to flout 'world public opinion' and called on member states to break off diplomatic relations, take steps to prevent South African ships using the ports of another state, boycott all South African goods and prevent passage facility to South African craft. The express intent of Resolution 1761 was 'to bring about the abandonment of those [apartheid] policies' but this did not preclude that South Africa might also be held accountable. Indeed, the reference to disregarding 'world public opinion' implied a global consensus that the law had been breached, while calling upon all member states to act in response can be seen as a means of seeking redress; thus, both limbs of the state accountability concept were satisfied. The second notable feature of Resolution 1761 is that it established a Special Committee with the mandate to keep the apartheid policies of South Africa under review when the General Assembly was not in session. There is a parallel here between establishing a special committee for the purpose of monitoring South Africa and the state review mechanism by the UN's human rights monitoring bodies, which it was earlier argued is an increasingly effective means for seeking accountability. The third point is that Resolution 1761 referred to the Security Council, which from 1960 joined the General Assembly in condemning apartheid.

390 'Question of Race Conflict in South Africa Resulting From Policies of Apartheid of the Government of the Union of South Africa' General Assembly Resolution 820 (1954).

391 Ibid.

392 'Question of Race Conflict in South Africa Resulting From Policies of Apartheid of the Government of the Union of South Africa' General Assembly Resolution 1248 (1958).

393 'Question of Race Conflict in South Africa Resulting From Policies of Apartheid of the Government of the Union of South Africa' General Assembly Resolution 1598 (1961).

In 1960, after complaints made by 29 states following the death of protestors as a result of the 'demonstrations and racial segregation in South Africa' and the 'racial policies of the Government',[394] the Security Council issued Resolution 134 calling on South Africa to 'abandon its policies of apartheid'. In 1963, and having noted an arms build up by South Africa, Security Council Resolutions 181 and 182 sought an embargo relating to the sale of arms and ammunition, with the express intent of ensuring international peace and security. Subsequent resolutions would be broader in scope; for example, in 1964 Security Council Resolution 190 called for the release of political prisoners and in 1972 Security Council Resolution 311 sought state contributions for funds to aid victims of apartheid. The final feature of General Assembly Resolution 1761 was that it called on the Security Council to 'consider action under Article 6 of the UN Charter', which in turn provides that 'a Member of the United Nations which has persistently violated the Principles contained in the present Charter may be expelled from the Organization by the General Assembly upon the recommendation of the Security Council'. It would in fact be another decade before such a step was considered by the Security Council, during which time the General Assembly continued to condemn the apartheid policies of South Africa.[395]

In its 1974 'Report to the Security Council' pursuant to Resolution 3322 and in Resolution 3207 on the 'Relationship Between the UN and South Africa', the General Assembly called upon the Security Council to review the relationship between the UN and South Africa, citing the 'flagrant violation of the principles of the UN Charter and the Universal Declaration of Human Rights'. The Security Council did not act because France, the UK and the US exercised their right of veto, similar to the situation in 1960 when they abstained from voting on Resolution 134.[396] The US and the UK had already ceased arms trade with South Africa by 1964 and thus the decision to veto any action under Article 6 suggests either that those states did not consider such an extreme step by the Security Council was warranted or that, at the time, apartheid was not considered a threat to peace and security in order to justify a response from the Security Council. It is possible that the US, the UK and France were influenced by other political factors. Certainly, the failure of the Security Council to respond stands in contrast to the recommendation in 1974 in General Assembly Resolution 3324E that 'the South African regime be totally excluded from participation in all international organizations

394 Official Records of the Security Council Fifteenth Year, Supplement for January, February and March 1960 and cited in Security Council Resolution 134 (1960).

395 For example, in 1966, a colloquium on apartheid was held by the General Assembly and 21 March was declared the International Day for the Elimination of Racial Discrimination. See also General Assembly Resolutions 2202 'The Policies of Apartheid of the Government of South Africa' (1966) and 2764 'The Policies of Apartheid of the Government of South Africa' (1971) that formally denounced the institution of homelands. In 1978 (General Assembly Resolution 33/23) and 1983 (General Assembly Resolution 38/11) South Africa was condemned at the World Conference Against Racism.

396 'Situation in South Africa' General Assembly Resolution 3324E (1974) preamble.

and conferences under the auspices of the United Nations so long as it continues to practice apartheid'. Such an extreme step implies that the General Assembly was seeking some form of penal sanction against South Africa. By 1977, the members of the Security Council were similarly of the opinion that something more was required in response to apartheid because Security Council Resolution 418 placed a mandatory arms embargo 'on all States', in contrast to the voluntary embargoes previously called for.

The embargo in Security Council Resolution 418 was expressly pursuant to Chapter VII of the UN Charter and thus in direct response to threats to international peace and security. However, three additional factors should be noted. First, Resolution 418 was adopted unanimously. Secondly, the embargo imposed against South Africa was the second and last time sanctions would be imposed by the Security Council during the Cold War.[397] Finally, then UN Secretary General Kurt Waldheim stated that, because apartheid was 'a gross violation of human rights and so fraught with danger to international peace and security', 'a response commensurate with the gravity'[398] was justified, implying that the embargo was both in response to the threat to international security and to the massive breach of human rights. The mixed response by member states and the delay in responding, given that apartheid legislation was enacted by 1950, show how political factors can influence state accountability, irrespective of the perceived importance of the norm and even though many member states had already condemned South Africa's apartheid policy either independently or through organisations other than the UN.

The first example of responses, other than by the UN, are those taken by international organisations. The Lusaka Manifesto was adopted by 13 out of the 14 African states present at the Conference of the Organisation of African Unity (OAU) and Assembly of Heads of State in 1969. Malawi did not vote in favour but was, at that time, receiving aid from South Africa – a consideration that (again) indicates how other factors can influence the accountability process.[399] The manifesto was unequivocal in its condemnation of not just the apartheid per se but South Africa, stating that 'South Africa should be excluded from the UN agencies, and even from the UN itself. It should be ostracised by the world community. It should be isolated from trade patterns and left to be self-sufficient'.[400] The manifesto is noteworthy because the strong language implied that more than just the end of apartheid was sought from South Africa. The combination of trade, diplomatic and political isolation was so severe as to exceed by far any reparation that may be imposed in terms of a finding of state responsibility, and presents a strong case that those states who signed the manifesto intended that South Africa

397 The first time was in relation to economic sanctions against Rhodesia in 1966: J. Farrall, *United Nations Sanctions and the Rule of Law* (Cambridge: Cambridge University Press, 2007).

398 *The United Nations and Apartheid* Document 90 at 348 cited in Jorgensen (n 288) 247.

399 R. Hall, 'The Lusaka Manifesto' (1970) 69 *African Affairs* 179.

400 Manifesto on South Africa UN Doc A/7754 (1969).

be held accountable. A second illustration where the response in question appeared actively to seek accountability is the subsequent Lagos Declaration for Action Against Apartheid adopted by the OAU in 1977. The World Conference, which was organised by the UN in cooperation with the OAU and the Federal Government of Nigeria, adopted the Declaration and committed 'full support to the legitimate aspirations of the South African people', including 'all appropriate assistance to the oppressed people of South Africa and their national liberation movement'.[401] Thus, in addition to the end of apartheid policies, a change of the State's government was desired.

The second non-UN response that will be cited here was the withdrawal of South Africa from the British Commonwealth in 1961. South Africa had earlier conducted an internal referendum in which 53 per cent of persons allowed to vote were in favour of the State becoming a republic with the result that South Africa was then required to reapply for membership, which it chose not to do after member states of the Commonwealth – including India – indicated that they would oppose the application owing to the state's apartheid policies. Hansard Records for the UK Parliament at the time illustrate not just the strong feeling against apartheid but that the culpable state was not simply considered to be the sum of its citizen parts – as illustrated in a speech by the Honourable Member Gaitskell who stated:[402]

> I should like to join with the Prime Minister, if I may, in saying to the people of South Africa, whatever colour they may be, that we hope that, in time, the racial theories and policies adopted by the Union today may be changed and brought into line with those practised in the rest of the Commonwealth, and that they will then return as welcome friends to the Commonwealth.

Thirdly, individual states imposed sanctions ranging from the arms embargo imposed in accordance with the many General Assembly and Security Council Resolutions noted above, to the variety of measures taken, for example by the US under the Comprehensive Anti-Apartheid Act 1986 implemented pursuant to Executive Order 12571 and expressly 'designed to bring about reforms' and 'the end of apartheid'. The US Congress overrode the veto of then President Reagan to suspend, amongst other things, aircraft landing rights contrary to US treaty obligations with South Africa. The fact that this was the first time the Presidential veto had been overridden since 1973 provided a strong indication of the commitment from the US Congress to the measures being taken.[403]

401 Lagos Declaration for Action Against Apartheid (1977) para 12 and see Report of the World Conference for Action Against Apartheid UN Doc E.77.XIV.2 (1977).

402 House of Commons Hansard (16 March 1961) col 1748.

403 P. Sethi and O. Williams, *Economic Imperatives and Ethical Values in Global Business: The South African Experience* (USA: Kluwer, 2000) 247.

Fourthly, sporting sanctions were imposed by individual states and the International Olympic Committee in 1962, to which South Africa's response was in stark contrast to the intransigent attitude it had shown in the face of political condemnation by UN bodies. As a result of the State's policies on segregation, the Olympic team could only include white athletes. The International Olympic Committee warned that this would result in South Africa being banned from the 1964 Olympic Games. In 1963, the South African Non-Racial Olympic Committee was established but this was insufficient to stop a ban being imposed on South Africa competing in the 1964 Olympic Games in Tokyo. South Africa selected a multi-racial side in advance of the 1968 Olympic Games in Mexico, but the ban on participation would remain in place until the Olympic Games in Barcelona in 1992.[404] The use of sporting sanctions recalls the issue as to how to hold a state accountable without also punishing the citizens of that state, which becomes more difficult to resolve given that certain individuals will be complicit in the breach and must also be required to answer for their actions. In the case of sporting sanctions it is the individual athletes who are principally affected by a participation ban. Before a multi-racial side was selected in 1968 the South African Olympic team was made up of white athletes and, because it was white citizens who had the vote and consistently kept the government in power, these athletes arguably possessed a degree of culpability. However, where the view is taken that effective redress should only affect liable parties, it becomes much harder to make the case that the use of sporting sanctions was justified after 1968 when the team included disenfranchised black athletes.

Unlike the earlier case studies where attempts at seeking redress from the state largely occurred once the breach in question was brought to an end, the response by the international community to apartheid in South Africa was contemporaneous. In fact, since the end of apartheid by 1994 when the Government of National Unity was established under Nelson Mandela, and in contrast to other situations where any attempt to seek redress was *ex post facto*, there has been relatively little intervention by the international community after the breach desisted. Throughout the 1990s, there was a proliferation of international tribunals and courts established to hold individuals criminally accountable for grievous breaches of international law, which arguably is a contributory means of also seeking redress from the relevant state, notably the *ad hoc* Tribunals for Rwanda and the Former Yugoslavia. This was not the approach taken post-apartheid where a Truth and Reconciliation Commission was instead established by the government without the assistance of the international community. In 1995, and pursuant to Section 4 of the Promotion of National Unity and Reconciliation Act, the Truth and Reconciliation Commission was given a mandate by the Government of National Unity not only to determine individual accountability but 'question whether such violations were the result of deliberate planning on the part of the State or a former

404 M. Krotee, 'Apartheid and Sport: South Africa Revisited' (1988) *Sociology of Sport Journal* 125.

state or any of their organs' and 'facilitate inquiries' into 'accountability, political or otherwise, for any such violations'. The Commission found that:[405]

> the State perpetrated, amongst others, the following types of gross violations of human rights in South and/or Southern Africa: torture ... the unjustified use of deadly force in situations where lesser measures would have been adequate ... the deliberate manipulation of social divisions in society with the intention of mobilising one group against another ... judicial killings, involving the execution of opponents for offences of a political and not a criminal nature ... extra-judicial killings in the form of State-planned and executed assassinations, attempted killings, disappearances, abductions and so-called 'entrapment killings'.

The conclusion was that 'the preponderance of responsibility' for the 'gross violations of human rights' must 'rest with the State' and recommendations were made for 'a process that contributes to economic developments that redress past wrongs as a basis for promoting lasting reconciliation'.[406] It is not within the scope of this discussion to explore the findings of the Truth and Reconciliation Commission, which are instead cited here because they contribute to the cumulative body of measures taken in response to apartheid and seeking more than merely to hold South Africa responsible for breaching its international obligations. The express link drawn by the Commission between South Africa's liability, the various atrocities perpetrated and the measures to be taken to dismantle the institutional State structure that meant apartheid was practised for so many decades support the argument that state accountability was sought in this case.

Several decades of cumulative responses taken by states, international organisations, other members of the international community and even the successive Government of South Africa certainly meant that the stated objective, being the end of apartheid, was achieved. In addition, the lack of any further response by the international community after apartheid was dismantled implies that nothing further was required by way of redress. Put differently, the end of apartheid was equivalent to holding South Africa accountable for apartheid.

5.2.4 Comparing responses to state aggression in the 20th century

This case study focuses on a specific *jus cogens* norm and compares the response to three separate instances where states have breached the prohibition of aggression. The question here is whether the reaction of the international community to,the invasion of the Republic of Korea in 1950, Israel's use of aggression against Iraqi nuclear installations and the invasion of Kuwait by Iraq in 1990, respectively, was

405 South African Truth and Reconciliation Commission 'Conclusions' (1999) para 66, 101.
406 Ibid, para 165.

simply the application of the collective security provisions of the UN Charter or whether the gravity of the breach inspired a response or responses that in turn meant the respective state was also held accountable.

In theory, all the prerequisites for holding states accountable for aggression can be found in the collective security framework established by the UN. Aggression was defined by the UN General Assembly in 1974 in Resolution 3314 on the 'Definition of Aggression' as the 'use of armed force by a State against the sovereignty, territorial integrity or political independence of another State or in any other manner inconsistent with the UN Charter'. Furthermore, the Security Council has the authority pursuant to Article 39 of the UN Charter to 'determine the existence of any threat to the peace, breach of the peace, or act of aggression' and to decide whether any of the measures listed in Articles 41 and 42 will be taken in response. Thus, and in theory, there is provision within the UN framework for determining that aggression occurred and that a particular state committed aggression as well as both the means and mode for seeking redress as a result.

Comparing the three examples of aggression selected for this case study will test the validity of that theory. In particular, three questions arise. First, aggression was not defined by the UN General Assembly until 1974 so it will be considered whether there are any differences in the response to aggression before and after that time – in other words, does labelling the use of force as aggression have any bearing on the nature of the response that follows. Secondly, any inconsistency in which party determined that there was aggression or any inconsistency in the nature of the response will be assessed to determine the continuing influence of politics in responding to the breach, despite the existence of a framework for responding to aggression. Thirdly, the responses to aggression, both pursuant to Articles 41 and 42 and in terms of any additional measures taken, will be examined to assess effectiveness in highlighting the gravity of the breach, which would be pivotal in arguing that accountability was attained. This last issue is pertinent because General Assembly Resolution 3314 states that wars of aggression give rise to the 'international responsibility' of states, suggesting that the appropriate response is to engage the breaching state's responsibility. This is incongruous with the seriousness of aggression being recognised as a *jus cogens* norm, and as captured in Article 5(2) of Resolution 3314 that designates wars of aggression 'a crime against international peace'. A further anomaly arises because engaging the breaching state's 'international responsibility' is only referred to as the consequence for a war of aggression in Article 5(2) and not as the consequence for general acts of aggression, as defined in Article 1. Whether or not this was a conscious distinction or whether, in practice, all acts of aggression have been treated in the same manner will also be analysed here.

5.2.4.1 Invasion of the Republic of Korea 1950

After failed negotiations for reunification, North Korea's armed forces crossed the 38th Parallel that separated North Korea from the Republic of Korea on 25 June 1950. The invasion was an act of aggression as it was subsequently defined in

Article 3(a) of Resolution 3314 that referred to 'an invasion or attack by the armed forces of a State against the territory of another State'. On the same day as the invasion the Security Council passed Resolution 82, which stated that the 'armed attack' by North Korea constituted a 'breach of the peace'. Two days later, on 27 June, Security Council Resolution 83 confirmed that the attack was a 'breach of the peace', noted that 'immediate and effective steps' were therefore required 'to secure peace and security' and recommended that member states provide such assistance to the Republic of Korea as was 'necessary to repel the armed attack and restore peace and security'. By 7 July , Security Council Resolution 84 had sought to coordinate the military assistance under UN authority and, ultimately, 16 states would contribute troops to a US-led force. On the one hand, the swift response suggested that states perceived the situation as particularly grave while, on the other hand, the speed with which the Security Council acted can, cynically, be explained by the limited window of opportunity available. The Security Council was able to condemn the attack and authorise military assistance because the USSR had absented itself from the Security Council in January 1950, protesting at China's seat being occupied by the Taiwan based Government. To cynics it would come as no surprise that after the USSR ended its protest in August 1950 there was no further action by the Security Council in this matter.

In contrast, the first response by the General Assembly was not until October 1950 and, although Resolution 410 on 'Relief and Rehabilitation' used the word aggression, the focus was primarily on restructuring the country and ensuring the independence of Korea once the active phase of hostilities finished.[407] This would change with General Assembly Resolution 498 on the 'Intervention of the Central People's Government of the People's Republic of China in Korea'. The General Assembly linked 'a lack of amity of the permanent members' to the Security Council having 'failed to exercise its primary responsibility for the maintenance of international peace and security', given that the situation had at the time been aggravated by the 'Chinese Communist intervention in Korea'. The General Assembly described the attacks by both China and North Korea as aggression, rather than 'a breach of the peace' as the Security Council had, and called upon all member states to support the military action already authorised by the Security Council. In addition, Resolution 498 called for the creation of good offices in order to ensure 'the achievement of UN objectives in Korea by peaceful means', which was very much in keeping with the traditional emphasis on peaceful dispute settlement, and an understandable response insofar as the invasion of Korea was the first time the General Assembly had been required to react to a situation of such severity; thus, no precedent existed in terms of an effective response. Accordingly, Resolution 498 was also used to establish a Collective Measures Committee to 'consider additional measures to be employed to meet the aggression' and the recommendations of the First Committee were adopted in Resolution 500 on the 'Additional Measures to be Employed to Meet the Aggression in Korea',

407 See also 'The Problem of the Independence of Korea' General Assembly Resolution 376 (1950).

recommending that all member states apply an embargo on arms and related commodities against both North Korea and China.

Arguably, steps were also taken in terms of making China answer for its role in assisting North Korea. In 1950, General Assembly Resolution 490 on the 'Question of the Representation of China in the General Assembly' established a Special Committee to consider the question of China's representation at the United Nations. The committee was due to report its findings in 1951 but in the interim China had invaded Korea and pledged its support to North Korea. Thus, immediately after Resolution 500 adopted additional measures in response to the invasion of Korea, the General Assembly passed Resolution 501, taking note of the Special Committee's Report but postponing any further consideration of the issue. It was not until 1961 that the General Assembly voted once again to deliberate on the question of China's representation.[408] To the extent that postponing consideration of China's representation at the UN was a means to hold China accountable for aggression by imposing a form of political isolation, and not just a manifestation of the Cold War politics at the UN, it was certainly severe and expressed, with as solid a consensus as could be expected in the context of the Cold War, that the actions by North Korea and China were not to be tolerated.

China was subjected to political isolation and North Korea was the object of military force led by the US and subject to an arms embargo until the end of the conflict in 1953. In both cases the lack of a definition of aggression did not prevent the Security Council and the General Assembly from agreeing that North Korea and China had acted in a way that both threatened international security and breached the peace. Furthermore, what was justified in response was more than the standard responses for settling disputes between states, although clearly the political context played a major role in how states did respond. For instance, as early as 1951 the Security Council removed the question of aggression in Korea from the list of matters with which it was seised pursuant to Resolution 90, while the General Assembly remained active in the matter as long as the conflict continued. Removal of the matter from the Security Council's agenda ensured that the General Assembly was able to stay seized in the matter without breaching Article 12 of the UN Charter, which does not permit the General Assembly to make recommendations when the Security Council is exercising its duty; however, it was unlikely that the Security Council would have been able to act once the USSR resumed its seat given the likelihood that either the US or the USSR, depending on the proposed action, would have exercised the veto power.

It will be seen that, in subsequent years, the UN has used more assertive language and taken more extreme measures when responding to aggression, although this does not mean that in 1950 the response to aggression against Korea was significant. The combination of criticism by the UN bodies, military force, the arms embargo and, arguably, political isolation from the UN sought more than simply to hold the states in question responsible. It is argued here that the motivation of

408 'Representation of China in the UN' General Assembly Resolution 1668 (1961).

the UN member states was, at least in part, to protect the interests of the international community.

5.2.4.2 Bombing of the Osiraq Nuclear Reactor 1981

The second example is Israel's air strike on the Osiraq nuclear reactor on 7 June 1981, and therefore after the UN General Assembly adopted its definition of aggression in Resolution 3314. In contrast to commentators such as D'Amato, who continue to argue over the legal validity of Israel's actions,[409] the Security Council adopted the position, on 19 June 1981, in Security Council Resolution 487 that the attacks were in 'clear violation of the Charter of the United Nations and norms of international conduct'. A determination that the attacks were in violation of international law, however, is not the same as determining that Israel committed an act of aggression, for which the Security Council could have referred to the definition of aggression in General Assembly Resolution 3314. Indeed, the wording used and the consequences listed in Resolution 487 imply that the Security Council was not prepared to treat the breach differently from other breaches of public international law, which come within the standard scope and rules of state responsibility. Of course, the more reticent wording is likely to be the reason that Resolution 487 was adopted unanimously by the Security Council, which in itself has condemnatory weight as it reflects a consensus amongst member states. The Security Council criticised 'the military attack by Israel' while, in contrast, General Assembly Resolution 36/27 on the 'Armed Israeli Aggression Against the Iraqi Nuclear Installations' used stronger language and condemned Israel for its 'acts of aggression'. It is argued here that the difference in tone is indicative that it was the General Assembly that was instrumental in seeking state accountability from Israel – as opposed to the Security Council, which acted in satisfaction of its mandate to protect international peace and security.

This argument is borne out by the specific consequences sought by each UN body. The Security Council was 'deeply concerned about the danger to international peace and security' that resulted from the instability of the nuclear reactor owing to the attack and Resolution 487 called 'upon Israel to refrain in the future from any such acts or threats thereof'.[410] In addition to non-recognition of the breach, the Security Council noted that 'Iraq was entitled to appropriate redress' and referred to compensation for the 'destruction' of Iraq's property, although it did not state that it was Israel's responsibility to provide compensation. Non-recognition and compensation for the damage caused are two of the consequences

409 A. D'Amato, 'Israel's Air Strike Upon the Iraqi Nuclear Reactor' (1983) 77 *American Journal of International Law* 584; A. D'Amato, 'The International Law Aspects of the Israeli Air Strike' (11 May 1987) cited in A. D'Amato, 'Israel's Air Strike Against The Osiraq Reactor: A Retrospective' (1996) 10 *Temple International and Comparative Law Journal* 259; see also L. Beres and Y. Tsiddon-Chatto, Reconsidering Israel's Destruction of Iraq's Osiraq Nuclear Reactor' (1995) 9 *Temple International and Comparative Law Journal* 437.

410 Security Council Resolution 487 (1981).

set out in Draft Articles 37 and 41 on state responsibility that apply where a state commits an internationally wrongful act. As noted, the consequences in engaging state responsibility can be part of an effective matrix of measures that ensure the state is likewise held accountable. In terms of redress for breaching the *jus cogens* prohibition of aggression, however, it is submitted that there must be some sort of recognition that the breach is graver than standard breaches of public international law. The question is whether specifically referring to the attacks as aggression and invoking the definition, as the General Assembly did, was sufficient in terms of providing the necessary recognition that would then suggest that Israel was being required to account for having committed an act of aggression.

In its first resolution on the matter, Resolution 36/27 on the 'Armed Israeli Aggression Against the Iraqi Nuclear Installations', the General Assembly described the attacks as 'armed Israeli aggression' and noted that Israel had refused to comply with Security Council Resolution 487. In comparison with Resolution 487, the General Assembly was unequivocal in its condemnation of Israel's 'threats to repeat such attacks' and its 'premeditated and unprecedented act of aggression in violation of the Charter of the UN and the norms of international conduct, which constitutes a new and dangerous escalation in the threat to international peace and security'.[411] In the same way that the tone of condemnation by the General Assembly was in stark contrast to that of the Security Council, so too were the proposed consequences that arguably exceeded the standard responses to an internationally wrongful act. First, and as with the Security Council's non-recognition of the breach, the General Assembly gave a solemn warning to cease and desist from future attacks. Secondly, all states (not just member states) were called upon not to supply Israel with the necessary equipment for such attacks. Thirdly, a plea was made to the Security Council to take 'effective enforcement action to prevent Israel from further endangering international peace and security' through its 'continued policies of expansion, occupation and annexation'. Fourthly, Israel's aggression toward Iraq may have been the catalyst but the General Assembly sought redress from Israel for all 'acts of aggression against Arab countries'; however, it is arguable that using the term 'aggression' in this context undermined the legal impact of Resolution 36/27, given that the word was used more as a descriptor than a legal determination that the attacks amounted to aggression as defined in General Assembly Resolution 3314. Finally, it was demanded that Israel 'in view of its international responsibility for acts of aggression pay prompt and adequate compensation'. Unlike Security Council Resolution 487 that referred generally to redress without requiring that it was Israel's responsibility, General Assembly Resolution 36/27 demanded that Israel pay 'adequate compensation for the material damage and loss of life suffered'.

411 At the same time, the General Assembly noted the role played by the US in supplying Israel with aircraft and weapons for this purpose 'Armed Israeli Aggression Against the Iraqi Nuclear Installations' General Assembly Resolution 36/27 (1981).

The General Assembly would repeat its condemnation in resolutions that were worded equally strongly in 1982, 1983, 1984 and 1985.[412] All subsequent resolutions on the matter, including for example Resolution 38/9 on the 'Armed Israeli Aggression Against the Iraqi Nuclear Installations', noted 'with deep concern Israel's continued refusal to comply' with the demands of both UN bodies. Yet, the refusal by the Security Council to take any enforcement action undermined the impact of these statements, which is apparent given Israel's continued intransigence. By 1987 the General Assembly no longer referred to the attacks on Iraq, focusing instead on the broader risk of Israel's nuclear armament. It is interesting to note that in the last of the resolutions condemning Israel's aggression against Iraq, which was Resolution 40/6 that was adopted in 1985, the General Assembly called upon 'all States *and organisations* ... to discontinue cooperating' with Israel. The General Assembly appears to have tried to overcome its lack of enforcement powers and undoubtedly its frustration in being unable to address what was perceived by the members as a grave breach, by maximising the impact of non-cooperation with Iraq. In calling on all states and organisations, the General Assembly was also clarifying that it considered that both states and organisations had an interest in maintaining the prohibition of aggression. Certainly, the gravity of Israel's actions was not only noted by states; within two months of the attack, the International Atomic Energy Agency, as 'the agency, under the aegis of the United Nations ... responsible for international activities concerned with the peaceful uses of atomic energy'[413], condemned the attacks as aggression and suspended relations between itself and Israel.[414]

By the time of Israel's attack on the Osiraq nuclear reactor, Resolution 3314 had been adopted by the General Assembly so that there was an accepted standard for condemning an attack as an act of aggression. Despite this, there was a difference in approach between the Security Council and the General Assembly as to whether the acts would be classified as aggression and what the response to the attacks should be. There is a contrast between the Security Council criticising the 'illegal attacks' and the General Assembly strongly condemning the aggression by Israel, but possessing a limited capacity to enforce the measures taken in response. This example has raised questions as to the utility of both bodies in responding to acts of aggression during the Cold War and the legitimacy of the permanent member system; however, these debates cannot be resolved here. Instead, one last example seeks to determine whether the impact that the political context has on the responses to acts of aggression has lessened after the Cold War.

5.2.4.3 Invasion of Kuwait 1990

The Security Council's response after Iraq invaded Kuwait in 1990 illustrated a significant change in the political environment of the UN, even before Russia

412 General Assembly Resolutions 37/18 (1982), 38/9 (1983), 39/14 (1984) and 41/12 (1985).
413 Agency Agreement with the United Nations IAEA Doc No INFCIRC/11 (1959).
414 International Atomic Energy Agency Resolution GC (XXV) 643 (1981).

succeeded to the seat previously occupied by the USSR on the Security Council in January 1992 and prior to the official end of the Cold War in 1991 with the collapse of the USSR. The Security Council played a pivotal role in not only bringing the attack on Kuwait to an end but in holding Iraq accountable, to an extent, for its actions. It is argued here that the emergence of the Security Council as a key accountability player in this case was possible for two reasons. First, a change in the political climate meant that historic tensions, which had previously frustrated any effective reaction by the Security Council, were no longer a barrier to co-operation amongst member states and, secondly, there was consensus on the Security Council that the threat the invasion posed to the interests of the international community necessitated an effective and decisive response, beyond mere political criticism.

On 2 August 1990, the same day that Iraq invaded Kuwait, the Security Council responded in a similar fashion to that in the previous examples, and adopted Resolution 660 to 'condemn the Iraqi invasion' as 'a breach of international peace and security' and call upon Iraq to withdraw its troops and begin negotiations with Kuwait. Non-recognition of the breach and the steps taken to bring about the peaceful settlement of the dispute are standard consequences when states commit an internationally wrongful act; thus there was little to suggest that the Security Council's initial response was influenced by the fact that Iraq had breached the *jus cogens* prohibition on aggression. In contrast, the General Assembly did refer to the invasion as an act of aggression, but owing to the active and ongoing role being played by the Security Council and in light of Article 12 of the UN Charter that was discussed previously, its response was limited to political condemnation. After acceding to a request by Kuwait to debate the 'Iraqi Aggression and the Continued Occupation of Kuwait in Flagrant Violation of the Charter of the United Nations' during its Forty-fifth session,[415] the General Assembly adopted two resolutions, namely Resolution 45/170 on the 'Situation of Human Rights in Occupied Kuwait' in 1990 and Resolution 46/135 on the 'Situation of Human Rights in Kuwait Under Iraqi Occupation' in 1991, which condemned the invasion and the 'Iraqi authorities and occupying forces for their serious violations of human rights ... in violation of the Charter of the United Nations, the International Covenants on Human Rights, other relevant human rights instruments and the relevant instruments of humanitarian law'. The wording of both resolutions indicated the gravity with which the General Assembly perceived Iraq's actions throughout the conflict. In contrast, it was not until four months after Resolution 660 was adopted that the Security Council appeared to share the views of the General Assembly as to the seriousness of the breach when it adopted Resolution 661, which deemed that the situation warranted the use of armed force. This delay was in contrast, for example, to the adoption of Resolution 83 within two days of the invasion of the Republic of Korea, which recommended that all

415 UN Docs A/45/233 and 45/455.

member states 'furnish such assistance' 'as necessary to repel the armed attack and restore peace and security'.

Before resorting to the use of force, the Security Council imposed a number of interim measures, in accordance with Article 41 of the UN Charter, including economic sanctions, an embargo on arms and related commodities being sent to Iraq and prohibiting any assistance by way of undertaking or financial assistance except for humanitarian purposes. In addition, Security Council Resolution 662 called on 'all States, international organisations and specialized agencies' not to recognise Iraq's purported annexation of Kuwait. The reference to 'all States' was in keeping with the stated purpose of the UN found in Article 2(6) of the Charter to 'ensure that States which are not Members of the United Nations act in accordance with these Principles so far as may be necessary for the maintenance of international peace and security'. In addition, the reference to 'all States, international organisations and specialized agencies' illustrates that more than just member states of the UN were considered to be affected by the attacks and have an interest in redress accordingly. In seeking to protect the interests of the international community, which were perceived to be at threat from the invasion, the Security Council unanimously adopted a series of resolutions over the next four months that expanded on the range of sanctions imposed against Iraq.[416] For example, in Resolution 670 the Security Council decided that all states were to forbid aircraft to use air space or landing facilities, except for humanitarian purposes. Security Council Resolution 670 is notable because the measures were to be implemented irrespective of whether to do so would be in breach of 'any existing rights or obligations conferred or imposed by any international agreement'. Clearly, member states considered the circumstances warranted a very liberal interpretation of the term 'such measures' in Articles 41 and 42, insofar as the Security Council perceived that a permissible response may have required the breach of states' treaty obligations. This implies the gravity with which Iraq's actions were viewed, although the only express reference that had been made to aggression, at that stage, was in Security Council Resolution 667, which referred to violence toward diplomatic officials and premises as being 'in flagrant violation of [Iraq's] international obligations which strike at the root of international relations'.

By November 1990 the interim measures not involving the use of force were sufficiently ineffective in responding to Iraq's ongoing occupation of Kuwait and failure to comply with the Security Council's demands, that Resolution 678 was

416 These were Security Council Resolution 664 (1990), Security Council Resolution 665 (1990), Security Council Resolution 666 (1990), Security Council Resolution 667 (1990), Security Council Resolution 670 (1990), Security Council Resolution 674 (1990), Security Council Resolution 677 (1990). The unanimous voting record changed when rotating members Cuba and Yemen voted against and China abstained from voting at all in relation to Security Council Resolution 678 (1990), which authorised the use of 'all necessary means', and thus force. Cuba also voted against Resolution 670 (1990) which related to use of air space, air landing facilities and called for detention of Iraqi registered ships.

adopted authorising 'all necessary means' to restore international peace and security and forcibly implement the Security Council's earlier demands. Military intervention into Kuwait commenced in January 1991 with a coalition of 27 states and after a six week period of grace was given to Iraq for compliance. UN member states were permitted to take all necessary steps required under Security Council Resolution 678, although all states were requested to provide the appropriate assistance, which further highlights that the entire community of states was perceived to hold a vested interest in responding. In addition to the invasion having undermined the fundamental interests of more than just Kuwait, three factors legitimated Resolution 678, in the sense that sanctioning the use of military force did not breach Article 2(4) of the UN Charter. First, Iraq failed to comply with the previous Security Council resolutions calling for the state to withdraw from Kuwait; secondly, the invasion was a threat to international peace and security; and, thirdly, the action was authorised by the Security Council pursuant to its powers under Chapter VII of the UN Charter.[417]

Military intervention by the coalition forces was short lived as on 27 February 1991 Iraq's Deputy Prime Minister and Foreign Affairs Minister communicated the State's intent to comply with the Security Council's prior resolutions.[418] Security Council Resolution 686 demanded, still pursuant to Chapter VII, that Iraq not only comply with earlier resolutions but that it also rescind the annexation of Kuwait, 'accept its liability under international law for any loss, damage or injury' and comply with the State's obligations under the relevant provisions of international humanitarian law. Rescission, compensation and orders for compliance are all forms of reparation under the doctrine of state responsibility and, as already discussed, General Assembly Resolution 3314 in fact provides that aggression is an internationally wrongful act. However, greater reference to the manner in which the Security Council's demands were satisfied suggests that the objective was more than merely engaging Iraq's international responsibility, more than simply maintaining international security and even more than ensuring a formal and sustainable ceasefire.

Not only was there to be restitution of the border between Iraq and Kuwait but both states were required to submit to the deployment of a UN observation unit to monitor the demilitarised zone. In addition, Iraq's compliance with its international obligations was to be monitored, including its obligations under the Treaty on the Non-Proliferation of Nuclear Weapons, which Iraq ratified in 1969. Iraq was also invited to ratify the Convention on the Prohibition of the Development, Production and Stockpiling of Bacteriological (Biological) and Toxic Weapons and on Their Destruction 1972, which, at that time, it had only signed – it did so in June 1991. And, finally, Iraq was to permit the access of organisations such as the International Committee of the Red Cross in order to determine the whereabouts and well-being of detainees. All of these forms of oversight were related to

417 For discussion see Shaw (n 356) 1253.

418 Security Council Resolution 686 (1991).

some degree to Iraq's internal affairs, so that it is arguable that in exercising its power under Articles 41 and 42 of the UN Charter, the Security Council infringed the Article 2(7) prohibition on intervention 'in matters that are essentially within the domestic jurisdiction of any state', although Article 2(7) goes on to provide that the principle of non-intervention does not 'prejudice the application of enforcement measures under Chapter VII'. Suffice it to note, without engaging in a debate as to the fine line between prejudicing the application of Chapter VII and abusing the power under Articles 41 and 42, that to the extent that the Security Council did impinge on Iraq's internal affairs pursuant to the terms of Security Council Resolution 686, this was tolerated, thereby implying that other states considered that Iraq's actions justified such a response.

A second indicator that the scope of the response by the Security Council implied that more was sought than simply holding Iraq responsible was the measure of compensation adopted by the Iraqi Compensation Commission, pursuant to Security Council Resolution 687. The Commission did not adopt the guidance of either the Hull Formula of 'prompt, adequate and effective' compensation or Article 2(2) of the Charter of Economic Rights and Duties of States that calls for 'appropriate' compensation, both of which are concerned with compensation for expropriation but provide an appropriate analogy given that an individual who loses his or her property during a time of conflict is likewise losing his or her property as an indirect result of the liable state's policy. Neither was compensation only sought to the extent necessary to ensure full reparation for the internationally wrongful act in accordance with rules of state responsibility. Instead, Resolution 687 determined that Iraq's contribution was to be 'based on a percentage of the value of its exports of petroleum' and taking 'into account the requirements of the peoples of Iraq'. This formula ultimately led Iraq to incur such significant levels of debt that by 2003 the State had to be 'exonerated' in order to finance internal reconstruction.[419]

The final distinguishing factor is that Iraq was required to subject the destruction of all its nuclear, chemical, biological and missile weapons to international supervision by a special commission established for this purpose and by the International Atomic Energy Agency. The embargo that had been imposed under Security Council Resolution 661 was to continue and, in addition, Iraq was to undertake that in the future it would not 'use, develop, construct or acquire' any such weapons. There is a parallel between the measures imposed on Iraq and those taken after the Second World War in dismantling the war making capacity of both Germany and Japan, which was referred to earlier as an example of one of the cumulative mechanisms used to hold the respective states accountable. In all three cases the response is not simply to punish the state, although it may be perceived as possessing penal attributes. The destruction of a state's ability both to defend and attack diminishes its sovereign capacity – far exceeding the

419 C. Tomuschat, 'Darfur – Compensation for the Victims' (2005) *Journal of International Criminal Justice* 579, 586.

consequences when a state's responsibility is engaged, which purport to restore the relationship between the victim and breaching states rather than alter the structural framework of the breaching state. An analogy would be to envisage the breaching state as a pile of bricks with each brick representing a sovereign quality. When a state abuses its power then it can be said that the brick that represents the relevant sovereign quality is flawed and undermines the whole structure. When the brick is removed the whole structure will collapse but it can be rebuilt with the remaining bricks. In so doing there is a new structure, which can be described as the accountable state, which in theory is a different conceptual entity. Thus, the removal of Iraq's defence and attack capabilities can be interpreted as an attempt to hold the state accountable by dismantling the structural element that facilitated Iraq's use of aggression when it invaded Kuwait.

The response to Iraq's invasion of Kuwait was remarkable. On the one hand, there was seldom any direct reference by the Security Council to the invasion as aggression and the Council was consistent in noting that the response was in accordance with the powers given to it under Chapter VII to ensure international peace and security. On the other hand, the combination of responses, mostly initiated by the Security Council, almost always acting unanimously, was clearly the most severe of the three examples discussed here and thus the example most likely to be an illustration of state accountability for breaching the *jus cogens* prohibition on aggression.

5.2.4.4 Conclusions on the responses to state aggression

These examples have highlighted, particularly in the Cold War context and in relation to the Security Council, that determining whether an attack amounts to aggression is not straightforward, despite the fact that a state's belligerent acts can be assessed against the definition adopted by the General Assembly in Resolution 3314. Of itself, the reluctance of states to use the term implies that an act of aggression is of greater severity than a belligerent act that does not meet the threshold in Resolution 3314. Certainly, the International Military Tribunal at Nuremberg perceived aggression to represent another layer of depravity, stating that a war of aggression 'is the supreme international crime differing only from other war crimes in that it contains within itself the accumulated evil of the whole',[420] while the inclusion of aggression on the ILC's list of *jus cogens* norms confirms that states recognise aggression to be a more serious breach because the interests of the entire international community are under threat. Aggression undermines the interests of the entire international community as it poses a threat to the very framework of international peace and security in which international relations are conducted. Given that the mandate of the Security Council is to protect that very framework it is somewhat ironic that, in the examples above, it was the Security Council, rather than the General Assembly, that was reluctant to label the respective attacks as

420 *Judgment of the IMT for the Trial of German Major War Criminals* (London: HMSO, 1946) 186.

aggression both before and after Resolution 3314. The political context was undoubtedly a significant factor in terms of how the Security Council responded, as illustrated by both the careful wording used after Israel's attack on the nuclear reactor in Osiraq and the short period of involvement following the invasion of Korea. The influence of Cold War political tensions between states was even more apparent when compared with the Security Council's proactive response after Iraq invaded Kuwait and was more in keeping with the Security Council's mandate to protect international peace and security, rather than protecting the individual political interests of Security Council members.

Three issues were raised at the start of these comparative studies on the responses to aggression that must be specifically addressed. First, there was no difference in terms of the response to aggression from before and after General Assembly Resolution 3314 was adopted in 1974, in contrast to the significant impact made by the decreased political tensions between permanent members of the Security Council toward the end of the Cold War. This in turn answered the second point being that political factors have proven remarkably influential in state accountability for aggression, at least as it was sought by the Security Council, which was often unable to achieve a consensus of response – in comparison to the General Assembly that was active in condemning the relevant states, despite the much greater number of states involved. The final point confirms the reoccurring proposition here that accountability is the cumulative result of a range of measures, which result in a more severe response than if it was the state's responsibility that had been engaged. In all three examples the response to aggression included the use of force, criticism from states and non-state actors, embargoes and other forms of reparation in keeping with the fact that aggression is also an internationally wrongful act.

As only three cases have been included, the conclusions above are necessarily tentative. Further case studies would inevitably provide a more comprehensive picture of state practice and provide a direction for future study. Just one example of a useful comparative study would be the lack of an active response by the UN to the invasion of Iraq by the US led forces in 2003. The legality of the invasion was disputed;[421] for instance, former UN Secretary General Kofi Annan has stated that the invasion was illegal[422] and Russia, France and China issued a joint statement that Resolution 1441, which was relied on by the US led coalition to justify the

421 In comparison to Security Council Resolution 678 (1990), which, it was argued above, was a permissible use of force because Iraq had failed to comply with the relevant Security Council resolutions and had annexed Kuwait, the US led coalition had no such justification given that Iraq had complied with Security Council Resolution 1441 (2002) that had called on Iraq to satisfy its disarmament obligations under Security Council Resolutions 687 and 688 (1991).

422 E. MacAskill and J. Borger, 'Iraq War was Illegal and Breached UN Charter, Says Annan' *The Guardian* (16 September 2004) available at http://www.guardian.co.uk/world/2004/sep/16/iraq.iraq.

invasion, 'excludes any automaticity in the use of force'.[423] Yet neither the Security Council nor the General Assembly responded to the invasion of Iraq. One possible reason may relate to the cost that would be incurred. For example, economic sanctions could have led to retaliatory policies by the US while in practical terms the cost of mounting an attack against the US was, and is, prohibitive. A second suggestion is that there was no state that could coordinate a response as the US did in relation to Korea and Iraq in 1990. An alternative explanation might be that there were attempts to seek some form of accountability beyond the UN framework, such as criticism of the US by individual states and human rights bodies that could be interpreted as a form of 'reputational accountability', whereby maintaining the US's reputation as a defender of democracy rather than an aggressor in international relations was an 'incentive' for the US to defend its actions.[424] All of these suggestions are untested and further analysis would be needed to determine the reasons why there has been little direct reaction to the US led invasion of Iraq. In turn, this and other case studies would allow a determination of the extent to which there are common attributes amongst the political factors that currently influence state practice in seeking accountability; in the same way that the response, if any, to breaches of aggression by the Security Council during the Cold War was predictable.

5.2.5 Australia's 'stolen generation'

It has been consistently noted throughout this book that the 20th century represented an epoch in the way public international law was construed. Rather than being seen solely as a vehicle for protecting the interests of states, the legal framework was reformulated to ensure that the interests of states are balanced with those of non-state actors, namely individuals – with the most significant development for these purposes being the substantive incorporation of a body of fundamental *jus cogens* norms into public international law and increasing recognition that there must be state accountability when those norms are breached. Contemporaneous to the reformulation of the international legal framework was a realignment of the political framework, owing primarily to the symbiotic processes of decolonisation and state building that have occurred over the past 100 or so years. This case study touches on both events when it considers Australia's accountability for the treatment of the indigenous Aboriginal population in post-colonial Australia and in particular the Australian Government's policy of removing Aboriginal and Torres Strait Islander children from their families – a group of children that would become known as the Stolen Generation. This case study aims to show that rapid change within the international legal framework has not necessarily been

423 'Joint Statement from the Peoples Republic of China, the Federation of Russia, and France' (2002).

424 R. Keohane, 'The Concept of Accountability in World Politics and the Use of Force' (2003) 24 *Michigan Journal of International Law* 1121.

followed in terms of the realities of the political framework because, on the one hand, Australia has been a pioneer of international human rights protection yet, on the other hand, its policy of forced child removal breached a number of these human rights, including fundamental protections recognised as *jus cogens*.

There is a stark contrast with the earlier case studies, in which the breaching states tended to be repressive and largely totalitarian regimes or else the breach needed to be viewed in the context of historical conflict, as with Israel. The forcible removal of children from a specific cultural group that some observers have even described in relation to the Stolen Generation as genocide,[425] in a country that is widely viewed as a progressive and liberal democracy and pursuant to a government policy that was sanctioned by law until as late as 1970 by which time human rights protection was an entrenched characteristic of the modern international framework, is not an atypical example of when states breach *jus cogens* norms. Thus, the particular focus here is on determining how instrumental these contextual factors were in terms of the nature and occurrence of Australia's accountability. In other words, this case study considers whether it was more or less likely that Australia would be held accountable for breaching *jus cogens* norms, because it is a liberal democracy.

Child removal legislation was first adopted, in the various territories that would comprise the Commonwealth of Australia from 1901, by the federal state of Victoria with the 1869 Aboriginal Protection Act, which was followed over the next 80 years with similar regulatory measures. These included the 1897 Aboriginal Protection and Restriction of the Sale of Opium Act in Queensland, the 1905 Aborigines Act and 1936 Native Administration Act in Western Australia, the 1915 Aborigines Protection Amendment Act in New South Wales and the 1918 Aborigines Ordinance in the Northern Territories.[426] All these statutes gave local governments wide powers in relation to the Aboriginal community, including the authority forcibly to remove children and to exercise rights of guardianship. The Report of the National Inquiry into the Separation of Aboriginal and Torres Strait Islander Children from Their Families would estimate that in the period from 1910 to 1970 alone 'between one in three and one in ten indigenous children were forcibly removed from their families and communities'[427] – a figure

425 For example Sir Ronald Wilson, President of Australia's Human Rights Commission, stated that 'it clearly was attempted genocide', a view also taken by the Social Justice Commissioner Mike Dodson following a national inquiry into the removals published in 1997: M. Perry, 'A Stolen Generation Cries Out' *Reuters* (1997) available at http://www.hartford-hwp.com/archives/24/088.html. The Australian Government denied this charge in its 12th Report to the UN Committee on the Elimination of Racial Discrimination (UN Doc CERD/C/SR.1395) paras 115–18.

426 M.F. Christie, *Aboriginal People in Colonial Victoria, 1835–1886* (Sydney: Sydney University Press, 1979).

427 Human Rights and Equal Opportunity Commission, Commonwealth of Australia *Bringing Them Home: Report of the National Inquiry into the Separation of Aboriginal and Torres Strait Islander Children from Their Families* (1997) National Overview.

that the former Australian Prime Minister Kevin Rudd would subsequently cite as forming part 'of the historical record' and 'a product of the deliberate, calculated policies of the states, as reflected in the explicit powers given to them under statute'.[428] Removal was legally sanctioned on a variety of grounds but even from the time the measures were introduced, members of Australia's parliaments have questioned the policy's legitimacy.[429] Examples of the condemnation levelled included a former Minster for Territories who pointed out at the Native Welfare Conference in 1951 that Australia's treatment of its indigenous people was inconsistent with the State's promotion of human rights at the international level;[430] during parliamentary debates from as early as 1914 the effect of the 1915 Aborigines Protection Amendment Act was described as legalising the 'reintroduction of slavery in NSW';[431] and in 1943 the incumbent Administrator of the Northern Territory stated that the restrictions imposed on the Aboriginal community remained in place 'even though they are at variance with the complete ideals of the Universal Declaration of Human Rights'.[432] Although the Commonwealth Government did not have the constitutional authority to legislate in respect of the Aboriginal community until 1967, Aboriginal and human rights groups had similarly urged the central authorities to exercise their considerable influence over the respective local authorities and withdraw the policy of forced removal from as early as the 1930s. Yet these calls went unheeded for several decades.

The plight of the Stolen Generation was not widely known, either in Australia or internationally, until after the offending policies were mostly outlawed by approximately 1970, following the election of the Whitlam Government in 1972 that campaigned on a platform of Aboriginal self-determination and through the research of historians starting with Read's 1981 account of *The Stolen Generations: The Removal of Aboriginal Children in New South Wales 1883 to 1969*.[433] In 1994, a conference was organised and attended by representatives from every territorial state where the issue of determining a suitable response to the atrocities was discussed and the conclusion reached was 'to make governments accountable for their actions'.[434] The first approach in seeking accountability was the initiation of civil compensation claims including *Kruger & Ors v Commonwealth of Australia* and *Bray &*

428 'Full Text of Kevin Rudd's Speech' *Herald Sun* (2008).

429 As discussed by the historian Peter Read who coined the phrase 'Stolen Generation': P. Read, 'Don't Let Facts Spoil This Campaign' *The Australian* (18 February 2008) available at http://www.theaustralian.com.au/news/opinion/dont-let-facts-spoil-this-campaign/story-e6frg6zo-1111115574447.

430 Note 427 above, National Overview.

431 *Parliamentary Debates 1914–15*, at 1951, 1953, 1957 (n 427) National Overview.

432 Australian Archives No AA ACT: CRS F1 1943/24 (n 427).

433 P. Read, *The Stolen Generations: The Removal of Aboriginal Children in New South Wales 1883 to 1969* (Department of Aboriginal Affairs, 1981) (reprinted 2006) available at http://www.daa.nsw.gov.au/publications/StolenGenerations.pdf.

434 The 1994 *Going Home Conference* was discussed in the *Bringing Them Home Report* (n 427) Inquiry Process.

Ors v Commonwealth of Australia – although these were ultimately unsuccessful.[435] Secondly, in response to increasing domestic criticism and with regard to the Australian Government's human rights, social justice and access and equity policies in pursuance of Sections 11(1)(e), (j), and (k) of the 1986 Human Rights and Equal Opportunity Commission Act, the Attorney General requested the Human Rights and Equal Opportunity Commission to inquire into and report on the allegations of forcible transfer and racial discrimination of the Aboriginal and Torres Strait Islander communities.

The terms of reference for the report requested the Commission to 'trace past laws, practices and policies which resulted in the separation of Aboriginal and Torres Strait Islander children from their families by compulsion, duress or undue influence, and the effects of those laws, practices and policies', effectively requesting that a determination be made as to whether the government had instituted a policy of forcible transfer that was directed towards a particular cultural group. In addition, the Commission was charged with identifying what steps needed to be taken in redress, including an examination of 'the adequacy of and the need for any changes in current laws, practices and policies', what legislative provisions were required to facilitate the access of victims to 'individual and family records' and 'assistance towards locating and reunifying families', the potential for compensation and advice on any required changes in current laws and policies to ensure the self-determination of Aboriginal and Torres Strait Islander peoples.[436] The reference to self-determination and the express provision made within the mandated scope of inquiry to refer to international laws, policies and practices illustrated that the work of the Commission was not simply focused on the State's liability under domestic law; the Commission was also required to determine breaches of public international law.

The 1997 Final Report of the National Inquiry was extensive and condemned both regional and central authorities for their respective roles in legalising and implementing a policy of forced child removal. The potential political fallout from the findings was significant and it was therefore unsurprising when the Australian Federal Government criticised the Commission and sought to defend itself by arguing that the Report failed to distinguish between legitimate and illegitimate instances of removal, in terms of the circumstances of the removal and the reasons for it.[437] This is not the place for a rigorous analysis of the report or its methodology and for the purposes of this discussion it is sufficient to note that despite challenging certain aspects of the report, the Australian Government has largely accepted that the forced removal of Aboriginal and Torres Strait Islander children from their families throughout the 20th century was made permissible and possible because it was sanctioned and carried out by the State. What does need to be

435 [1997] HCA 27.

436 Note 427 above, Terms of Reference.

437 Minister for Aboriginal and Torres Strait Islander Affairs to the Senate Legal and Constitutional References Committee *Inquiry into the Stolen Generation: Federal Government Submission* (2000).

considered for the purpose of this inquiry is whether the government's policy – either substantively or as it was implemented – breached the *jus cogens* prohibitions on racial discrimination, genocide or crimes against humanity, which includes the forcible transfer of populations pursuant to Article 6 of the Nuremberg Charter and Article 7 of the Rome Statute. As with the earlier case studies, this is a crucial factor in order to determine whether any response to the breach was owing to the *jus cogens* status of the norm.

Among the justification and reasoning for removal of Aboriginal children that was given by authorities at the time, including physical protection and mental health well-being, the historian Peter Read noted that there were certain pragmatic factors that suggested more malevolent motives also existed. For example, in southern Australia there was a shortage of viable land that could be farmed by settlers and, in order to decrease the Aboriginal population on arable land reserves so as to resolve 'this great problem', the Aborigines' Protection Board Chief Inspector considered that 'the only solution' was 'the removal of the children. In the course of the next few years there will be no need for the camps and stations; the old people will have passed away, and their progeny will be absorbed in the industrial classes of the colony'.[438] By 1910, local governments had instituted the policy of forced removal and children were either institutionalised or placed into domestic service, with one figure estimating that 49 per cent of all removed children were required to work in this way.[439] The National Inquiry Report also cited the more blatant decisions of the Aborigines' Protection Board to remove children merely 'for being aboriginal',[440] noting that the 'the ultimate purpose of removal was to control the reproduction of indigenous people with a view to merging or absorbing them' into the non-indigenous post-colonial Australian (and predominantly white) community.

The Commission concluded that it was as a result of government policy that children were removed from their families either by compulsion, which was defined as 'the officially authorised use of force or coercion and illegally exercised force or coercion', both legal and illegal forms of duress and undue pressure including the use of church or community officials who were able to exercise their influence and persuade Aboriginal parents to relinquish their children to the guardianship of the State.[441] The Commission listed the main elements of forcible removal that were proven as the 'deprivation of liberty by detaining children and confining them in institutions', transfer being pursuant to state policy that was 'directly discriminating on racial grounds'; the abolition of parental rights by making children wards of the Chief Protector or Aborigines' Protection Board or by assuming custody and control of the children; abuses of power in the removal

438 Note 429 above.

439 Ibid.

440 Note 427 above, Part 2 Chapter 3.

441 Ibid, Scope of Inquiry.

process; and the breach of guardianship obligations on the part of Protectors, Protection Boards and other 'carers'.[442]

In terms of how policies of forced removal violated public international law, the Commission noted that the relevant legislation had 'established a legal regime for those children and their families which was inferior to the regime which applied to non-indigenous children and their families', breaching the State's positively incurred obligations under the Universal Declaration of Human Rights; in particular 'the right to liberty and security of person (Article 3), the equal protection of the law (Article 7), the right to a fair and public hearing by an independent and impartial tribunal in the determination of their rights and obligations (Article 10), freedom from arbitrary interference with their privacy, family, home and correspondence (Article 12), the right to a free elementary education and the right of parents to choose the kind of education to be given to their children (Article 26)'.[443] Having found that 'the Australian practice of indigenous child removal involved systematic racial discrimination', the Commission then adopted a more controversial stance by stating that the Government's policy also amounted to 'genocide as defined by international law'.[444] This view was not universally held; for example, the earlier 1987 Royal Commission into Aboriginal Deaths in Custody had concluded that the relevant child removal policies were adopted 'not for the purpose of exterminating a people, but for their preservation'.[445] In order, therefore, to substantiate its finding that the forced removals amounted to genocide, the Commission argued that:[446]

> ... the predominant aim of indigenous child removals was the absorption or assimilation of the children into the wider, non-indigenous, community so that their unique cultural values and ethnic identities would disappear, giving way to models of Western culture. In other words, the objective was 'the disintegration of the political and social institutions of culture, language, national feelings, religion, and the economical existence of' indigenous peoples.

The Commission also cited the earlier judgment of the High Court of Australia in *Polyukovich v Commonwealth* and in particular the dissenting view of Justice Brennan that, at a minimum, the policy of forcible removal for the purpose of raising indigenous children separately from their culture could be labelled as genocide in the legal sense – at least from 1946 when the term was coined by Lemkin.[447] Irrespective of whether the allegation of genocide could be independently upheld by an international investigatory body, there was sufficient evidence that the forced removals

442 Ibid, Reparation.

443 Ibid.

444 Ibid.

445 Royal Commission into Aboriginal Deaths in Custody *National Report* (1987–1991) Volume 5 para 36.3.7.

446 Note 427 above, Reparation.

447 *Polyukovich v Commonwealth* [1991] HCA 32.

breached the prohibition on discrimination and amounted to a crime against humanity, given the sustained nature of the government's policy that included acts of deportation and physical transfer. On that basis, the focus can now shift to identify any response to those breaches and to consider whether Australia was made to account for the harm it committed against the Stolen Generation.

As already noted, there was little response to the plight of the Aboriginal community at the time the removal of children was occurring. This omission was remarkable given that contemporaneous to the discriminatory policies of the Australian Government from 1945 onwards, the apartheid policies of the South African Government were being strongly condemned by the international community – and is especially poignant in light of the fact that Australia considered itself to be 'an important player in moves to isolate South Africa so long as race remained part of its selection policy'.[448] The complex reasons why one state would come under international scrutiny and another would escape inquiry, regardless that both adopted and were implementing policies of racial discrimination, could form the basis of a completely separate inquiry. Speculative answers include Australia's strategic relationships with the UK and the US as a key ally in the World Wars and as a Pacific bastion during the Cold War, as well as the cultural and democratic affiliations between Australia and those states with the greatest power in international relations during the 20th century. Realistically, both explanations hold some weight, although it must be acknowledged that these propositions equally apply to the position of South Africa in international relations at the time. In addition, and in light of Australia's *ex post facto* assumption of accountability that will be canvassed below, it is probable that the failure to respond was symptomatic of the incongruence noted at the outset of this case study between the rapid development of international law during the 20th century and the political ability and willingness of states to implement (or not) the increased scope of express legal duties and obligations. This argument is made on the basis that Australia has not sought to avoid accountability; rather, it has been the state itself (and not the international community) that in the past 20 years has been instrumental in the accountability process.

The Final Report of the National Inquiry concluded that Australia was legally obliged to provide an effective remedy and reparation to the victims, by referring to principles of customary international law, Article 2(3) of the International Covenant on Civil and Political Rights, Article 39 of the Convention on the Rights of the Child, Article 19 of the Declaration on the Protection of All Persons from Enforced Disappearances, the Declaration of Basic Principles of Justice for Victims of Crime and Abuse of Power, Article 6 of the International Convention on the Elimination of All Forms of Racial Discrimination and the United Nations Sub-Commission on Prevention of Discrimination and Protection of Minorities' Basic Principles and Guidelines on the Right to Reparation for Victims of Gross

448 Australian Government 'Fact Sheet 255 – Australia and the Issue of Apartheid in Sport' (2010) available at http://www.naa.gov.au/about-us/publications/fact-sheets/fs255.aspx.

Violations of Human Rights and Humanitarian Law. The commission set out what was needed for there to be an effective remedy in the report, with the two components that were listed equating to the two limbs of state accountability as conceptualised here. The first aspect was an acknowledgement of liability in the form of an apology and other acts of commemoration, including introducing the history of the Stolen Generation into state school curricula. Secondly, the commission sought redress by way of compensation and appropriate assistance to facilitate land, culture and language restitution, both in the form of financial aid and legislative recognition of the right of the Aboriginal community to exercise self-determination. To the extent that both recommendations were fully implemented, it could be soundly argued that Australia was held accountable because there was recognition of liability and redress commensurate with the gravity of the norms breached. However, recent history shows that the State has not acted on all of the recommendations in the Report and thus it cannot be said that there was an effective remedy as envisaged by the commission, although this does not preclude finding that there has been accountability after greater consideration of the steps that were in fact taken by the Australian Government.

In terms of apologising, both central and local governments have made amends, although a federal state apology did not occur until a decade after the report was issued and only after the change in power from the Liberal Government that was in office in 1997 to the Labour Government that assumed this role in 2007. The Liberal Government refused to make an apology on behalf of the State for reasons including that current generations should not be made to account for the acts of past governments, that the removal of Aboriginal children was not in fact illegal under Australian law and that any apology would in some way open the State up to future compensation claims. Despite the Federal Government's initial refusal to apologise, redress was offered at the territorial state government and grass roots community level. The first national Sorry Day was commemorated in 1998 and every year since hundreds of thousands of Australians have made acts of commemoration, including signing over 400 'Sorry Books', while in 2000 over 250,000 people embarked on a walk of solidarity across the city of Sydney. Starting in 1997 territorial state governments have adopted motions within their respective legislatures either apologising (in the sense that the word 'apology' was used) or expressing sincere regret in the case of Tasmania at the forced removal of Aboriginal and Torres Strait Islander children. These apologies acknowledged not only the harm caused but, for example in the 27 May 1997 apology by the Government of Western Australia entitled 'Aborigines, Family Separation', that the removal of children was 'a consequence of Government policy' or in the words of the Queensland State Apology on 26 May 1999 that the government was sorry for 'the past policies under which indigenous children were forcibly separated from their families'. The combined effect of these acts of commemoration and apologies was to establish a profound expression of moral accountability.

By 2008, and in light of increased pressure not only domestically but also internationally as discussed below, then newly elected Australian Prime Minister Kevin Rudd gave a formal apology for the policy of forced removal of Aboriginal and

Torres Strait Islander children. On behalf of 'the Prime Minister of Australia', 'the Government of Australia' and 'the Parliament of Australia', Rudd stated:

> ... we apologise for the laws and policies of successive Parliaments and governments ... especially for the removal of Aboriginal and Torres Strait Islander children from their families, their communities and their country.[449]

There could be no clearer statement that the State in all its manifestations accepted liability for instituting a policy of forced child removal and thus by implication that it had breached and sought to make amends for violating the prohibition of such acts and omissions under public international law.

The provision of a national apology by the government was not, however, accompanied by any nationwide provision for compensation, which was rejected by all political parties at the time a motion was introduced before the Australian Senate endorsing the State's apology. In 2000, the 'Senate Legal and Constitutional References Committee's 2000 Inquiry into the Federal Government's Implementation of Recommendations Made by the Human Rights and Equal Opportunity Commission' issued its report entitled 'Healing: A Legacy of Generations', which recommended the establishment of a 'Reparations Tribunal'. As of 2010, the Tasmanian Labour Government had acted by adopting the 2006 Stolen Generations of Aboriginal Children Act that established a fund of AU$5 million to compensate members of the Stolen Generation, while the Western Australian Government instituted a AU$114 million redress scheme in 1997. In terms of civil claims for compensation, the Federal Court of Australia has yet to uphold an award on the grounds that there was no legal wrong that caused the damage. A 2007 decision by the Supreme Court of Australia in *Trevorrow v State of South Australia* was the first case to award compensation to a victim of the Stolen Generation,[450] when the applicant was granted AU$525,000 in compensation, which was then upheld in 2010 on an appeal by the South Australian Government. However, given that the application was filed in 1997 (taking 13 years to be judicially confirmed) and that the compensation was awarded for the breach of a duty of care owed by the authorities in relation to the process of removal, rather than on the basis of the removal itself being unlawful, this case is not a strong precedent for future compensation claims.

The focus on forms of redress that were voluntarily undertaken by Australia does not mean that there has been no response by the international community although, and as with all the case studies, the reaction has primarily been led by the UN. In 2000, the UN Committee on Racial Discrimination noted the conclusions of the National Inquiry into the Separation of Aboriginal and Torres Strait Islander Children from Their Families, before expressing concern that 'the Commonwealth Government does not support a formal national apology and

449 'Full Text of Kevin Rudd's Speech' *Herald Sun* (2008).

450 *Trevorrow v State of South Australia (No 5)* [2007] SASC 285.

that it considers inappropriate the provision of monetary compensation for those forcibly and unjustifiably separated from their families'.[451] The UN Committee rejected the argument that Australia could avoid its obligation to make redress 'on the grounds that such practices were sanctioned by law at the time and were intended to "assist the people whom they affected"'.[452] Having noted that the State's culpability arose from the establishment and maintenance of a legal structure that allowed the abuse to occur (a determination of liability), the committee recommended that Australia 'consider the need to address appropriately the extraordinary harm inflicted by these racially discriminatory practices' (redress).[453] The findings of the committee certainly encouraged political accountability, as they were not legally binding, while the moral accountability of the state was simultaneously being promoted with a wave of global awareness of the plight of the Stolen Generation; the scope of publicity including movies such as *Rabbit Proof Fence*, popular songs by prominent rock groups such as Midnight Oil and exposure given to the issue at the 2000 Sydney Olympic Games. The impact of the adverse international publicity and the criticism by the UN Committee on the Elimination of Racial Discrimination was apparent in terms of promoting accountability when Australia subsequently bowed to pressure in 2008 and followed through with the Human Rights and Equal Opportunity Commission's recommendation that it offer a formal national apology. Later that same year, the Human Rights Council adopted Resolution 7/33 on 'A Global Call for Concrete Action Against Racism, Racial Discrimination, Xenophobia and Related Intolerance', in which it 'welcome[d] the landmark and historic formal apology by the Government of Australia for the past laws and policies that inflicted profound grief, suffering and loss on its indigenous peoples', recognising that the state was liable but also accountable for the breach. It is submitted here that Australia's proactive response to criticism from the international community (including both state and non-state actors), is an indicator of the political and moral currency of state accountability within international relations, even if the concept's legal status remains unclear and even though Australia's liberal democratic tradition arguably meant that it was susceptible to condemnation and losing the goodwill of the community of states.

This case study has sought to reflect upon whether the breach of *jus cogens* norms by a liberal and democratic state leads to any distinguishing features in terms of the nature and approach to holding that state accountable. The role of the international community in holding Australia accountable for policies of forcibly removing Aboriginal and Torres Strait Islander children was certainly minimal in comparison with the proactive response taken by Australia itself. The first explanation for the lack of international reaction, despite the seriousness of the breach,

451 Concluding Observations by the Committee on the Elimination of Racial Discrimination: Australia CERD/C/304/Add.101 (2000) para 13.

452 Ibid, para 13.

453 Ibid, para 13.

was that the international community did not consider Australia had done anything wrong; however, isolated instances of criticism and recognition that it was the *jus cogens* prohibition on racial discrimination that was breached were noted above and suggest otherwise. Secondly, there was considered to be no need for the international community to react except when the measures taken by Australia were perceived as insufficient, as when the UN Commission on Racial Discrimination called on the State to implement the recommendations of the National Inquiry Report. Thirdly, the fact that Australia was a liberal democracy and otherwise had a strong record in terms of complying with its obligations under international law, which was strengthened by the fact that it initiated a credible inquiry into the breach and reacted to the findings, meant that the State was afforded the opportunity to address its accountability internally. It is argued here that a combination of the last two suggestions is the most accurate explanation. In turn, this case study introduces a new feature of how state accountability is sought in practice, whereby states hailing from a liberal democratic tradition are afforded greater discretion to ensure there is accountability for the respective breach. On the one hand, this could be interpreted as political favouring between democratic – even Western – states. The other view is that democratic states are more likely to perceive accountability and the protection of fundamental norms as vital to the maintenance of international relations and are therefore considered to be more willing actively to ensure accountability without the interference of the international community.

5.3 Conclusion

The primary objective of this chapter was to determine whether there is an informal practice in holding states accountable for breaching *jus cogens* norms. The case studies suggest that there is indeed an *ad hoc* practice whereby states that breach *jus cogens* norms are made to (or voluntarily choose to) account for their actions, notably in relation to the apartheid in South Africa and the amends made by Australia to the Stolen Generation. The argument that accountability was attained is not as strong in the three comparative examples of state aggression but, when the General Assembly and the Security Council did respond, there was a correlation between the gravity of the breach and the nature of the redress, especially following Iraq's invasion of Kuwait. The many issues that can frustrate attempts at seeking state accountability were apparent in all the case studies but were particularly inhibiting in the earlier historical examples pertaining to crimes against humanity allegedly perpetrated by the USSR and Turkey.

The argument that the occurrence of state accountability in practice increased as the 20th century progressed can be effectively illustrated in envisaging a sort of accountability graph. The vertical axis would indicate the date of the breach with more recent examples such as the invasion of Iraq at the top of the axis. The horizontal axis would represent the extent to which the response can be linked to some level of state consensus that the breach of the specific norm undermined the interests of the entire international community so that the greater the link between consensus and response the further along the horizontal axis the incident would be plotted. For example, the response to the apartheid in South Africa would be placed at the far right of the horizontal axis because both state and non-state actors declared their abhorrence at the practice and the varied measures taken in response were sustained and brought about the end of apartheid. Australia would likewise be placed at the far right of the horizontal axis, having acknowledged that it breached the prohibition on racial discrimination, which as a party to the VCLT and various human rights instruments implied that Australia recognised the gravity of the breach, and that in turn was apparent from the public and formal apology made by the state. When all the case studies are plotted on the graph, the points form an upward trajectory and a strong correlation emerges between how recently the incident occurred and recognition of the gravity of the breach, or even that the norm in question was *jus cogens*.

On the basis that an informal, albeit inconsistent, practice of state accountability can be seen as occurring, some consideration is needed as to whether state accountability in practice is the same as state accountability as theorised here. In particular, the evaluative characteristics adopted for the purpose of conceptualising state accountability are recalled. First, it was proposed that holding a state accountable would require more than reparation for the breach of the state's obligations owed to another state. In other words, a combination of the General Assembly and the Security Council condemning Iraq's actions, the US led coalition that invaded Kuwait and engaged in combat with Iraqi troops, the severe compensation regime imposed and the ongoing monitoring of Iraq's weapon capabilities was argued to far exceed the consequences if Kuwait had sought to engage Iraq's responsibility before the ICJ. The second proposed criterion was that accountability may be legal, political and even moral, which was arguably the case when South Africa ended its policy of apartheid after decades of intransigence. The cynical view would be that the nature of accountability in that case was political because South Africa had no choice but to end apartheid or continue to face isolation by the community of states. A more optimistic interpretation is that the sustained abhorrence by the entire international community eventually encouraged South Africa to accept and understand that the apartheid violated fundamental human rights – a view confirmed with reference to Australia where the government's formal apology followed a series of apologies by territorial authorities and acts of public commemoration that illustrated the awareness and desire of the State as a whole to make amends. The final two criteria were that accountability was most likely when a variety of responses was employed, provided they were not illegal. In all the case studies, regardless of whether or not accountability was achieved, redress was sought in a number of ways, including criticism, sanctions, military force, forms of oversight, reparations, non-recognition of the breach, memorials and even the criminal trial of liable individuals after the Armenian massacres in Turkey, although this had very little impact in terms of the state's accountability in that case.

In addition to the evaluative criteria that were proposed as characteristics of conceptual state accountability, three issues were raised at the start of the case studies that specifically pertain to what the concept means in practice. These were: what form does redress take (which has been addressed above), what party determines the occurrence of a breach and what party implements redress and determines when the state is held accountable. These final few remarks consider whether any resolution of these issues can be been gleaned from this limited study. In practice, the Security Council and the General Assembly are primary players in determining whether a state has breached public international law, although a broader consensus is sought from states before – and in the course of – responding to the breach. For example, all states (not only UN members) and even non-state actors were called on to respond to the apartheid in South Africa and to the use of aggression by Korea and Iraq. In terms of determining that redress should be sought from the breaching state (and the form it should take), the requisite level of consensus was based less on the number of states and more on the perceived power that those states possessed. So, for example, a consensus among the few Security Council members was of significant weight in mobilising action against Iraq, while very little was sought in terms of redress from the USSR despite the almost global condemnation by states and non-state actors owing to both the state's power in terms of maintaining a global political equilibrium and because the USSR's self-imposed political isolation meant it was relatively uninfluenced by the opinion of other states. The benefit of a consensus based on numbers is that the response has greater credence as it is more likely to transcend politics and be seen as independent of ulterior motives and, in addition, it can be distinguished from a response within the context of engaging state responsibility. On that basis, the possibility was explored that the end of the Cold War may see *ex post facto* attempts to hold Russia accountable for crimes against humanity by the USSR – given the consensus that the USSR was culpable and the removal of political barriers that had historically existed.

The view that there could not be a response without some form of state consensus associates redress with the principle of collective security, rather than state accountability, but the Foucauldian framework of analysis employed in this book invites a broader interpretation. International peace and security do not need to relate solely to military security or peaceful state borders and can include other collective interests of the entire international community. Insofar as such an approach is taken, those instances where states expressly determine and respond to a threat to international peace and security may, in certain circumstances, also be seen as a determination and redress on the basis of a breach of *jus cogens* norms. An increasing array of potential examples of state accountability in practice serves to strengthen the conclusion that a concept of state accountability has increasing credibility in international relations. This point was illustrated in particular by referring to Australia's accountability for state policies that discriminated against its indigenous population. It was argued that Australia was the chief protagonist in holding itself accountable because as a democratic and liberal state it considers accountability to be a key characteristic of good governance and necessary for the state's effective participation in international relations. State accountability may not yet be *lex lata* under public international law but just a few examples taken from state practice have shown that the concept has increasing support as *lex feranda*.

Conclusion: An accountability epoch?

On the basis of the substantive analysis that looked at both the juridical viability of the concept and its application in state practice, the final chapter concludes that: (1) state accountability has no normative standing; (2) state practice is indicative rather than determinative of state accountability; (3) state accountability is a legal, political and moral concept; (4) state accountability represents a continuum of answerability; and (5) that state accountability is sought on the basis of a norm's substance and not its *jus cogens* status.

In the context of referring to the study and development of public international law, Hammer claimed that 'the goal need not be the creation of a norm *per se* but rather the delineation of factors that merit consideration by the international system',[454] a claim which captures the motivation behind this study. It has not been the aim to prove that the normative content of international law has or has not expanded or to clarify what the normative content of *jus cogens* is. To adopt such an approach and argue that state accountability is *lex lata* would fail to recognise the reality that states breach international law, irrespective of whether the law in question is recognised as *jus cogens*, and that the more pressing concern is how the international community responds to such breaches. Therefore, the goal in this book was to provide greater consideration of the issues that exist in terms of making states answer for breaching public international law and to highlight that the need and desire for effective state accountability is an increasing preoccupation for the international community. Issues such as the nature of redress, what accountability means in practice and whether the state for accountability purposes is any different from the state as defined under the Montevideo Convention were all analysed here in order to argue that a norm of state accountability is evolving within international relations and to give some indication as to what its conceptual characteristics are.

454 L. Hammer, *A Foucauldian Approach to International Law: Descriptive Thoughts for Normative Issues* (London: Ashgate, 2007).

The factors that merited consideration were not simply legal concerns and because the discussion was not so much concerned with pure legal theory as it was with the potential evolution of public international law and its impact on international relations, a mix of methodologies and perspectives, notably the approaches of Foucault and Koskenniemi, was justified. While there are benefits in viewing state accountability strictly as a legal construct, namely the legitimacy that attaches when a principle is considered a norm of public international law, there is also the danger that the concept would then be unworkable in terms of its application – that overly bureaucratising accountability would undermine its effectiveness.[455] Therefore, evidence of state accountability was sought not only in terms of juridical support, notably from among the different international courts and tribunals, academic scholars and the practice and opinion of international organisations and other non-state actors, including the UN and its human rights monitoring bodies, but also in terms of state practice. The overview of juridical support and state practice was persuasive in cumulatively illustrating that the notion exists in a fragmentary and indeterminate conceptual form and increasingly could even be seen as *lex feranda* – but it also confirmed the assumption, made at the outset, that state accountability is not *lex lata* at this point in time. In other words, this discussion has identified more of a paradigmatic shift throughout the 20th century in how the international community responds when states breach international law, rather than a determinate legal principle that governs the response.

The risk when a theory or concept is attempted to be moulded into a legal principle is apparent with reference to both rules of *jus cogens* and the doctrine of state responsibility. While both principles have far greater normative standing than a concept of state accountability, their effectiveness in the maintenance and protection of public international law was shown to be limited. That statement is not a criticism; rather, it is an observation that where a theoretical concept assumes a legal form, its utility will be constrained in accordance with that form. In turn, there is the risk that any issue that falls outside the subject scope of the particular doctrine will not be addressed, which begs the question of whether it would in fact be desirable to find that state accountability is evolving *lex lata,* given the parameters that would be placed on state accountability as a legal principle. One example of a potential limitation could be if a legal principle of state accountability dictated that only the UN Security Council could determine whether or not the state in question had breached a *jus cogens* norm. The political factors that influence the Security Council in exercising its powers under the UN Charter were apparent in the various case studies; and should a determination of liability for accountability purposes likewise be frustrated then the whole objective in broadening the scope of redress from states within the framework of public international law, is thus defeated. As long as state accountability is not limited in accordance with a strictly

455 H. Slim, 'By What Authority? The Legitimacy of Accountability and NGOs' (2002) *Journal of Humanitarian Assistance*.

determined legal form then other parties, such as the UN General Assembly, are more likely to act; and the case studies have shown that at this time the greater the number of parties able to, and that do in fact, respond the greater the chance that accountability will result. Before making any final comments on whether, at this time, it is preferable that the concept of state accountability remains *lex feranda*, it is appropriate first to give an overview of the arguments developed here, the conclusions drawn and the conceptual characteristics of state accountability that have emerged throughout the discussion.

The book has effectively comprised two halves, with the first half dealing with the theoretical substance that underpins state accountability and the second seeking out evidence of juridical support and state practice that would indicate at what evolutionary stage the concept currently rests. In the theoretical component, it was argued that independent of cultural and other subjective perspectives, accountability could be defined as a two-step process (being a determination of liability and some form of commensurate redress), while the accountable state was understood as the structural framework that allowed the breach to occur rather than merely an inflexible application of the elements contained in Article 1 of the Montevideo Convention. The constituent elements were then brought together and the concept of state accountability was presented as an interpretive framework to be used in order to determine the extent to which an *ad hoc* or informal practice of holding states accountable already exists and to identify whether a broader approach to making states answer for breaching international law than is currently provided for pursuant to the doctrine of state responsibility, is juridically viable. The most significant indicator that the framework of international law would not only tolerate but would arguably facilitate state accountability as *lex lata* was increased recognition throughout the 20th century that certain fundamental interests are shared by the entire international community and the designation by states of a category of *jus cogens* norms to protect those interests. *Jus cogens* norms were shown here to provide the link between state accountability as an academic legal concept and state accountability as an evolving political norm in international relations and, on that basis, *jus cogens* was described as a legal rather than a linguistic convenience. It was shown throughout the discussion that an indeterminate concept of state accountability has been accommodated in various ways by states, international courts and organisations and even the very framework of public international law, for example, where political or moral forms of redress have been used to compensate for a lack of legal 'punishment'. It is submitted that the reason for this increased flexibility is to ensure that states are somehow made to answer when their acts and omissions threaten the interests of the entire international community.

Before considering whether state accountability as it was conceptualised in the first section could be identified to any extent in terms of practical application, the question of why accountability was even an issue when the doctrine of state responsibility already exists, was addressed. State accountability was shown to be different from the doctrine of state responsibility but it was noted that when the ILC attempted to codify the doctrine it had sought to cover much of the perceived gap in state answerability that is theoretically addressed by the state accountability concept. Attempts to expand the doctrine either by introducing a principle of criminal state responsibility or a more conservative serious breach regime are indicators that a broader and more comprehensive conceptualisation of state redress has some juridical support. Finally, the practical viability of holding states accountable when no such principle exists under international law and there is no formal framework for that purpose, similar to that of the state responsibility doctrine and the ICJ, was explored through a series of five case studies. The obstacles that were identified as frustrating state accountability do not preclude its existence; they simply confirm the nebulous and evolving nature of the concept, and although no perfect model of state accountability was shown to exist in practice there was sufficient evidence to articulate some of the concept's formative characteristics. Before turning to the particular features of state accountability that emerged from the case studies, the broad conclusions reached during the analysis will be restated.

1 State accountability has no normative standing

State accountability has no normative standing in international law. There is thus no institutional form against which state practice can be analysed and judged. On the one hand, this means that contextually relevant factors can be taken into account and accountability is not simply measured against a strict legal standard, which is also in keeping with the Foucauldian perspective that has underpinned the analysis here. On the other hand, without a determinate legal form, there is the risk that states are able to justify less beneficently motivated actions on the grounds of seeking state accountability. To adopt Koskenniemi's language, the conceptual indeterminacy of state accountability has allowed its empirical reality to be determined,[456] although the necessary consequence of this conceptual indeterminacy is that the stronger argument is for state accountability as *lex feranda* and not *lex lata.*

2 State practice is indicative rather than determinative of state accountability

A lack of consistency does not undermine the fact that there is an *ad hoc* practice occurring whereby states are made to account for breaching international law. However, the varied reasons why some states have been held accountable and others have not illustrates that practice cannot, by itself, be determinative of the concept's normative standing. In particular, the case studies highlighted the significant influence of political factors, as seen in the contrasting responses by the Security Council that were linked with Cold War tensions between UN

456 M. Koskenniemi, *From Apology to Utopia – The Structure of International Legal Argument* (Cambridge: Cambridge University Press, 2006).

member states. Ultimately, the inconsistency in state practice confirms that the concept is indeterminate but this does not mean that state accountability does not exist. Kirgis's argument that customary international law is increasingly determined by a 'sliding scale' of practice and *opinio juris*, which changes for each emerging norm, is useful here because it highlights that the evolution of international law is not formulaic and that greater regard to the evolutionary context is required.[457]

One of the benefits of adopting a Foucauldian methodology that views the wider context as relevant is that, while the dominance of states is an important factor, the role played by non-state parties is also taken into consideration. The UN and particularly the Security Council were key in responding to acts of aggression by Iraq, Israel and Korea while human rights oversight bodies, such as the Human Rights Council, have been seen to play an important part in requiring states to justify any failure to uphold their obligations under public international law. Thus, state practice was instrumental in the conclusions reached but where non-state actors helped to 'force a clarification of state practice or have a state affirm its position regarding a [evolving] norm because of external pressure' this was taken into account.[458]

3 State accountability is a legal, political and moral concept

The third conclusion relates to the features that are attributed to the concept in the next section. State accountability is not strictly legal and it has been argued here that the concept currently has political and even moral characteristics. In other words, where legal accountability is not feasible at this time, political (and to a lesser extent moral) accountability will be sought. The relationship between the three forms of accountability can be illustrated in two ways. First, accountability can be viewed as a circle and the full space of this circle would represent total accountability, while the surface area of the circle is split into thirds signifying moral, political and legal accountability – although the relative proportion of representation may vary. An international lawyer advocating Kelsen's pure theory of law would most probably argue that state accountability should be wholly legal. However, it can be seen that such an outcome is currently unlikely, given that state practice was shown here to be heavily influenced by political factors, and because state accountability is a concept and not a legal principle. Accordingly, and to varying degrees, state accountability will be a mix of legal, political and moral accountability. The second way to illustrate the relationship between the forms of accountability is by referring to the case studies. It was argued that South Africa was held accountable, but only after having noted the variety of responses and their cumulative impact over several decades. Legal accountability was clearly

457 F. Kirgis, 'Custom on a Sliding Scale' (1987) 81 *American Journal of International Law* 146.
458 Note 454 above, 58.

sought because South Africa's domestic laws were deprecated and the state was called on to conform with the UN Charter[459] as, for example, in General Assembly Resolution 1598 on the 'Question of Race Conflict in South Africa Resulting From Policies of Apartheid of the Government of the Union of South Africa', so that ultimately the end of apartheid policies illustrated that legal accountability was achieved. However, the fact that South Africa's intransigence continued for many years made it clear that attempts to hold the state legally accountable were, for a long period, ineffective. Concurrent with attempts on the part of the international community to ensure South Africa's compliance with the law, there were various other responses to apartheid and it is argued here that these mechanisms led to varying degrees of political and moral accountability. Individual states and regional organisations criticised and sought to isolate South Africa in its international relations as a means of political accountability, while the use of sporting sanctions and trade embargoes communicated to the state and its citizens that apartheid was ethically unsustainable, in the opinion of the greater international community, as a form of moral accountability. On the basis that state accountability is not strictly legal, the concept can be understood as holding the state accountable as a separate entity for having breached public international law (rather than being held accountable for any breach by the state's organs) without having to resolve issues such as the mens rea of an inanimate entity, the impossibility of a state physically acting or electing not to, and the notion of imprisoning or punishing a state – all of which have thus far proved insurmountable when, for example, state accountability is viewed through the lens of criminal responsibility as a legal principle.

4 State accountability represents a continuum of answerability

State accountability is determined contextually and thus can be conceived of as a continuum of answerability, whereby the nature of accountability alters depending on both the context and the breach so that, just as there is no one standard of evil, there can be no one standard of redress. On that basis, there is no reason to suggest that a state cannot be held accountable if every member of a rogue government that abused its power and breached public international law was brought to criminal trial, which is theoretically possible with the International Criminal Court. Alternatively, the combination of reducing a state's territory, restricting its logistical war-making capacity and suspending the state from military treaties could likewise be seen as accountability – as Professor Tomuschat believed was the case in holding Germany accountable after the Second World War.[460] Indeed, the response might not even be described in terms of seeking accountability at all

459 'Question of Race Conflict in South Africa Resulting From Policies of Apartheid of the Government of the Union of South Africa' General Assembly Resolution 1598 (1961).

460 In an interview with the author at Humboldt University (April 2009).

and the attainment may be an unintended by-product. Such a scenario is more likely to unfold where the prohibition of aggression is breached and where the response is therefore to secure international peace and stability, as was the case in the examples of Korea and Iraq in 1990. A point not considered, but which is relevant here, is that the growth in transitional justice mechanisms adopts the very same approach, whereby the nature of redress will depend on the context in which redress is sought. The UN Office of the High Commissioner for Human Rights, in seeking to 'provide practical guidance to field missions and transitional administrations in critical transitional justice' stated clearly that it is 'imperative … to carefully consider the particular rule of law and justice needs in each host country'.[461]

5 State accountability is sought on the basis of a norm's substance, not its *jus cogens* status

The *jus cogens* status of a norm had little direct bearing, in the case studies undertaken here, on whether states responded when such norms were breached. That is not to say that the content of the norm was irrelevant; rather, that any express, formal recognition of the norm as *jus cogens*, for example by the ILC or before one of the international courts, was incidental. The fact that juridical support for a broader concept of answerability than is currently provided for under public international law is evidenced by the international courts, international organisations and academic scholars referring to *jus cogens* confirms that the concept of *jus cogens* is not superfluous to this discussion. Indeed, it was argued that it is the idea that a body of norms exists to protect the interests of the international community as a whole, and which must therefore be maintained, that has been the catalyst for an increasing state accountability practice – *jus cogens* was the tool used here to rationalise and articulate that phenomenon.

The case studies relied on the definition of *jus cogens* norms given by the ILC, rather than advancing a novel normative construct or attempting to resolve any of the debates as to either the content or source of such norms. Furthermore, it was noted in Chapter 3 that the reader did not need to agree with the notion of *jus cogens* norms in order to follow the argument being made because an examination of state accountability in practice could in fact help prove or disprove existence, provided it was established that the response was motivated out of recognition that the breached norm was *jus cogens*. The fact that the strongest evidence of state accountability in practice was also where the relevant norm is listed by the ILC as *jus cogens* is not the same as arguing that accountability was only sought because the norm was recognised as *jus cogens*. Indeed, it is argued that formal recognition that the relevant norm was *jus cogens* has had little impact in terms of state practice and that there have been many motives for responding, as was probably the case

461 'Report of the Secretary General on the Rule of Law and Transitional Justice in Conflict and Post-Conflict Societies' UN Doc S/2004/616 (2004) para 14.

in the rapid reaction by the Security Council to Iraq's invasion of Kuwait that was arguably due, even in part, to the significant interest in protecting Kuwait's oil and petroleum resources.[462] Where states have responded to large-scale human rights breaches and thus sought to protect the interests of more than just states, it has usually been without express regard to the strict *jus cogens* designation of the norm that was breached. Thus, for example, the terms 'peremptory' or *jus cogens* norm do not appear in either General Assembly Resolution 3314 that defined aggression or the Apartheid Convention but there was a significant response by states to breaches of both prohibitions. Indeed, in the case of the Armenian massacres, it seemed that determining that it was a specific norm that was breached appeared to hinder rather than assist the pursuit of accountability.

6 Characteristics of state accountability

Relying on a combination of Foucauldian methodology, juridical contemplation and state practice, this discussion has identified a concept of state accountability and has argued that it is evolving so that states are made to answer when they breach public international law. Specifically, state accountability is not the same as state responsibility, collective security or criminal state responsibility, although it was argued that the former two doctrines may also be a means for holding states accountable. State accountability does not have normative standing and the indeterminate nature of the concept has been noted from the outset. However, three characteristics have emerged from the discussion that give some clarity to the concept's current form.

6.1 A mix of motivations

In the majority of the case studies, there was no evidence that the party that determined liability and imposed redress, usually the UN, was expressly seeking to hold the state in question accountable. The nebulous nature of the concept makes it difficult to articulate at a theoretical level, let alone in practice. Therefore, it is most likely that in practice the objective of state accountability will either be unintended (so that it could be the maintenance of international security in the Middle East that was sought); implied (so that the stated goal was compensation for the victims of persecution by the Soviet regime or rehabilitation of the indigenous population); or incidental (so that the aim was to bring the policy of apartheid to an end).

462 H. Elnajjar, 'Oil Interests and the US Invasion of Iraq' Paper Presented at the Annual Conference of the American Sociological Association (2009) available at http://www.allacademic.com/meta/p21288_index.html.

6.2 A mix of accountability seekers

Unlike collective security, which is principally the domain of the Security Council, and the state responsibility doctrine, which resolves inter-state disputes, state accountability is the concern of all members of the international community. The General Assembly may provide the most credible determination of a state's liability, owing to its concentration of state representation. However, it has been seen that the general public, international organisations and individual states are all influential in requiring states to answer when they are perceived to have breached public international law. This was illustrated when a link was made between international and domestic criticism of the US's detention facilities in Guantánamo Bay, Cuba and the executive order signed by President Obama in January 2009 for closure of the facility by 2010.[463] The only caveat, in terms of determining liability, which arises out of pragmatism, is that some sort of safeguard is required to prevent a concept of state accountability from being abused in the same way that President D'Escoto of the UN General Assembly considered to have occurred with the R2P doctrine.[464] To avoid the concept of state accountability from being brought into disrepute, it is submitted that states should not be allowed to make a determination of liability unilaterally – or, as was the case of Australia, any unilateral determination should be subject to international scrutiny. Ideally, a collective determination system is needed. The logistics involved in formally establishing such a determination mechanism would be significant, and were noted by Special Rapporteur James Crawford as prohibitive in the context of codifying the state responsibility doctrine.[465] Furthermore, the dangers of overly bureaucratising the process of accountability have been recognised above. Yet it is argued here that, based on sufficient evidence in the representative case studies, the UN General Assembly and the UN Security Council are able to fulfil this function when the political will exists and therefore what is required is a stronger commitment to state accountability rather than a greater range of tools with which to implement the concept.

6.3 A mix of responses

Not only is the concept of state accountability legal, political and moral in nature but so too are the forms of redress that may be used. The case studies highlighted a range of responses. These include the more traditional responses when states breach public international law, such as the forms of reparation when a state's

463 'Executive Order: Review and Disposition of Individuals Detained at the Guantánamo Bay Naval Base and Closure of Detention Facilities' Section 2 (2009). Emphasis added.

464 'Statement of the President of the UN General Assembly at the Opening of the Thematic Dialogue of the General Assembly on the Responsibility to Protect' (2009) available at http://www.un.org/ga/president/63/statements/openingr2p230709.shtml.

465 'Third Report of the Special Rapporteur, James Crawford' UN Doc A/CN.4/507/Adds 4 (2000) para 372.

responsibility is engaged, the application of collective security and the use of means, both involving and not involving force, under Articles 41 and 42 of the UN Charter. Non-traditional means of redress were also identified through the application of the interpretive framework including criticism and condemnation as a form of 'reputational accountability'[466] (in encouraging Australia to offer a national apology) and stigmatisation, sporting sanctions (as imposed on South Africa) and political isolation (such as the case of China at the UN after it assisted North Korea). Other mechanisms, which did not feature as strongly in the case studies, include the use of Universal Peer Review and Human Rights Council monitoring, as well as the criminal trials of individual state leaders. It is the cumulative effect of the redress imposed on a state that establishes, first, that the response is more than it would be if it were the state's responsibility that had been engaged; second, that the gravity of breaching what is recognised as a *jus cogens* norm is acknowledged; and, ultimately, that the state was accountable.

7 Moving from *lex feranda* to *lex lata*?

Impunity is the unavailability of redress under international law. It is therefore inappropriate to talk about impunity when states breach *jus cogens*, because it has been shown here that a practice exists of holding states accountable. A more accurate description would add the appropriate caveats, which are that the practice of accountability is *ad hoc* and that the nature of redress is not always legal. There is little doubt that public international law has undergone radical change in the past century but one development that has yet to crystallise as a legal principle is a broader conception of state accountability. However, the recognition, for example, of a category of norms that are sometimes described as *jus cogens* indicates that the interests of more than merely states have proven influential in both the development and the implementation of public international law. Furthermore, if state accountability is understood as arising from sometimes legal and – probably in part – political or even moral redress, which recognises that the breach had the potential to affect the interests of the entire international community, then there is both state practice and juridical indicators signalling that the concept is evolving into a legal principle.

There are costs involved if state accountability evolves as a legal norm. Therefore, instead of 'making legal culture more dense'[467] by arguing for normative recognition of state accountability at this time, this discussion sought to deconstruct what can best be described as the current accountability epoch, and reconstruct state accountability as an interpretive framework that could be used to identify any opportunities within the existing framework of international law and politics for

466 R. Keohane, 'The Concept of Accountability in World Politics and the Use of Force' (2003) 24 *Michigan Journal of International Law* 1121.

467 D. Kennedy, 'Contestation of the Outcomes and Procedures of the Existing Legal Regime' (2003) *Leiden Journal of International Law* 915.

ensuring that states are made to answer for breaching *jus cogens* norms. In short, the problem was how to ensure states are made to answer when they breach *jus cogens* norms. The argument that was made here is that the opportunity exists to conceive a broader response than that envisaged under public international law at this time but which is nevertheless compatible with the existing legal framework. The proposed solution is for state accountability to evolve as *lex feranda* with the potential that one day it is recognised as *lex lata.*

Bibliography

Articles

Balint, J. 'The Place of Addressing Internal Regime Conflicts' (1996) 59 *Law and Contemporary Problems* 103.

Bassiouni, M. 'International Crimes: *Jus Cogens* and *Obligatio Erga Omnes*' (1996) 59 *Law and Contemporary Problems* 63.

Bassiouni, M. 'Searching for Peace and Achieving Justice: The Need for Accountability' (1996) 59 *Law and Contemporary Problems* 9.

Bassiouni, C. and Derby, D. 'Final Report on the Establishment of and International Criminal Court for the Implementation of the Apartheid Convention and Other Relevant International Instruments' (1981) 9 *Hofstra Law Review* 523.

Beres, L. and Tsiddon-Chatto, Y. 'Reconsidering Israel's Destruction of Iraq's Osiraq Nuclear Reactor' (1995) 9 *Temple International and Comparative Law Journal* 437.

Berman, P. 'Seeing Beyond the Limits of International Law' (2006) 84 *Texas Law Review* 1265.

Bilinsky, Y. 'Was the Ukrainian Famine of 1932–1933 Genocide?' (1999) 1 *Journal of Genocide Research* 147.

Bodansky, D and Crook, J. 'The ILC's State Responsibility Articles: The ILC and State Responsibility' (2002) 96 *American Journal of International Law* 773.

Borneman, J. 'Events of Closure, Rites of Repetition: Modes of Accountability' *Conference on Settling Accounts: Truth, Justice and Redress in Post-Conflict Societies* (Harvard University, 2004).

Borneman, J. 'Public Apologies as Performative Redress' (2005) 25 *Johns Hopkins SAIS Review of International Affairs* 53.

Brown Weiss, E. 'Invoking State Responsibility in the Twenty-First Century (Symposium: The ILC's State Responsibility Articles)' (2002) 96 *American Journal of International Law* 798.

Brown Weiss, E. 'Bottom Up Accountability' (2007) 37 *Environmental Policy and Law* 259.

Brownlie, I. 'General Course on Public International Law' (1995) *Hague Recueil* 9.

Charney, J. 'Third State Remedies in International Law (1989) 10(1) *Michigan Journal of International Law* 57.

Charney, J. 'Universal International Law' (1993) 87 *American Journal of International Law* 529.

Christenson, G. 'Jus Cogens: Guarding Interests Fundamental to International Society' (1988) 28 *Virginia Journal of International Law* 585.

Cobbah, J. 'African Values and the Human Rights Debate: An African Perspective' (1997) *Human Rights Quarterly* 323.

Cohen, R. 'How Kofi Annan Rescued Kenya' 55(13) *The New York Review of Books* (August 14, 2008).

Cohen, S. 'State Crimes of Previous Regimes' (1995) 20 *Law and Social Inquiry* 6.
Commission on the Responsibility of the Authors of the War and the Enforcement of Penalties 'Conclusions' (1920) *American Journal of International Law* 95.
Crawford, J. 'The ILC's Articles on Responsibility of States for Internationally Wrongful Acts: A Retrospect (Symposium: The ILC's State Responsibility Articles)' (2002) 96 *The American Journal of International Law* 874.
Crawford, J. and Olleson, S. 'The Continuing Debate on a UN Convention on State Responsibility' (2005) 54 *International and Comparative Law Quarterly* 959.
Dadrian, V. 'The Turkish Military Tribunal's Prosecution of the Authors of the American Genocide: Four Major Court-Martial Series' (1997) 11 *Holocaust and Genocide Studies* 28.
Dadrian, V. 'The Historical and Legal Interconnections Between the Armenian Genocide and the Jewish Holocaust: From Impunity to Retributive Justice' (1998) 23 *Yale Journal of International Law* 503.
D'Amato, A. 'Israel's Air Strike Upon the Iraqi Nuclear Reactor' (1983) 77 *American Journal of International Law* 584.
D'Amato, A. 'Israel's Air Strike Against the Osiraq Reactor: A Retrospective' (1996) 10 *Temple International and Comparative Law Journal* 259.
De Hoogh, A. 'The Relationship Between *Jus Cogens*, Obligations *Erga Omnes* and International Crimes: Peremptory Norms in Perspective' (1991) 42 *Austrian Journal of Public and International Law* 183.
Dupuy, P. 'A General Stocktaking of the Connections Between the Multilateral Dimension of Obligations and Codification of the Law of Responsibility' (2002) 13 *European Journal of International Law* 1053.
El-Khodary, T. and Tavernise, S. 'In the Fog of Urban War, Crimes and Ethics Blur' (25 January 2009) *New York Times.*
Fitzmaurice, G. 'The Law and Procedure of the International Court of Justice' (1953) *British Yearbook of International Law* 1.
Fitzmaurice, G. 'The General Principles of International Law Considered from the Standpoint of the Rule of Law' (1957) 92 *Recueil des Cours de L'Académie de Droit International de La Hague.*
'Full Text of Kevin Rudd's Speech' *Herald Sun* (2008).
Gibney, M. and Roxstrom E. 'The Status of State Apologies' (2001) 23 *Human Rights Quarterly* 911.
Gilbert, G. 'The Criminal Responsibility of States' (1990) 2 *International and Comparative Law Quarterly* 345.
Grey, C. 'The Choice Between Restitution and Compensation (1999) 10 *European Journal of International Law* 413.
Guevara, C. (Cuban representative to UN) 'Colonialism is Doomed' *19th General Assembly of the United Nations* (1964).
Hall, R. 'The Lusaka Manifesto' (1970) 69 *African Affairs* 179.
Kaplan, M.'Using Collective Interests to Ensure Human Rights: An Analysis of the Articles of State Responsibility' (2004) 79 *New York University Law Review* 1902.
Keohane, R. 'The Concept of Accountability in World Politics and the Use of Force' (2003) 24 *Michigan Journal of International Law* 1121.
Kielsgard, M. 'Restorative Justice for The Armenians, Resolved: It's The Least We Can Do' (2008) *Connecticut Journal of International Law* 1.
Kirgis, F. 'Custom on a Sliding Scale' (1987) 81 *American Journal of International Law* 146.
Koh, H. 'Transnational Legal Process' (1996) 75 *Nebraska Law Review* 181.

Koskenniemi, M. 'The Fate of Public International Law: Between Technique and Politics' (2007) 70 *The Modern Law Review*.

Koskenniemi, M. 'The Politics of International Law' (1990) 1 *European Journal of International Law* 4.

Kozyrev, A. 'Russia: A Chance for Survival' (1992) 71 *Foreign Affairs* 11.

Krotee, M. 'Apartheid and Sport: South Africa Revisited' (1988) *Sociology of Sport Journal* 125.

Lowe, V. 'The Iraq Crisis: What Now?' (2003) 52 *International and Comparative Law Quarterly* 859.

Meron, T. 'On a Hierarchy of International Human Rights' (1986) 80 *American Journal of International Law* 1.

Milanovic, M. 'State Responsibility for Genocide: A Follow-Up' (2007) 18 *European Journal of International Law* 669.

Mullerson, R. 'The Continuity and Succession of States, by Reference to the Former USSR and Yugoslavia' (1993) 42 *International and Comparative Law Quarterly* 473.

Myers, F. 'Harold MacMillan's "Winds of Change" Speech: A Case Study in the Rhetoric of Policy Change' (2000) 3 *Rhetoric & Public Affairs* 555.

Nagan, W. and Hammer, C. 'The Changing Character of Sovereignty in International Law and International Relations' (2004) 43 *Columbia Journal of Transnational Law* 141.

Naqi, S. 'The Process of Accountability' (2008) *International Business Management* 1.

Nash, M. 'Contemporary Practice of the United States Relation to International Law' (1996) 90 *American Journal of International Law* 442.

Olleson, S. and Crawford, J. 'The Continuing Debate on a UN Convention on State Responsibility' (2005) 54 *International and Comparative Law Quarterly* 959.

Parker, K. and Neylon, L. 'Jus Cogens: Compelling the Law of Human Rights' (1989) 12 *Hastings International and Comparative Law Review* 411.

Pollock, F. 'Locke's Theory of the State' (1904) 2 *Proceedings of the British Academy* 237.

Rezie, R. 'The Ukrainian Constitution: Interpretation of the Citizens' Rights Provisions' (1999) 31 *Case Western Reserve Journal of International Law* 169.

Schabas, W. 'United States Hostility to the ICC: It's All About the Security Council' (2004) 15 *European Journal of International Law* 701.

Schabas, W. 'Darfur and the "Odious Scourge": The Commission of Inquiry's Finding on Genocide' (2005) 27 *Leiden Journal of International Law* 871.

Schachter, O. 'International Law in Theory and Practice' (1982) *Recueil des Cours de L'Académie de Droit International de La Hague* 175.

Schwarzenberger, G. 'The Forms of Sovereignty' (1957) 10 *Current Legal Problems* 264.

Schwelb, E. 'Some Aspects of International *Jus Cogens* as Formulated by the International Law Commission' (1967) 61 *American Journal of International Law* 946.

Serbyn, R. 'Lemkin on Genocide of Nations' (2009) *Journal of International Criminal Justice* 123.

Siedlecka, E. 'Ombudsman to Join Katyń Claims in Strasbourg Court' *Gazeta Wyborcza* (2008).

Simma, B. and Alston, P. 'The Sources of Human Rights Law: Custom, Jus Cogens and General Principles' (1988) 12 *Australian Yearbook of International Law* 82.

Slim, H. 'By What Authority? The Legitimacy of Accountability and NGOs' (2002) *Journal of Humanitarian Assistance*.

Tomuschat, C. 'Die internationale Gemeinschaft' (1995) 33 *Archiv des Völkerrechts* 1.

Tomuschat, C. 'General Principles of international Law' (1999) *Recueil des Cours de L'Académie de Droit International de La Hague*.

Tomuschat, C. 'Darfur – Compensation for the Victims' (2005) *Journal of International Criminal Justice* 579.

Tunkin, G. 'International Law in the International System' (1975) 147 *Recueil des Cours de L'Académie de Droit International de La Hague*.

UK Materials on International Law (1991) 62 *British Yearbook of International Law*.

UK Materials on International Law (1993) 63 *British Yearbook of International Law*.

Velayutham, S. 'The Discharge of Accountability and Responsibility in Asian Societies: An Evaluation' (1999) 27 *Asian Profile* 361.

Vermeer-Kunzli, A. 'A Matter of Interest: Diplomatic Protection and State Responsibility *Erga Omnes*' (2007) *International and Comparative Law Quarterly* 553.

Verdross, A. 'Forbidden Treaties in International Law' (1937) 31 *American Journal of International Law* 571.

Verdross, A. 'Jus Dispositivism and Jus Cogens in International Law' (1966) 60 *American Journal of International Law* 55.

Von Sternberg, M. 'A Comparison of the Yugoslavian and Rwandan War Crimes Tribunals: Universal Jurisdiction and the "Elementary Dictates of Humanity"' (1996) *Brooklyn Journal of International Law* 110.

Weil, P. 'Towards Relative Normativity in International Law' (1983) 77 *American Journal of International Law* 412.

Weil, P. 'Le Droit International en Quête de Son Identité' (1992) 237 *Recueil des Cours de L'Académie de Droit International de La Hague*.

Western, J 'A Divided City: Cape Town' (2002) 21 *Political Geography* 711.

Wouters, J. 'Perspectives for *International Law* in the Twenty-First Century: *Chaos* or a World Legal Order' (2000) *Ethical Perspectives* 1.

Yasuaki, O. 'International Law In and With International Politics: The Functions of International Law in International Society' (2003) 14 *European Journal of International Law* 105.

Books

Akehurst, M. *Akehurst's Modern Introduction to International Law* (7th edn) (London: Routledge, 1997).

Alston, P. (ed.) *Human Rights Law* (Aldershot: Dartmouth, 1996).

Bernauer, T. and Carrette, J. (eds) *Michel Foucault and Theology: The Politics of Religious Experience* (Aldershot: Ashgate, 2004).

Blay, S. *The Unification of Germany in International and Domestic Law* (Atlanta: Rodopi, 1997).

Brownlie, I. *International Law and the Use of Force by States* (Oxford: Clarendon Press, 1963).

Brownlie, I. *State Responsibility* (Oxford: Clarendon Press, 1983).

Bruck, O. *Les Sanctions en Droit International* (Paris: A. Pedone, 1933).

Cassese, A. *International Law* (Oxford: Oxford University Press, 2005).

Charlesworth, H. and Chinkin, C. *The Boundaries of International Law* (Manchester: Manchester University Press, 2000).

Christie, M. F. *Aboriginal People in Colonial Victoria, 1835–1886* (Sydney: Sydney University Press, 1979).

Churchill, W. *The World Crisis, 1911–1918* (London: Free Press, 2005).

Conquest, R. *The Harvest of Sorrow: Soviet Collectivization and the Terror-Famine* (New York: Oxford University Press, 1986).

Crawford, J. *The International Law Commission's Articles on State Responsibility: Introduction, Text and Commentaries* (Cambridge: Cambridge University Press, 2002).

Crawford, J. *The Creation of States* (Oxford: Oxford University Press, 2006).

Dadrian, V. *The History of The Armenian Genocide* (6th edn) (Providence: Berghan Books, 1995).

Dinstein, Y. (ed.) *International Law at a Time of Perplexity – Essays in Honour of Shabtai Rosenne* (Dordrecht: Martinus Nijhoff Publishers, 1989).

- Shaw, M. 'Genocide and International Law' 818.

Doebbler, C. *International Human Rights Law: Cases and Materials* (Washington: CD Publishing, 2004).

Du Pré, R H. *Separate but Unequal – The 'Coloured' People of South Africa – A Political History* (Johannesburg: Jonathan Ball Publishers, 1994).

Farrall, J. *United Nations Sanctions and the Rule of Law* (Cambridge: Cambridge University Press, 2007).

Fitzmaurice, M. (ed.) *Issues of State Responsibility Before International Judicial Institutions* (Oregon: Hart Publishing, 2004).

- Evans, M. 'State Responsibility and the European Court of Human Rights' 139.

Foucault, M. *Power/Knowledge: Selected Interviews* (Sussex: Harvester Press, 1980).

Foucault, M. *Discipline and Punish: The Birth of the Prison* (New York: Vintage Books, 1995).

Germain, R. and Kenny, M. (eds) *The Idea of Global Civil Society: Politics and Ethics in a Globalizing Era* (UK: Routledge, 2005).

- Amoore, L. and Langley, P. 'Global Civil Society and Global Governmentality'.

Hammer, L. *A Foucauldian Approach to International Law: Descriptive Thoughts for Normative Issues* (London: Ashgate, 2007).

Jelin, E. *State Repression and the Labours of Memory* (Minneapolis: University of Minnesota Press, 2003).

Jorgensen, N. *The Responsibility of States for International Crimes* (Oxford: Oxford University Press, 2003).

Kelsen, H. (trans Trevino, J.) *General Theory of Law and State* (Cambridge: Harvard University Press, 2005).

Kelsen, H. *Peace Through Law* (Chapel Hill: University of North Carolina Press, 1944).

Kelsen, H. (trans Knight, M.) *Pure Theory of Law* (New Jersey: Law Book Exchange Ltd, 2002).

Kelly, M. (ed.) *Critique and Power: Recasting the Foucault/Habermas Debate* (Cambridge: MIT Press, 2004).

- McCarthy, T. 'The Critique of Impure Reason: Foucault and the Frankfurt School' 243.

Kleffner, J. *Complementarity in the Rome Statute and National Criminal Jurisdictions* (Oxford: Oxford University Press, 2008).

Koskenniemi, M. *From Apology to Utopia – The Structure of International Legal Argument* (Cambridge: Cambridge University Press, 2006).

Langer, W. *The Diplomacy of Imperialism 1890–1902* (New York: Knopf, 1935).

Lauterpacht, H. *The Function of Law in the International Community* (Oxford: Clarendon Press, 1933).

Luard, E. *A History of the United Nations* (London: Palgrave Macmillan, 1982).

McAuley, M. *Soviet Politics 1917–1991* (Oxford: Oxford University Press, 1992).

Morgenthau, H. *Ambassador Morgenthau's Story* (New York: Doubleday Page, 1919).

Oppenheim, L. *International Law: A Treatise* (8th edn) (London: Longmans, 1955).

Oppenheim, L. and Roxburgh, R. (eds.) *International Law – A Treatise* (3rd edn) (London: Longmans, 1920).

Paulus, A. *Die internationale Gemeinschaft im Völkerrecht* (Munich: Beck, 2000).

Randelzhofer, A. and Tomuschat, C. (eds) *State Responsibility and the Individual* (Great Britain: Kluwer Law International, 1999).

- Tomuschat, C. 'Individual Reparation Claims in Instances of Grave Human Rights Violations: The Position Under General International Law' 1.

Ratner, S. and Abrams, J. *Accountability for Human Rights Atrocities in International Law* (2nd edn) (Oxford: Oxford University Press, 2001).
Ratner, S. and Abrams, J. *Accountability for Human Rights Atrocities in International Law* (3rd edn) (Oxford: Oxford University Press, 2009).
Röling, B. and Cassese, A. *The Tokyo Trial and Beyond: Reflections of a Peacemonger* (Cambridge: Polity Press, 1994).
Sakwa, R. *The Rise and Fall of the Soviet Union, 1917–1991* (UK: Routledge, 1999).
Sanford, G. *Katyń and the Soviet Massacre of 1940: Truth, Justice and Memory* (London: Routledge, 2005).
Sarooshi, D. *International Organizations and Their Exercise of Sovereign Powers* (Oxford: Oxford University Press, 2005).
Service, R. *The History of Twentieth Century Russia* (New York: Penguin, 1998).
Sethi, P. and Williams, O. *Economic Imperatives and Ethical Values in Global Business: The South African Experience* (USA: Kluwer, 2000).
Shaw, M. *International Law* (6th edn) (Cambridge: Cambridge University Press, 2008).
Smith, B. (ed.) *The American Road to Nuremberg: The Documentary Record 1944–1945* (New York: Basic Books, 1982).
Sztucki, J. *Jus Cogens and the Vienna Convention on the Law of Treaties* (Vienna: Springer-Verlag, 1974).
Taylor, T. 'Guilt, Responsibility and the Third Reich' *Churchill College Overseas Fellowship Lectures* (1970).
Tomushcat, C. and Thouvenin, J-M. (eds) *The Fundamental Rules of the International Legal Order* (Boston: Martinus Nijhoff Publishers, 2006).
- Czalinski, W. '*Jus Cogens* and the Law of Treaties' 83.
- Hillgruber, C. 'The Right of Third States to Take Countermeasures' 265.
- Kadelbach, S. '*Jus Cogens*, Obligations *Erga Omnes* and Other Rules – The Identification of Fundamental Norms' 1.
- Schmahl, S. 'An Example of *Jus Cogens*: The Status of Prisoners of War' 41.
- Talmon, S. 'An Obligation Without Real Substance?'98.
- Tomuschat, C. 'Concluding Observations' 425.

Trask, R. *The United States Response to the Turkish Nationalism and Reform 1914–1939* (Minneapolis: University of Minnesota Press, 1971).
Viscount Bryce, J. and Toynbee, A. *The Treatment of Armenians in the Ottoman Empire* (London, HMSO, 1916).
Weber, M. *The Profession and Vocation of Politics (1919 Lecture)* (Cambridge: Cambridge University Press, 1994).
Wellens, K. (ed.) *International Law: Theory and Practice – Essays in Honour of Eric Suy* (The Hague, Martinus Nijhoff, 1998):
- Graefrath, B. 'International Crimes and Collective Security' 237.

Wolfrum, R. and Deutsch, U. (eds) *The European Court of Human Rights Overwhelmed by Applications: The Problems and Possible Solutions'* (Berlin: Springer-Verlag, 2009):
- Tomuschat, C. 'The European Court of Human Rights Overwhelmed by Applications: Problems and Possible Solutions' 1.

Documents

General Assembly Resolutions

'Additional Measures to be Employed to Meet the Aggression in Korea' General Assembly Resolution 500 (1950).

'Affirmation of the Principles of International Law Recognised by the Charter of the Nuremberg Tribunal' General Assembly Resolution 95 (I) (1946).

'Armed Israeli Aggression Against the Iraqi Nuclear Installations' General Assembly Resolution 36/27 (1981).

'Armed Israeli Aggression Against the Iraqi Nuclear Installations' General Assembly Resolution 38/9 (1983).

'Armed Israeli Aggression Against the Iraqi Nuclear Installations' General Assembly Resolution 40/6 (1985).

'Criminal Accountability of UN Officials and Experts on Mission' General Assembly Resolution 62/63 (2008).

'Definition of Aggression' General Assembly Resolution 3314 (1974).

'Follow-up to the Report of the United Nations Fact-Finding Mission on the Gaza Conflict' General Assembly Resolution 64/253 (2010).

'Illegal Israeli Actions in Occupied East Jerusalem and the Rest of the Occupied Palestinian Territory' General Assembly Resolution 10/14 (2003).

'Intervention of the Central People's Government of the People's Republic of China in Korea' General Assembly Resolution 498 (1951).

'Israeli Practices Affecting the Human Rights of the Palestinian People in the Occupied Palestinian Territory, Including East Jerusalem' General Assembly Resolution 63/98 (1998).

'Policies of Apartheid of the Government of South Africa' General Assembly Resolution 1761 (1962).

'Policies of Apartheid of the Government of South Africa' General Assembly Resolution 37/69 (1982).

'Problem of the Independence of Korea' General Assembly Resolution 376 (1950).

'Question of Race Conflict in South Africa Resulting From Policies of Apartheid of the Government of the Union of South Africa' General Assembly Resolution 721 (1953).

'Question of Race Conflict in South Africa Resulting From Policies of Apartheid of the Government of the Union of South Africa' General Assembly Resolution 820 (1954).

'Question of Race Conflict in South Africa Resulting From Policies of Apartheid of the Government of the Union of South Africa' General Assembly Resolution 917 (1954).

'Question of Race Conflict in South Africa Resulting From Policies of Apartheid of the Government of the Union of South Africa' General Assembly Resolution 1248 (1958).

'Question of Race Conflict in South Africa Resulting From Policies of Apartheid of the Government of the Union of South Africa' General Assembly Resolution 1598 (1961).

'Question of the Representation of China in the General Assembly' General Assembly Resolution 490 (1950).

'Question of the Representation of China in the General Assembly' General Assembly Resolution 501 (1951).

'Relationship Between the UN and South Africa' General Assembly Resolution 3207 (1974).

'Relief and Rehabilitation' General Assembly Resolution 410 (1950).

'Report to the Security Council' General Assembly Resolution 3322 (1974).

'Representation of China in the UN' General Assembly Resolution 1668 (1961).

'Request for the Codification of Principles of International Law Governing State Responsibility' General Assembly Resolution 799 (VIII) (1953).

'Responsibility of State for Internationally Wrongful Acts' General Assembly Resolution 59/35 (2004).

'Restoration of the Lawful Rights of the People's Republic of China in the United Nations' General Assembly Resolution 2758 (1971).

'Situation of Human Rights in Kuwait Under Iraqi Occupation' General Assembly Resolution 46/135 (1991).
'Situation of Human Rights in Occupied Kuwait' General Assembly Resolution 45/170 (1990).

Documents of the International Courts

'Annual Report of the ICTY' (2008) UN Doc A/63/210-S/2008/515.
Preparatory Commission for the International Criminal Court 'Elements of the Crimes' UN Doc PCNICC/2000/INF3/Add.2 (2000).

Documents of the International Law Commission

'Conclusions of the Work of the Study Group on the Fragmentation of International Law: Difficulties Arising from the Diversification and Expansion of International Law' UN Doc A/61/10 (2006).
'Conference on the Law of Treaties' UN Doc A/CONF/39/11/Add.2 (1968).
'Draft Articles on the Responsibility of States for Internationally Wrongful Acts' UN Doc A/Res/56/83 (2001).
International Law Commission Yearbook of the International Law Commission (1963).
International Law Commission Yearbook of the International Law Commission (1966) Volume II.
International Law Commission Yearbook of the International Law Commission (1976) Volume II.
International Law Commission Yearbook of the International Law Commission (1983) Volume II.
International Law Commission Yearbook of the International Law Commission (1998) Volume II.
'Report of the International Law Commission on the Work of its Fifty-Third Session' UN Doc A/56/10 (2001).
'Seventh Report of the Special Rapporteur Gaetano Arangio-Ruiz' UN Doc A/CN.4/469 (1995).
'Third Report of the Special Rapporteur, James Crawford' UN Doc A/CN.4/507/Adds 4 (2000).

Other UN Documents

'Comments Under Article 19' UN Doc A/CN.4/488.
'Concluding Observations for Canada' UN Doc CERD/C/CAN/CO/18 (2007).
'Concluding Observations for the United States' UN Doc CERD/C/USA/CO/6 (2007).
Concluding Observations by the Committee on the Elimination of Racial Discrimination: Australia CERD/C/304/Add.101 (2000).
'Concluding Observations of the Human Rights Committee: Consideration of Reports Submitted by States Parties Under Article 40 of the Covenant, United States of America' UN Doc CCPR/C/USA/CO/3 (2006).
'Final Act of the International Conference of Human Rights' UN Doc E/68/XIV.2 (1968).
'Fourth Periodic of the Russian Federation Report' UN Doc CCPR/C/SR.1426 (1995).

'General Comment No 19: The Right to Social Security Under Article 9' UN Doc E/C.12/GC/19 (2008).
'Iraqi Aggression and the Continued Occupation of Kuwait in Flagrant Violation of the Charter of the United Nations' UN Doc 45/455 (1990).
'Letter Dated 26 March 2007 from the Secretary-General Addressed to the President of the Security Council' UN Doc S/2007/168 (2007).
Manifesto on Southern Africa UN Doc A/7754 (1969).
'Progress Report' UN Doc A/C.6/31/SR (1976).
'Remarks at the Opening of the 2009 Session of the Committee on the Exercise of the Inalienable Rights of the Palestinian People' UN Doc SG/SM/12097 GA/PAL/112 (2009).
'Report of the United Nations Fact-Finding Mission on the Gaza Conflict' UN Doc A/HRC/12/48 (2009).
'Second Report by the Russian Federation' UN Doc CAT/C/17/Add.15 (1996).
'Thirteenth Periodic Report Under Article 9 Submitted by the Russian Federation Addendum' UN Doc CERD/C/263/Add.9 (1995).

Other International Documents – Americas

'Settlement of Claim between Canada and the Union of Soviet Socialist Republics for Damage Caused by Cosmos 954' (2 April 1981).
'Executive Order: Review and Disposition of Individuals Detained at the Guantánamo Bay Naval Base and Closure of Detention Facilities' (2009).
Senate Resolution 106 'Calling on the President to Ensure that the Foreign Policy of the United States Reflects Appropriate Understanding and Sensitivity Concerning Issues Related to Human Rights, Ethnic Cleansing, and Genocide Documented in the United States Record Relating to the Armenian Genocide' (2007).

Other International Documents – Europe

'Bulletin of the European Communities' (1980) 13(4).
'Commemoration of the Holodomor, the Ukraine Artificial Famine (1932-1933)' European Parliament Resolution (2008).
'Commission Regulation of 26 January 2009 Amending Council Regulation No 314/2004 Concerning Certain Restrictive Measures in Respect of Zimbabwe' EC Doc No 77/2009 (2009).
'Conclusion on Zimbabwe' Council of the European Union (22 July 2008).
'Conclusion on Zimbabwe' Council of the European Union (15 September 2008).
'Council Decision of 22 July 2008 Implementing Common Position 2004/161/CFSP Renewing Restrictive Measures Against Zimbabwe' EC Doc 2008/605/CFSP (2008).
'Correspondence between the Chairman of the Council of Ministers of the USSR and the Presidents of the USA and the Prime Ministers of Great Britain during the Great Patriotic War of 1941 - 1945' Document No.151 (Moscow: Progress Publishers, 1953).
'Draft Opinion on the International Legal Obligations of Council of Europe Member States in Respect of Secret Detention Facilities and Inter-State Transport Of Detainees' EC Opinion No 363/2005 EC Doc No CDL-DI 001 Rev (2006).
'European Conscience and Totalitarianism' Council of Europe Parliamentary Assembly Resolution 213 (2009).

'European Parliament Resolution on the Alleged Use of European Countries by the CIA for the Transportation and Illegal Detention of Prisoners' Doc 0045 (2009)
'Need For International Condemnation of Crimes of Totalitarian Communist Regimes' Council of Europe Parliamentary Assembly Resolution 1481 (2006).
'Report on Turkey's Progress Towards Accession' Council of Europe Parliament Doc No 2006/2118 (2006).
'Report on Turkey's Progress Towards Accession' Council of Europe Parliament Doc No 2006/1390 (2007).
'Resolution on a Political Solution to the Armenian Question' Council of Europe Parliamentary Assembly (1987).
'Resolution on the Alleged Use of European Countries by the CIA for the Transportation and Illegal Detention of Prisoners' Council of Europe Parliamentary Assembly (2009).
'Resolution on the Situation in the Gaza Strip' Council of Europe Parliamentary Assembly (2008).

South Africa

South African Truth and Reconciliation Commission 'Conclusions' (1999).

Reports

'Final Report of the Special Rapporteur on the Right to Restitution, Compensation and Rehabilitation for Victims of Gross Human Rights Violations' UN Doc E/CN.4/2000/62 (2000).
'Final Report into the 1932-33 Famine in the Ukraine' International Commission of Inquiry (1990).
'Forgotten Voices: A Population Based Study on Attitudes About Peace and Justice in Northern Uganda' International Centre for Transitional Justice and the Human Rights Centre, University of California Berkeley (2005).
'Fourth Report (from the) Foreign Affairs Committee: Session 1989–90: German Unification: Some Immediate Issues' (HMSO: London, 1990).
'History of the United Nations War Crimes Commission and the Development of the Laws of War' UN War Crimes Commission Report (London: HMSO, 1948).
Human Rights and Equal Opportunity Commission, Commonwealth of Australia *Bringing Them Home: Report of the National Inquiry into the Separation of Aboriginal and Torres Strait Islander Children from Their Families* (1997).
'Promotion and Protection of Human Rights Report of the Independent Expert to Update the Set of Principles to Combat Impunity, Diane Orentlicher: Updated Set of Principles for the Protection and Promotion of Human Rights Through Action to Combat Impunity' UN Doc E/CN.4/2005/102/Add.1 (2005).
'Question of the Impunity of Perpetrators of Human Rights Violations (Civil And Political) Revised Final Report Prepared By Mr Joinet Pursuant To Sub-Commission Decision 1996/119' UN Doc E/CN.4/Sub.2/1997/20/Rev.1 (1997).
'Report No 2505 82nd Congress Concerning the Katyń Forest Massacre' Committee on House Administration US House of Representatives Document 100-183 (1952) (Washington: US Government Printing Office, 1988).
'Report of Bassiouni, M. to the Ad Hoc Working Group of Experts for the Commission on Human Rights' UN Doc E/CN.4/1426 (1981).

'Report of Human Rights Council on the Eighth Session' UN Doc A/HRC/8/52 (2008).
'Report of the Human Rights Council on the Promotion and Protection of Human Rights While Countering Terrorism' UN Doc A/HRC/12/22 (2008).
'Report of the Political Affairs Committee Rapporteur Mr Göran Lindblad on the Need for International Condemnation of Crimes of Totalitarian Communist Regimes' European Parliament Doc 10765 (2005).
'Report of the Secretary General on the Rule of Law and Transitional Justice in Conflict and Post-Conflict Societies' UN Doc S/2004/616 (2004).
'Report of the Special Rapporteur on the Situation of Human Rights in the Sudan: Addendum Status of Implementation of the "Compilation of Recommendations of the Experts Group to the Government of The Sudan for the Implementation of Human Rights Council Resolution 4/8" Pursuant to Human Rights Council Resolutions 6/34, 6/35, 7/16, and 9/17' UN Doc A/HRC/11/14/Add.1 (2009).
'Report of the Special Representative of the Secretary-General on the Issue of Human Rights and Transnational Corporations and Other Business Enterprises, John Ruggie: Addendum State Obligations to Provide Access to Remedy For Human Rights Abuses by Third Parties, Including Business: An Overview of International and Regional Provisions, Commentary and Decisions' UN Doc A/HRC/11/13/Add.1 (2009).
'Report of the World Conference for Action Against Apartheid' UN Doc E.77.XIV.2 (1977).
'Report on the Question of the Impunity of Perpetrators of Human Rights Violations' Special Rapporteur Louis Joinet (E/CN.4/Sub.2/1997/20/Rev.1) (2005).
'Revised and Updated Report on the Question of the Prevention and Punishment of the Crime of Genocide' UN Sub-Commission on Prevention of Discrimination and Protection of Minorities UN Doc E/CN.4/Sub.2/1985/6 (1985).
Royal Commission into Aboriginal Deaths in Custody *National Report* (1987–1991).
'Study Concerning the Right to Restitution, Compensation and Rehabilitation for Victims of Gross Violations of Human Rights and Fundamental Freedoms' UN Doc E/CN.4/Sub.2/1993/8 (1993).

Jurisprudence

International Court of Justice – Advisory Opinions.

Advisory Opinion Concerning the Legal Consequences on Construction of a Wall in the Occupied Palestinian Territory ICJ Reports (2004) 82, 98
Advisory Opinion in the Case of the Legality of the Threat or Use of Nuclear Weapons ICJ Reports (1995) 66
Advisory Opinion on Reservations to the Convention on the Prevention and Punishment of the Crime of Genocide ICJ Reports (1951) 20
Advisory Opinion on the Legal Consequences for States of the Continued Presence of South Africa in Namibia (SW Africa) Notwithstanding Security Council Resolution 276 ICJ Reports (1971) 72, 73, 104

International Court of Justice – Contentious Cases

Application of the Convention on the Prevention and Punishment of the Crime of Genocide (Bosnia and Herzegovina v Yugoslavia (Serbia and Montenegro) (Further Requests for the Indication of Provisional Measures) ICJ Reports (1993) 14, 20, 38, 71, 75, 77, 116
Application of the Convention on the Prevention and Punishment of the Crime of Genocide (Bosnia and Herzegovina v Yugoslavia (Serbia and Montenegro) (Initiative to the Court to Reconsider Ex Officio Jurisdiction over Yugoslavia) ICJ Reports (1993) 14, 20, 38, 71, 75, 77, 116

Application of the Convention on the Prevention and Punishment of the Crime of Genocide (Bosnia and Herzegovina v Yugoslavia (Serbia and Montenegro) (Judgment 2007) ICJ Reports (1993) 14, 38, 116
Application of the Convention on the Prevention and Punishment of the Crime of Genocide (Bosnia and Herzegovina v Yugoslavia (Serbia and Montenegro) (Preliminary Objections 1996) ICJ Reports (1993) 20, 71, 75, 77
Asylum Case (Columbia v Peru) (Request for Interpretation of the Judgment of 20 November 1950 in the Asylum Case) ICJ Reports (1950) 121
East Timor (Portugal v Australia) ICJ Reports (1991) 68
Fisheries Jurisdiction Case (UK v Iceland) (Merits) ICJ Reports (1974) 121
Jurisdictional Immunities of the State (Germany v Italy) (Application of the Federal Republic of Germany) ICJ Reports (2008) 19, 31
Military v Paramilitary Activities In and Against Nicaragua (Merits 1986) ICJ Reports (1984) 37, 106
North Sea Continental Cases (Federal Republic of Germany v Denmark; Federal Republic of Germany v Netherlands) (Merits 1969) ICJ Reports (1967) 2, 63
Nuclear Tests Case (Australia v France; New Zealand v France) ICJ Reports (1974) 68
South West Africa Cases (Ethiopia v South Africa; Liberia v South Africa) (Preliminary Objections 1962) ICJ Reports (1960) 46, 68
South West Africa Cases (Ethiopia v South Africa; Liberia v South Africa) (Second Phase 1966) ICJ Reports (1960) 63
Temple of Preah Vihear (Cambodia v Thailand) ICJ Reports (1959) 85
United States Diplomatic and Consular Staff in Tehran ICJ Reports (1979) 80

Permanent Court of International Justice

Factory at Chorzów (Germany v Poland) (Merits) PCIJ Series A No 17 1928 85
Mavrommatis Palestine Concessions Case (Merits) PCIJ Series A No 2 1924 80

International Ad Hoc *Criminal Tribunals*

Prosecutor v Furundzija (Judgment) IT-95-17/I-T (1998) 50, 69
Prosecutor v Kambanda (Sentence) IT-97-28-S (1998) 15
Prosecutor v Karadžić and Mladić (Indictment) IT-95-18-1 (2002) 76
Prosecutor v Kunarac (Judgment) IT-96-23-T 22 (2001) 50
Prosecutor v Kunarac (Appeal) IT-96-23-A (2002) 50
Prosecutor v Tadic (Appeal Judgment) IT-94-1-AR7 (1999) 89

European Court of Human Rights

Aksoy v Turkey European Court of Human Rights (1996) 25
Assenov v Bulgaria European Court of Human Rights (1998) 25
Aydin v Turkey European Court of Human Rights (1997) 25
Cyprus v Turkey European Court of Human Rights (2001) 90
Ilhan v Turkey European Court of Human Rights (2000) 25
K-H W v Germany European Court of Human Rights (2001) 71
Keenan v UK European Court of Human Rights (2001) 25
Timofeyev v Russia European Court of Human Rights (2003) 117

Inter-American Courts and Commission

Beazley v USA Inter-American Commission on Human Rights (2003) 83
Fairen Garbi and Solis Corrales Inter American Court of Human Rights (1988) 24
Godínez Cruz Case Inter American Court of Human Right (1989) 24
Velasquez Rodriguez Inter American Court of Human Rights (1988) 24
Velasquez Rodriguez Inter American Court of Human Rights (Preliminary Objections) (1987) 24

Other

Al Adsani v United Kingdom 123 ILR (2003) 61
Attorney General of Israel v Eichmann 36 ILR (1968) 71
Demjanjuk v Petrovsky 776 F.2d 571 (6th Circuit) (1985) 71
East German Expropriation Case (Order of the Second Senate of the German Federal Constitutional Court) BVerfG 955/00 (2004) 27, 69
Janes Claim (USA v Mexico) 4 RIAA 82 (1926) 87
Judgment of the IMT for the Trial of German Major War Criminals (London: HMSO, 1946) (1946) 43, 140
Maastricht Judgment BVerfG 89/155 (1993) 30
Polyukovich v Commonwealth [1991] HCA 32 147
'Rainbow Warrior Affair' (New Zealand v France International Arbitration Award) 20 RIAA 217 (1990) 88
Re Treaty on the Basis of Relations Between the Federal Republic of Germany and the German Democratic Republic BVerfG 78 ILR 149 (1972) 117
Trevorrow v State of South Australia (No 5) [2007] SASC 285 150
Trial of Friedrich Flick and Five Others US Military Tribunal LRTWC Volume IX 1 (1947) 42
Zimbabwe Human Rights NGO Forum v Zimbabwe Communication No 245/2002 (2006) 26

Hansard

House of Commons Hansard (16 March 1961) col 1748.
House of Lords Hansard (14 April 1999) col 826.

Reference sources

Merriam-Webster Collegiate Dictionary (11th edn) (USA: Merriam-Webster, 2003).
Merriam-Webster's Dictionary of Law (UK: Book Service Ltd, 2000).
Oxford Dictionary of Law (6th edn) (Oxford: Oxford University Press, 2003).

Websites

Armenian Genocide Museum (2009): www.genocide-museum.am/eng/states.php
Associated Foreign Press (2009): www.france24.com/en/20081216-un-plan-condemnation-mugabe-fails-because-south-african-opposition-zimbabwe
Association of Ukrainians in Great Britain (2009): www.augb.co.uk
Australian Government 'Fact Sheet 255 – Australia and the Issue of Apartheid in Sport' (2010): www.naa.gov.au/about-us/publications/fact-sheets/fs255.aspx

BBC (2009): www.news.bbc.co.uk/1/hi/world/africa/7925240.stm www.news.bbc.co.uk/1/hi/world/europe/8094664.stm

Cassese, A. 'A Judicial Massacre' (2007) *The Guardian* (2009): www.guardian.co.uk/commentisfree/2007/feb/27/thejudicialmassacreofsrebr

Charter, D. 'Serbia Cleared of Genocide Charge Over Killing of 8,000 at Srebrenica' (2007) *The Times* (2009): www.timesonline.co.uk/tol/news/world/europe/article1444140.ece

Commission for the Prosecution of Crimes Against the Polish Nation (2010): www.ipn.gov.pl/portal/en/2/77/Decision_to_commence_investigation_into_Katyn_Massacre.htm

Elnajjar, H. 'Oil Interests and the US Invasion of Iraq' Paper Presented at the Annual Conference of the American Sociological Association (2009): www.allacademic.com/meta/p21288_index.html

European Community (2009): www.ec.europa.eu/enlargement/countries/index_en.htm

Fischer, B. 'The Katyń Controversy: Stalin's Killing Fields' (2007) Centre for the Study of Intelligence, Central Intelligence Agency Publication (2010): www.cia.gov/library/center-for-the-study-of-intelligence/csi-publications/csi-studies/studies/winter99-00/art6.html

Fox News (2010): www.whitehouse.blogs.foxnews.com/2010/03/05/turkey-troubles/

French Government (2010): www.diplomatie.gouv.fr/en/country-files_156/kenya_209/situation-in-kenya-2008

MacAskill, E. and Borger, J. 'Iraq War was Illegal and Breached UN Charter, Says Annan' (2004) *The Guardian* (2009): www.guardian.co.uk/world/2004/sep/16/iraq.iraq

Perry, M. 'A Stolen Generation Cries Out' *Reuters* (1997) (2010): www.hartford-hwp.com/archives/24/088.html

Read, P. 'Don't Let Facts Spoil This Campaign' (2008) *The Australian* (2010): www.theaustralian.com.au/news/opinion/dont-let-facts-spoil-this-campaign/story-e6frg6zo-1111115574447

Read, P. *The Stolen Generations: The Removal of Aboriginal Children in New South Wales 1883 to 1969* Department of Aboriginal Affairs (1981) (reprinted 2006) (2010): www.daa.nsw.gov.au/publications/StolenGenerations.pdf

Scheffer, D. 'Testimony Before the Senate Foreign Relations Committee' (1998) *US Department of State* (2009): www.state.gov/www/policy_remarks/1998/980723_scheffer_icc.html

Turkish Ministry of Culture (2009): www.kultur.gov.tr/EN/BelgeGoster.aspx?17A16AE30572D313AAF6AA849816B2EF21AE406D1C1546DE

United Nations (2009): 'Statement of the President of the UN General Assembly at the Opening of the Thematic Dialogue of the General Assembly on the Responsibility to Protect' (2009): www.un.org/ga/president/63/statements/openingr2p230709.shtml

'UN Experts Call for Rebuilding Zimbabwe's Health/Food Systems' (2008): www.un.org/apps/news/story.asp?NewsID=29385&Cr=zimbabwe&Cr1=

UN Office for the Coordination of Humanitarian Affairs (2009): www.irinnews.org/Report.aspx?ReportId=82370

'Victor Yushchenko, President of Ukraine: Official Website' (2009): www.president.gov.ua/en/news/8296.html

White House, 'Press Briefing to Preview The Nuclear Security Summit' (April 9 2010): www.whitehouse.gov/the-press-office/press-briefing-preview-nuclear-security-summit-gary-samore-white-house-coordinator-

Index

Aboriginal and Torres Strait Islander children 142–51
accountability: bottom up 18; human rights 20–6, 35, 37, 42, 65, 83; interpretation 9–28; top down 18–22
actio popularis 68
aggression: as a *jus cogens* norm 5, 42, 62, 70, 72; definition 129–33; General Assembly Resolution 3314 62, 130–8, 140–1, 162
Armenia 100–10
apartheid 12, 120–8
Australia 142–52

China: invasion of Korea 131–3; recognition of Taiwan 31, 131
Council of Europe 54–6; condemnation of crimes of the USSR 110–12; questioning of Turkey 108–10

Darfur 22, 38, 104–5
Draft Articles on State Responsibility 43, 71, 74–92, 134

erga omnes 63, 67–8, 77, 82–4
European Court of Human Rights 18, 71, 90, 117
European Parliament: condemnation of crimes of the USSR 109–12; Venice Commission 55–7
European Union: definition of accountability 15–21; definition of state 30–1; recognition of Armenian massacre 109–19; recognition of crimes by the USSR 110–19
extraordinary rendition 55–7

First World War 19, 41, 47–8; context of the Armenian massacre 103–10
Foucault, Michel 3, 29, 156

Gaza 52–3; Goldstone Report of the United Nations fact-finding mission on the Gaza conflict 54–5
Genocide Convention Case 14, 32, 38, 44, 46, 75–7, 84, 86–7, 89, 116
Germany 19, 29, 31, 36, 41–2, 45, 47–51, 71, 93, 102, 116–7, 139
Guantanamo Bay detention facility 58–9, 163

Holodomor famine 110–19; International Commission of Inquiry 110–12
Human Rights Committee 58, 69, 118
Human Rights Council 21–3, 53, 58, 151, 159, 164

Inter-American Commission on Human Rights 24, 83
Inter-American Court of Human Rights 19, 24–5, 35
International Court of Justice 1, 14, 19, 35–8, 41, 44, 46, 51–2, 64, 66, 68, 71, 75–82, 86, 89, 91, 95–6, 116, 121, 153, 158
International Law Commission 7, 43–5, 48, 63, 69–75, 78, 81, 84–6, 90–2, 105, 111, 120; Draft Articles on State Responsibility 43, 71, 74–92, 134; Report on the Fragmentation of International Law 63
Intervention 36–40, 59, 106, 138, 155–6
Iran: Nuclear Security Summit (2010) 95, 108; Tehran Hostages crisis (1979) 80–1
Iraq: bombing of Osiraq nuclear reactor 133–5, 152–5; invasion of Iraq (2003) 152–5; invasion of Kuwait (1990) 135–40, 152–5

Israel: bombing of Gaza 52–3; bombing of Osiraq nuclear reactor 133–5, 152–5; Israeli Supreme Court and the Eichmann case 71

jus cogens 61–74; Article 53 VCLT 61–74, 78, 104, 121, 153

Katyn massacre 115–20
Korea 132–3, 152–5
Kosovo 30, 77; Independent International Commission on Kosovo 37; Kosovo status settlement 30
Kuwait 135–40, 152–5

League of Nations 35, 43, 78, 112–3

Mexican Claims Commission cases 87
Montevideo Convention 28–32

NATO 16, 96, 107–8
Nicaragua case 37–8, 41, 86, 106
North Korea 132–3, 152–5
Nuclear Security Summit (2010) 95, 108
Nuremberg Tribunal 5, 9, 31, 42–5, 48–9, 63, 78, 140, 146

Obama, Barack 163
Organisation of African Unity 126; Lagos Declaration 127; Lusaka Manifesto 126
Osiraq nuclear reactor 133–5, 152–5

Permanent Court of International Justice 35, 38
Poland 117–20
Pope John Paul II 112

Rainbow Warrior affair 88
responsibility to protect 38–9; International Commission on Intervention and State Sovereignty 38–9
Russia 110–20

Second World War 39, 41, 47–8, 78, 93, 114, 139, 161; Potsdam Agreement 41–2, 49, 93, 116
Serbia 14, 30, 44, 46, 75–7, 86–7, 89, 116
state responsibility 74–93; Chorzow Factory Principle 14, 74, 88; Draft Articles on State Responsibility by States 43, 71, 74–92, 134; Draft Article 19 and criminal state responsibility 45, 79, 90–1, 121; Draft Article 40 and the serious breach regime 71, 79–80, 91; Draft Article 48 and obligations owed to the international community as a whole 79, 81–2
stolen generation 142–52
South Africa 120–9; Truth and Reconciliation Commission 128–9; winds of change speech 123

Turkey 100–9
Taiwan 31, 131
Treaty of Sevres 106–7
Treaty of Versailles 19, 41, 47, 106

United Nations 11, 31, 125–6, 132, 137; Secretary General Ban Ki Moon 52; Secretary General Kofi Annan 39, 51, 141; UN Committee on Economic, Social and Cultural Rights 21, 23; UN Committee on Racial Discrimination 118, 150
United States of America 17, 22, 30–1, 39, 51–2, 83
USSR 110–20; space damage 44
universal peer review 22, 58, 164

Venice Commission 55–7
Vienna Conference on the Law of Treaties 63, 66
Viscount Boyce 101

Zimbabwe 16–17